Language Play,
Language Learning

Guy Cook

Oxford University Press

OXFORD
UNIVERSITY PRESS

Great Clarendon Street, Oxford OX2 6DP

Oxford University Press is a department of the University of Oxford.
It furthers the University's objective of excellence in research, scholarship,
and education by publishing worldwide in

Oxford New York

Auckland Cape Town Dar es Salaam Hong Kong Karachi
Kuala Lumpur Madrid Melbourne Mexico City Nairobi
New Delhi Shanghai Taipei Toronto

With offices in

Argentina Austria Brazil Chile Czech Republic France Greece
Guatemala Hungary Italy Japan Poland Portugal Singapore
South Korea Switzerland Thailand Turkey Ukraine Vietnam

First published 2000
2012 2011 2010 2009 2008
10 9 8 7 6 5 4 3

ISBN: 978 0 19 442153 9

Printed in China

Contents

To Toby

Acknowledgements

While I was writing this book, I had the great advantage of working with an outstanding group of research students at the London University Institute of Education: David Barrett, Silvia Barros, Lynne Cameron, Seiko Harumi, Max Hui-Bon-Hoa, Terezinha Lobianco, Kieran O'Halloran, Beate Poole, and Elena Putyrskaya. Their enthusiasm and dedication have been an inspiration to me, and our many hours of discussion have greatly enriched my understanding of language and communication.

I am grateful too, to Elena Cook and Karen Ross, both for discussion, and for patiently disentangling me from my own bibliography. I have benefited immensely from dialogues with Rob Batstone, David Block, and Elaine Tarone, and from their detailed comments on earlier drafts. Especial thanks are also due to Cristina Whitecross at OUP for her patience and efficiency in the preparation of the manuscript for publication.

The greatest single influence on my writing is Henry Widdowson. In struggling to shape my own ideas into this book, I have relied more than I could express upon his advice, friendship, and support.

Lastly, thanks to my children, two-year-old Toby and eight-year-old Roxana, for their inspiring interruptions.

The authors and publishers are grateful to those who have given permission to reproduce the following extracts and adaptations of copyright material:

p.20 *PEEPO!* by Allen and Janet Ahlberg (Kestrel 1981). Copyright Janet Ahlberg, 1981. Reprinted by permission of Penguin Books Ltd.

p.26 'Rhyme in children's early reading' by Goswami from *Rhymes, Reading and Writing* edited by Roger Beard. Copyright 1995 Roger Beard.

p.34 'The Hippopotamus' from *Collected Poems 1909–1962* by T. S. Eliot reproduced by permission of Faber & Faber.

p.42 'My Pet Dinosaur' by Charles Thomson from *I'm Brilliant* edited by Paul Foster published by HarperCollins Publishers Ltd and reproduced with their permission.

p.45 *From Two to Five* by Kornei Chukovsky edited/translated by Miram Morton. Copyright 1963 The Regents of the University of California. Reprinted by permission of the University of California Press.

p.46 *Tree and Leaf* by J. R. R. Tolkien published by HarperCollins Publishers Ltd and reproduced with their permission.

Introduction   Not only for children

A group of seven-year-old girls stand in the playground at break time. They are free of the organized activity which was imposed on them only a few minutes ago. Outside the classroom, between blocks of lessons, they can do more or less as they please. On this occasion, they choose to play a skipping game. Two girls turn the rope while a third skips, chanting at the same time. Other girls stand round, appraising the situation, waiting for their turn. The chant is as relentless as the turning of the rope. It has a heavy, regular beat (falling on the underlined syllables below) and it follows a simple melody, with the second half of each line an octave higher than the beginning.

Eenee meenee dissaleenee,
You are the one and only
Educated, liberated,
I like you.

Dan Dan maybe,
Down by the roller coaster
Sweet sweet chariot,
No place to go.
Do do the dishes,
Lazy, lazy,
Stole a piece of candy,
Greedy, greedy
Jumped out the window,
Flipping crazy

Eenee meenee dissaleenee,
You are the one and only
Educated, liberated,
I like you.

Though most of the phrases have meaning in themselves, the overall effect can be described as nonsense. There is a hotchpotch of language from a variety of sources. As well as nonsense words, exclamations, and critical rebukes, there are phrases which seem to come from pop songs, children's stories, domestic life, communal singing, and adult discussions. The effect is a collage of disjointed and elliptical phrases, drawn from many places in children's passive experience of language. Yet the overriding consideration seems to be not coherent meaning, but rhythm. By juxtaposing monosyllabic and polysyllabic words within the framework of the steady beat, the chant necessitates rapid accelerations and decelerations of speech rate. It is a virtuoso display of bodily and linguistic control. To be regarded as successful by the onlookers, the girls should skip and say the rhyme as fast and as many times as possible.

This skipping game serves no immediate purpose, and answers no externally-generated demands. Like the school lessons which it follows, it is an organized activity, with its own rules and obligations, its own rewards and punishments, but it is one of the children's own choosing, and is regarded by them as essentially different from school work. Its carefully controlled rhythm and bizarre fleeting images are a considerable source of delight, and for a brief spell of time, the game creates its own miniature social world of spectators, competitors, judges, and assistants. Like society itself, it is both collaborative and competitive. It binds these children together, distinguishing them from other groups, but also enables each child to show off her individual skills. There are winners and losers, and some are much better at it than others.

Around the playground, other children are using language in similar ways, making and breaking ephemeral social bonds. Very often there is a focus on the patterning of linguistic forms or chance coincidences of sound. One child is telling jokes:

What came after the Bronze Age and the Stone Age?
The Saus Age.

Another issues a taunt:

Tell him, smell him,
Take him out and sell him!

Another answers an insult with a rhyme:

Twinkle, twinkle little star,
What you say is what you are.

to be answered in turn by

If you say it back to me,
You're a hairy chimpanzee.

Another, one of a small circle, points to each of his companions in turn, using the rhythm of a 'counting-out' rhyme to eliminate one child at a time, and decide who is to be 'it' in their game:

Mickey <u>Mouse</u> <u>in</u> his <u>house</u>,
<u>Pulling</u> <u>down</u> his <u>trou</u> <u>sers</u>,
<u>Look</u> <u>Mum</u>, <u>dirty</u> <u>bum</u>,
<u>You</u>   <u>are</u>   <u>not</u>   <u>it</u>.

At home later in the day, these same children will continue to seek out uses of language which, while perhaps less social and more serious than the playground jokes and rhymes, are equally superfluous to the 'real' world of necessary action. They use language to create make-believe worlds; they sing songs, follow stories on television or video, read or listen to stories told or read aloud to them by adults. All of these activities generate their own self-contained worlds. Often, they bring into existence, however briefly, fictional characters and events. They can be assembled and disassembled, started, suspended, or abandoned in an instant, with no lasting consequences for any of those involved.

We tend to take this kind of behaviour among children so much for granted, that we fail to wonder why it is so widespread. The examples I have given are from England in the 1990s,[1] but it is evident that children everywhere, left to their own devices, devote their time to play, and it is well documented that such uses of language by children have a very long history, and are found all over the world. There is no cultural gap to be bridged here. The details of the game or story may belong to a particular time and place, but there will be no problem in recognizing *the kind of* activity I am describing.

For this very reason—that it is both widespread and commonplace—we tend not to be surprised by the existence of children's play. We do not wonder why human young put so much of their physical, emotional, and mental energy into following unnecessary rules and procedures; or why we adults generally enjoy watching them do so. We do not wonder why children capable of using language for sensible communicative purposes should so often use it to make meaningless patterns of sound, or to create imaginary worlds. Yet there are many other forms of childhood behaviour which could have evolved in our species, with obvious advantages for all concerned. Children could, when they have nothing to do, switch off like machines, or sleep, or use their free time and linguistic ability more profitably to learn about the real rather than fictional worlds. Yet their play, with or without language, is just something which—like their language acquisition—we usually take for granted.

When I was a child, I spake as a child, I understood as a child, I thought as a child: but when I became a man, I put away childish things.
(I Corinthians 13: 11)

Although we take children's play for granted, at least we recognize its nature, and see that it is there. When we turn our attention to adult behaviour, we are likely to assume that play has disappeared, or at least shrunk to a minor role, overwhelmed and replaced by the more serious and necessary aspects of adult affairs. Yet is this actually the case? Are all the adult activities, and the uses of language to which we devote time and accord value, any more necessary than children's play, or is it just that we take them more seriously?

Given that we adults consider our concerns to be rather more 'real' than those of children, it is strange that some of our favourite activities do not strike us as out of character. After all, there are many leisure activities in which features of children's play continue quite *overtly*. Large numbers of adults use their leisure time to play organized games. For some of these games, crowds assemble to watch, encourage, and assess—rather as the girls formed a circle round the skipping game, if on a somewhat larger scale. In football matches (where there may be 100,000 spectators[2]) large sections of the crowd chant their reactions in unison, using verses which, like children's playground lore, often parody famous instances of more respectable genres:

Blue Moon, you started singing our tune
You won't be singing for long
Because we beat you 5–1.

At home, many adults devote their evenings to watching images of people pretending to be other people in situations which have never existed, talking about things which have never happened. Others queue and pay to watch similar but larger images in darkened auditoria. In both cases—watching TV and going to the cinema—members of these audiences follow and discuss the real lives of these 'actors' ('players' as they used to be called) with overwhelming interest and devotion.

In contrast to these forms of adult play, other supposedly serious activities are conducted through language which continue—one might almost say *covertly*—to manifest a fascination with the manipulation of linguistic form. The most popular tabloid newspapers[3] are devoted to representing events in weak puns. In big-business advertising, the promotion of goods is carried out not by listing their qualities, durability, uses, and cost, but through fictional cameos, plays on words, and rhyming and rhythmic jingles. Even some of the most serious discourses, such as political rhetoric, prayer, liturgy, and literature, use repetitive and rhythmic language which is markedly play-*like*—even though these forms are considered to be anything but playful by their users. From our interested adult perspective, they may seem a far cry from the skipping game in the playground—but then children, just as much as adults, take their play seriously, and one can imagine the girls in the skipping game discussing their activity at length, or mulling over a defeat or victory with emotions and opinions as serious as those of any political, religious, or literary adult commentator or analyst.

Here is a phenomenon worth investigating, and one which has on the whole been neglected, or at least sidelined, in the study of language and language learning.[4] In this book I shall bring together a range of normally dissociated activities under the heading of language play, though there is clearly a great deal of work to be done to specify more precisely both the similarities and the differences between them. The claim of this book is that although language play is manifested through a variety of different activities, these are expressions of a single underlying phenomenon, which is of particular relevance to mental adaptation, for individuals, for societies, and for the species. Though it appears superfluous, it is not actually so. Disconnection from reality, disruption and subversion of social structures, and the introduction of random elements, have particular benefits for all of us, and that is perhaps why we are so fond of them, even when they are forbidden. They are there to be exploited to our advantage in many areas of human activity, including language learning. The general purpose of this book is to offer an exploration, and at least a partial explanation, of why and how this might be so.

The book is in three parts: descriptive, theoretical, and pedagogic.

Part One, **The interlocking levels**, looks at the extraordinary importance and extent of language play in human life. No definition is offered at this stage, but it is assumed that language play involves the patterning of linguistic form, the creation of alternative realities, and the social use of both of these for intimacy and conflict. Play at each of these levels—linguistic form, semantic meaning, and pragmatic use—is examined in turn, as well as the ways in which play at one level creates play at the others. Chapter 1, *The forms of language play*, examines reasons for the attractiveness of rhythm and repetition, by considering their role in children's verse. Although both help in the development of language and literacy, this cannot entirely account for their fascination, which continues throughout life. Some larger explanation is needed to account for their power over adults. Chapter 2, *The meanings of language play*, examines the extent and importance of fiction for both children and adults, its intimate relation with the patterning of linguistic form, its vague and indeterminate meanings, and its contribution to creative and hypothetical thought. Chapter 3, *The uses of language play*, considers how—through activities such as insulting, joking, and ritual—linguistic patterning and alternative realities are used in both the private and the public sphere to effect competition and collaboration, and as a means of social organization.

Part Two, **Theories and explanations**, takes up the questions raised in Part One, attempting to characterize language play, and examines some of the theories which have been advanced both for play in general, and for language play in particular. Chapter 4, *The nature of play*, assesses the conflicting claims of evolutionary and sociocultural accounts of play. Are the forms and functions of human play essentially similar to those of animals, or has it developed unique characteristics? Is it largely genetically determined, or has cultural activity assumed a disembodied life of its own? Both approaches, though for different reasons, see play as providing insights into such serious activities as warfare, art, and politics. Chapter 5, *The play of nature*, examines how play shares features with creative processes beyond the human sphere which involve the interaction of chance, externally-determined forces, and choice. One such process is the evolution of life itself, resulting as it does from the interplay of random genetic mutation, environmental pressures, and, increasingly, human intervention. Developing this theme, the chapter offers a theory and definition of language play, and speculates upon its contribution to the adaptive capacities of individuals, societies, and the species as a whole.

Part Three, **Language learning**, considers the implications of an understanding of language play for language teaching and learning. Chapter 6, *The current orthodoxies*, questions the fashionable and widely-held views that language learning is best effected through concentration upon 'meaning' rather than 'form', and through activities which are 'useful' rather than 'useless', 'real' rather than 'contrived'. The importance and prevalence of play in human life undermines the validity of these dichotomies, and also suggests that human beings both enjoy and benefit from dissociation from reality. Chapter 7, *Future prospects*, points the way towards the reinstatement of many pedagogic activities which have fallen out of favour under the sway of the current orthodoxies. It draws upon the argument of the whole book for a new departure in language pedagogy, exploiting the universal human liking for competition, fiction and artifice, repetition, and the manipulation and analysis of form.

Different readers have different interests, and inevitably some will be more attracted to one of these sections than another. Perhaps, in the modern world, where the pressures of work are so insistent and there is so little time to play, the tendency to pick at academic books is growing. They can seem, after all, to contribute neither to work nor to play. Fewer people have the time to read each part, and the result is that readers are increasingly selective, paying attention only to those sections or even pages which seem relevant to their needs. For some the main interest of language play will be its relevance to language teaching. For these readers, Parts One and Two may well seem a long preamble to their main concern. For other readers, with no particular interest in the heated debates around language teaching, the opposite may be true. They may see no reason to venture beyond Part Two. Yet the purpose of this book is precisely to argue that things which seem irrelevant to each other are often connected, that what seems to be a waste of time can often be extremely useful, that apparently efficient use of time and language is not always in our best interests. I hope that—if you do read right through to the last page—you will agree that while each part, though it could have been read in isolation, is necessary for a full appreciation of the others, and of the essential contribution of language play to the quality of our lives.

Notes

1 Recorded by the author in north London, 1996.
2 If we include the television audience, numbers of spectators for some matches are estimated to be as high as four billion! Although it is mass communications and the sheer size of modern populations which lead to such enormous numbers, there is nothing particularly new about the phenomenon of large crowds for sporting events. In Ancient Rome, the Circus Maximus could accommodate 250,000 people (Russell 1993: 241).
3 In September 1993, with a British population of approximately 58 million, the combined daily sales of the popular tabloid newspapers *The Sun*, *The Mirror*, and *The Daily Star*, were 7,246,911 (easily exceeding the combined sales of the serious broadsheet newspapers).
4 There are, of course, many exceptions to this generalization. Notable for arguing the centrality and importance of language play are Farb 1973; Stewart 1979; Kristeva 1989; Lecercle 1990, 1994; Burke 1994; Beard 1995; Dowker 1997; Crystal 1998 (published as I was finishing the manuscript for this book).

PART ONE
The interlocking levels

1 The forms of language play: rhythm and repetition in children's verse

So much has been written in linguistics about children's language that it might seem there is little which could possibly be added, either in terms of description or of speculation. In this chapter, however, I should like to take a slightly different bearing from that which is customary, one which will point us forward to an understanding of why the playful uses of language do not end with childhood, but continue throughout our lives.

Phrases like 'children's language' or 'child language' are most commonly used to refer to the language which children produce, and how adults perceive it. However, as we can see by analogy with 'children's fiction' or 'children's programmes', they could equally refer to the language which surrounds children, and how *they* perceive *that*. In this latter interpretation, the object of study would include the language which children receive as well as that which they produce: the lore of older children, traditional rhymes and stories, books read aloud, and broadcast and recorded language. Most studies in linguistics, however, have opted for the former perspective, and in line with a general emphasis upon language production at the expense of reception, have tended to neglect these elements of the child's linguistic environment.[1]

In functionalist linguistics, there are extensive studies of adult speech to children, and of child–child interaction. Yet these tend to dwell upon language which elicits direct response from the child, rather than upon language in which the child is silently absorbed.[2] The usual practice is to look at situations in which children are busy 'doing' something with a short-term and evident outcome, rather than upon language which is less immediately 'useful', and whose longer term function may not be immediately apparent. The focus is more often upon adult–child or child–child dialogues, than upon adult monologues to children (for example, reading aloud), or upon child monologues (such as those which precede sleep, see Weir 1962; Nelson 1989).[3] It is in such less immediately functional uses of language, however, that play is particularly prominent.

In current cognitive linguistics, on the other hand, there is by definition consideration of what is happening internally in the child's mind, and, following Chomsky, attention is concentrated upon the unfolding of an internally generated programme, only suggested by what is actually said. Yet here we find two further constraints upon the kind of language which is to be considered. The first is the assumption (inevitably following the belief that language is modular) that, in essence, acquisition is only about the independent development of grammatical and phonological competence considered in isolation, rather than in interaction with the child's physical, social, and personal development. The second constraint is the assumption —which follows to some extent from the first—that this acquisition of grammar and phonology comes to an end in or around the sixth year, and that at that point in a child's development there is some kind of qualitative break when the process of acquisition is, as it were, complete. These constraints lead to the results observed by Locke (1993:5) who notes that on the one hand, there is little attention in the literature of this tradition to the environment of very young 'prelinguistic' children. On the other hand, there is an equivalent lack of attention to the language of older children: to literacy, vocabulary, and discourse skills, or to the relation between language acquisition and the development of imagination and ideas. All of these areas fall outside Chomsky's narrow definition of 'language', which effectively confines acquisition studies to the development of the formal linguistic system in a first language between the ages of roughly two and six.

There is then, for a number of reasons, a lack of proportionate attention in both formalist and functionalist studies to an aspect of the child's language environment which (if we define child language as language *to* as well as *from* children) is of immense importance. This is listening to verses, songs, jokes, and stories, watching videos and TV programmes, observing the games and listening to the 'lore' of older children.

Two connected factors, both characteristic of language play, should, I believe, mark out these activities for particular attention. One is the wide distribution and constant repetition of the same texts; the other is the unusual attention and affection which some of these inspire. It is these two characteristics which are not captured by analyses based only on observations of children's language behaviour. This is because such 'objective' approaches tend to treat all data on an equal footing, and to avoid speculation on which uses of language are most salient or valuable to the child. In language corpora, for example, a favourite verse is in danger of appearing only once, however much it is loved, and however often it is repeated (Cook 1998).[4] In the case of the language to which children listen, moreover, there is often no observable, quantifiable linguistic behaviour. The child stands or sits in rapt silence. Yet one might with reason imagine, judging subjectively by children's stated preferences and concentrated expressions, that from their point of view, it is these otherwise passively received texts which form one of the most important parts of their linguistic environment. They may not always *participate* in the language, but they are certainly *engaged* (Widdowson 1984).

To a degree, this neglect of the receptive effect of language arises from the aspiration of linguistics to establish its scientific credentials, to advance hypotheses which can be supported by evidence of one kind or another, and are open to falsification. There are differences, of course, in the kind of evidence admitted. Some concentrate upon the observation of behaviour, others follow introspection and reach conclusions based upon rational deduction rather than inductive empiricism. Yet all 'scientific' approaches must be stumped by the question of what is happening within the mind of a young child listening silently to a story or a rhyme, or standing as the onlooker of a new game. For there is no behavioural evidence of what is happening in these situations, and there can be no introspective evidence either, since the child is too young to reflect and comment upon what is happening. Any answer to this absorbing question must remain speculative and unsupported by rigorous evidence, which may explain why studies of stories and verses are considered to belong within literary studies, under a heading such as 'Children's Literature' (Hunt 1990; Townsend 1990), rather than with linguistics, applied linguistics, or psychology. Yet despite its resistance to any scientific answers,[5] the question of the linguistic and cognitive function of this aspect of a child's linguistic experience remains worth asking —and attempting to answer.

Pre-linguistic play: rhythm and interaction

In this spirit of legitimate speculation, let us begin by considering how two 'tickling rhymes' which are used widely with English-speaking children from a very young age must appear to the child who has not yet begun to speak. They are:

This little pig[6] went to market,
This little pig stayed at home,
This little pig had roast beef,
This little pig had none,
(And this little pig went 'wee, wee, wee, wee' all the way home.)

and

Round and round the garden
Like a teddy bear.
One step, two step,
And tickle you under there!

Though in many ways precursors of the stories of later years, neither of these rhymes is an example of language which is absorbed passively by the child listener. They are both highly and overtly interactive, ending with the adult tickling the child. They also demand some collaboration from the child as the adult speaker of the first rhyme takes hold of one of the child's toes with each line, and, in the second rhyme, uses two fingers to 'walk' around 'the garden' of the child's palm. (In the case of the youngest listeners, at first the adult may have to open and hold the baby's palm.) In addition, the 'pig' rhyme is not entirely for fun, since it is often used to accompany and enliven the drying of the child's toes after a bath, and is thus an example of a functional activity with language play built on to it.

From an adult point of view the rhymes seem to use language playfully at the three levels of linguistic form, semantic meaning, and pragmatic use. They pattern sounds and structures; they deal with fictional characters and events; they further the relationship of adult speaker and child recipient, ending with a kind of rudimentary proto-joke as the story is suddenly diverted into a surprise tickling. Yet from the baby's point of view, they cannot be said to operate straightforwardly at any of these levels, for the simple reason that the child (whatever inherited principles of Universal Grammar may or may not be present in his or her mind) has not yet acquired the phonology and grammar of the particular language in which the verses are spoken.[7] Nor, presumably, will the child be able to perceive the patterning of these levels in the verses—although he or she may be beginning to acquire these levels *by* repeatedly hearing such verses. For the same reason, the child at this age does not understand the verses as stories about fictional characters and events, not only because he or she does not know the grammar and vocabulary, but also because he or she is unlikely to know all the concepts they denote, such as 'roast beef', 'went to market', 'round the garden', etc. Indeed, we may suppose that in order to identify such concepts and distinguish fictional from factual events, it is necessary first to know a language; it is not that children *first* acquire a language and *then* are exposed to stories in it as a result, but rather the reverse.

Yet although the very young child does not yet understand these verses as language, he or she does seem to perceive two aspects of what is happening which are closely related to language: rhythm and intonation, on the one hand, and interpersonal interaction as expressed by eye contact, facial expressions, and touch, on the other. Both are instances of the paralanguage which inevitably accompanies spoken interaction.

What exist are, as it were, the two opposite ends of a spectrum stretching from meaningless but patterned sound at one end, to pragmatic contextualized interpersonal meanings at the other, with nothing, or very little, as yet, in between. At the patterned-sound end of the spectrum, the verse is composed of speech sounds, but is devoid, from the child's point of view, of linguistic form or precise semantic meaning. At the pragmatic end of the spectrum, the child is in successful communication with an adult, in a way which resembles the kind of interaction which takes place between people who *do* know a language in common, and use it to consolidate their relationship, express affection, tell stories, and play games. Eyes meet, hands touch, there are recognizable turns (the rhyme and the laughter), and a feeling of well-being as a result. At this stage, then, the rhymes have both a quasi-musical and a pragmatic aspect. They are simultaneously social interaction and a rhythmic, incantatory stream of sound, associated with repeated actions.

1 From the baby's view

Rhythm, melody	--	Interaction,	relationship
		(eye contact,	
		touch,	
		turn-taking)	

2 From the adult's view

Rhythm, intonation	Phonemes, morphemes, lexis, syntax	--------	Interaction,	relationship

Figure 1.1: The communication spectrum

At this stage in the child's life it would be wrong to call these tickling rhymes *language play*, if by this term we refer to the patterning of phonology and grammar (and through them the manipulation of meanings and relationships), which the child has not yet acquired. More accurately, we might call them *pre-linguistic play*. They are a stream of sound which is in some ways similar to music, though also, in other important ways, significantly different from it. Like music, they have rhythm and melody. However, pitch variation is less, musical resonance is absent, and contrasts are linear, all melody rather than harmony. The baby has an innate ability to make finer distinctions among speech sounds than among other sounds (Locke 1993:84, 93), including musical ones (Raffman 1993), an ability which presumably enables the child to perceive phonemic and other contrasts more readily. However, we may assume that at this stage the verse is as yet only rhythm and intonation, without a semantic meaning, though directly linked, as it were, to a pragmatic one. It is not yet language, though it will become more like language each time the child hears it.

Although the two tickling rhymes we are considering here may only appear to the baby as rhythmic speech sound and social interaction, it is noticeable that their rhythmic breaks not only coincide with linguistic boundaries, they also emphasize those boundaries *much more* than they would be emphasized in everyday speech. Grammar, rhythm, and actions all echo each other. The first two stresses fall upon the phrase 'this little pig', which is the theme of each clause. The next stress falls upon the varying predicators, which are the rhemes. In addition, the repetition of this phrase with different predicators highlights (as in a substitution table for language teaching) its existence as a grammatical unit (noun phrase) and functional unit (subject) within the clause. In technical metrical terminology, this phrase forms the first hemistich (or half-line) before the caesura (or slight pause) in the middle of the line. The 'Rest' at the end of each line clearly separates the clauses (of this rhythmic feature, more below); to make them even more distinct, each clause is also linked to the touching of a particular toe, and its boundary marked by the transition to the next one!

(/ = stress)

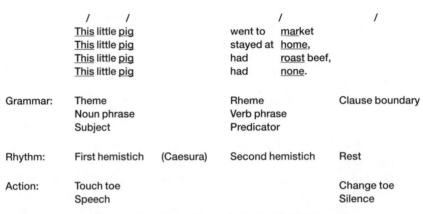

Figure 1.2: Mapped boundaries in 'This Little Pig'

In 'Round and Round the Garden', actions also aid meanings, since fingers go 'round and round' the child's palm, take steps, and tickle with the relevant words. The fact that the fingers are a teddy bear's legs, and the child's palm the garden, is a kind of make-believe or metaphor, whose meaning must be recovered from elsewhere, and once again, the rest at the end of each line emphasizes a boundary of both sense and grammar. So everything in our two verses conspires to lead the child from the verse as rhythm and social interaction towards the verse as grammar and lexis and meaning.

One may suppose that, over a crucial period of time in early life, exposure to simple rhythms emphasizing grammatical boundaries, heavy stresses (both on syllables which are stressed in speech and, occasionally, on those which are weak and might be lost), relevant ritualistic actions, and constant repetition, all play a significant role in aiding the child to cross the mysterious border between the perception of speech as meaningless sound and the perception of the same speech as referring to, and communicating, states of affairs in the actual or a fictional world. The verses also provide children with a model to imitate (followed sometimes to exasperating extremes) and an opportunity to improve through practice their control over vocalization. For such recitations, we may presume, the familiarity engendered by constant repetition, rhyme, and the steady simple beat serve as mnemonics, allowing children to produce language way above their current capacity, apparently with a great deal of pleasure. In much the same way, adults performing drama or reciting poetry enjoy producing language richer than that which they can invent themselves, and language learners gain satisfaction from the reading or recitation of ready-made texts, which allow them the sensation of being more fluent speakers of the language than they actually are.

We can gain some inkling of how such rhymes must appear to the pre-linguistic child by comparing them to the so-called 'gibberish rhymes' used by older children—and occasionally by adults. Being composed of nonsense words, for us these rhymes only have phonological form and pragmatic meaning. In other words, although the speakers of these verses *do* have the linguistic resources to make sense with language, they choose not to use it in this way, as in the following counting-out rhyme used by seven and eight-year-olds. (I have underlined the stressed syllables.)

Eenee	meenee	macker	racker	
Dare -	O	domer	lacker	
Chicka	bocker	lolli	popper	
Oo,	boo,	bush,	air.	Out![8]

These are speech sounds but—in the sense that they have no semantic denotation or precise reference—they are used, in effect, as if they were music. Even if they do not make sense,[9] they conform to some of the rules of the language. The rhyme above, for example, does not violate the syllabic and phonemic structures of English.

So gibberish rhymes are not as anarchic as they may at first seem. They have both formal regularity and social purpose, but no referential meaning. They appear to us, perhaps, as the piggy rhyme appears to the baby. In this sense, they are comparable to the use of foreign or archaic language in religious worship, when it is not understood by its users; or even to legal language as it appears to recipients who are not trained to understand it. However, the love of older children for gibberish rhymes, and that of children and adults in general for obscure and mysterious language, raises a problem which we shall need to pursue in a later chapter. If the function of rhythmic but semantically imprecise or meaningless speech sounds were only a stepping-stone in acquisition, there would be no need for it to persist in later life. We have examined why babies may enjoy such uses, but not why that enjoyment remains with us throughout our lives, or why this rhythmic but semantically vague sound is so often used in the intimate relationships and public ceremonies which are most important to us.

Reasons for responses to rhythm

In all societies, adults use verse of some kind to young children, and young children respond to it enthusiastically. There is evidence that infants pay more attention to verse than they do to other kinds of language (Glenn and Cunningham 1983). The issue which then arises—as with play in general—is whether this use and response to verse may be some kind of universal human behaviour, independent of the child's linguistic and cultural environment, naturally selected perhaps during the process of evolution. If so, there follows a further question: why should such a liking for verse have developed in our species? We tend to think of the socially significant genres of language use as being determined more by culture than biology. However, there is no reason in principle why—despite their diversity—part of our knowledge of at least some of them (song, verse, narrative, gossip, jokes, for example) should not be innate.

Such claims for an instinctive response to rhythmic language immediately run up against the obstacle of the diverse nature of verse in different languages. The claims only appear to hold if we define verse in the most general of ways. For while verse in all languages may be, as Gerard Manley Hopkins defined it,[10] 'speech wholly or partially repeating the same figure of sound', the nature of these 'figures of sound' varies with language type, and exploits, at least in adult poetry, different kinds of linguistic contrasts. In tone languages (such as Chinese) the units may be arrangements of different types of tone; in syllable-timed languages (such as Ancient Greek), they may be patterns of longer and shorter syllables; in isochronic languages (such as English) they are patterns of stressed and unstressed syllables.

Most modern poetry in English is of this last type, which is known as 'foot verse'.[11] The line can be divided into units combining stressed (/) and unstressed (x) syllables in various ways. These are the 'feet' of traditional poetic scansion. Among the most frequent in English verse are iambs (x /), trochees (/ x), and anapaests (x x /). The many ways of combining the various feet in lines and poems of varying lengths yield an enormous number of verse forms—both conventional and unconventional.

If the verse used with small children were as various in form as that of adult poetry, then the case for its universality would seem considerably weakened: the differences both across and within languages seeming far more significant than the similarities. Yet it is here that a scholarly disagreement about the scansion of English nursery rhymes—which might at first seem to be of only limited specialist interest—takes on a particular significance. This is the argument between those who believe that children's verse in a particular language should be scanned in the same way as adult verse forms of that language, and those who believe that it has its own distinctive, culture-independent—and therefore potentially innate—form. In English this disagreement comes down to whether the English nursery rhymes should be analysed as the foot verse (described above) or as something different.

Although there have been various attempts to scan the English nursery rhymes into foot verse (for example, Guéron 1974), such analysis has a tendency to become excessively complicated and unconvincing, suggesting that the rhymes are being made to conform to a system which is quite alien to them. A far easier and more elegant solution is to see the English nursery rhymes not as 'foot verse' at all, but as 'stress verse'.

In stress verse, a steady beat emphasizes the syllables on which it falls. Between the beats, up to four unstressed syllables either bunch up together (if there are several) or stretch out (if there are only a few) to maintain a steady rhythm (Malof [1970] 1978). Our two tickling rhymes (like many other nursery rhymes in English) are most satisfactorily scanned as following an absolutely regular 4/4 rhythm (of the same kind as is found in music) with a very heavy initial beat in each bar, and the option of a 'rest' (R) in which the beat continues through a pause. The best way to verify the plausibility of such a reading is to beat time while saying the verse with exaggerated regularity. In 'This Little Pig' the beat of the rhythm falls as follows:

1	2	3	4
<u>This</u> little	<u>pig</u> went to	<u>mar</u>ket	R
1	2	3	4
<u>This</u> little	<u>pig</u> stayed at	<u>home</u>	R
1	2	3	4
<u>This</u> little	<u>pig</u> had	<u>roast</u> beef	R
1	2	3	4
<u>This</u> little	<u>pig</u> had	<u>none</u>	R

(In the fifth line—'And this little pig went "wee, wee, wee, wee" all the way home'—the rhythm is abandoned, together with the counting of the toes.)

'Round and Round the Garden' can also follow a 4/4 rhythm,[12] as follows:

	1	2	3	4
	<u>Round</u> and	<u>round</u> the	<u>gar</u>	<u>den</u>
	1	2	3	4
	<u>Like</u> a	<u>teddy</u>	<u>bear</u>	R
	1	2	3	4
	<u>One</u>	<u>step</u>	<u>two</u>	<u>step</u>
	1	2	3	4
And	<u>tickle</u> you	<u>under</u>	<u>there</u>.	R

In stress verse, although the stressed and unstressed syllables do not necessarily occur in regular patterns, they may still create a rhythmic effect. When there are many unstressed syllables between beats there is a speeding up, as in:

1	2	3	4
<u>Cock</u> a doodle	<u>doo</u>, my	<u>dame</u> has lost her	<u>shoe</u>
1	2	3	4
My <u>master's</u> lost his	<u>fiddling</u> stick, and	<u>does</u>*n't know what to*	<u>do</u>.

Conversely, there is a slowing-down effect when two beats occur with no unstressed syllables between them, as in:

1	2	3	4
<u>Do</u> you know	<u>what</u>? said	*<u>Mad</u>*	<u>Mi</u>ckey
1	2	3	4
I <u>sat</u> in some	<u>glue</u> and I	<u>feel</u> all	<u>sticky</u>.[13]

Stress verse has many characteristics in common with music, which foot verse does not. It can be assigned a time signature indicating the number of beats to a line, and syllable length varies in a way analogous to the length variation between musical notes (quavers, crotchets, minims, etc.). Stress verse is also distinguished by rests (R)—similar to musical rests—in which the speaker must pause while the beat falls, but no words are spoken. In the 18th and 19th centuries it was widely believed that the phylogenetic origin of language was in music (Downing 1995; Humboldt [1836] 1988:60). Though to go this far seems fanciful, it is perhaps less far-fetched to suggest that this convergence of the two in the rhymes of infancy indicates at least a common *onto*genetic point of departure for both.

Confused attempts to read English nursery rhymes as foot verse (Guéron 1974) have obscured the simplicity of these rhythms used in children's verse, and also the extraordinarily widespread occurrence of one particular verse form: the 16-beat children's verse in 4/4 time.[14] This is not only the norm for nursery rhymes in English; it is also found among very diverse languages and cultures. Burling (1966), for example, found the form in a wide range of languages, including Arabic, Bengkulu (a Malayo-Polynesian language), Mandarin Chinese, Serrano (a North American language), Trukese and Ponupean (two Micronesian languages), and Yoruba. The duration of a four-beat line is approximately three seconds: a length which research by Turner (1992:76) suggests is universal in the canonical verse forms of all cultures! Such evidence points not only to a possibly innate basis for a general response to stress verse, but to something much more specific: an innate predilection for four lines of 4/4 stress verse.[15]

Whether or not this form is universal or innate, it is certainly widespread and enduring. In English, testimony to the apparently irrepressible appeal of this form is not only its occurrence in traditional rhymes, but also its constant *re*currence in the most popular writing for under-fives, as well as in the creations of older children themselves.[16] Commercially successful children's writers make frequent use of the form. Britain's best-selling children's authors, Janet and Allen Ahlberg, for example, are particularly fond of it— and perhaps this predilection is a major factor in their success.[17] To give one instance out of many, their book *Peepo* (chronicling in verse the routine of a baby in the 1940s) begins

> Here's a little baby, One, two, three,
> Stands in his cot, What does he see?
> He sees his father sleeping In the big brass bed
> And his mother too With a hairnet on her head

It continues in this regular form throughout.[18] Rhymes invented by children themselves also use this verse form, including those whose scatological or sexual impropriety confirms that they are the children's own creation. They exploit the 16-beat form for parody and subversion, as the ribaldry of the playground replaces the innocence of the traditional pre-school rhymes heard at home (Opie 1993):

> Buffalo Billy had a ten-foot willy
> He showed it to the girl next door　　(R)
> She thought it was a snake, and hit it with a rake
> And now it's only five foot four.[19]　　(R)

(Here, as in 'This Little Pig', the rests at the end of a line must be counted as a beat.)

It is interesting to speculate as to why this particular form is so widespread. The rhythm is simple, of course, and for that reason easier for young children to discern; but we should beware of dismissing it too glibly with this explanation. The causality can even be reversed. Is it that, because it is simple, we easily connect with it, or that because we connect with it, it appears to be simple? The question remains as to why children respond to this rhythm (and indeed to rhythm in general) so readily, and with so much enjoyment. The speculation that they are innately disposed to do so leads only to the further question of why this should be.

For the child, as we have seen, one function of rhythm may be to provide a path into language. Frederick Turner (1992), reviewing evidence that verse rhythms stimulate the brain to release pleasurable endorphins, comments that this phenomenon suggests that our liking for verse has other advantages for our species, which continue into adulthood.

> The brain (. . .) is able to reward itself for certain activities which are, presumably, preferred for their adaptive utility.
> (*op. cit.*: 68)

Among such advantages, he suggests, are an increased ability for social co-ordination and an increase in memory power. It may also be, he argues, that as rhythmic language apparently stimulates a greater co-ordination of the left and right hemispheres of the brain, thus integrating cognitive capacities which are unevenly distributed between the two, it enables richer cerebral activity.

Rhythm is a prominent and constitutive feature of dance, music, and language; in children's verse these three vehicles of rhythm often occur together. Although adults frequently use and perceive the three separately, we may suppose that for very young children, the boundaries are not so clear. As already remarked, for the baby, verses such as 'This Little Pig' and 'Round and Round the Garden' are only sound, rhythm, melody, and interaction. Like dance, and like many rhymes used by older children, they are often accompanied by set sequences of movements (Opie and Opie 1985). As many have argued (Raffman 1993), the ability to discriminate certain musical intervals, harmonies, and rhythms (including the 4/4 rhythm) appears, like the ability to distinguish speech sounds, to have an innate basis.

It may even be that a specialized mental module endows us with the principles of a 'generative grammar' of music (Lerdahl and Jackendoff 1983) comparable to the language module posited by Chomsky. A predilection to enjoy and participate in dance is similarly universal.

Like the four-line, four-beat verse, some instances of musical universals used by children may be surprisingly very particular. The composer Leonard Bernstein (1976:16), arguing eloquently for the comparability of musical and linguistic structures, suggests an innate basis for a particular melody which occurs in children's taunts, which he claims to be universal. An example is 'I'm the King of the Castle', sung as follows:

Figure 1.3: Children's taunt: 'I'm the King of the Castle'

Perhaps certain basic rhythms and melodies are the necessary opening to the development of more sophisticated and more culturally-specific variations in both music and language.

Of course, rhythm is not only a feature of dance, music, and verse. It is an intrinsic part of our internal and external lives. It is with us pre-natally, in the regularity of our mothers' heartbeats, and immediately post-natally in the rhythms of sucking and rocking. In later life, it continues in the rhythms of heartbeat, breathing, sexual climax, and giving birth (all rhythms which indicate or originate life). Such intrinsic rhythms seem to have been exploited to evolutionary advantage. Rhythm is a way of effecting co-ordinated action and augmenting a sense of fellowship, whether between individuals, among small groups or in large congregations—clearly an ability of immense importance to human societies. Without rhythm we should be unable to dance or declaim together, or enter into a whole range of activities which symbolize or actually effect social collaboration. There are rhythms in many ceremonies, parades, military drills, in manual work and in games. In language, rhythm continues to play a central part in some of the most emotive and socially significant discourse types: especially prayer, poetry, and song. Like play and games, the rhythms of these universal human activities are social, but also internally regulative. They allow us both to control and release our emotions. Rhythm is a source of comfort. In dance, chanting, poetry, and song, it may also alter the rhythms of our breathing, inducing both release of emotion and alteration of consciousness (Glucklich 1997:107–8).

The appeal of rhythm, therefore, seems to have its root in a realm common to music, dance, and language, and to human experience in general. Certain childhood rhythms and melodies are surprisingly common across cultures. Even if not universal, their widespread occurrence suggests an innate disposition in the child both to perceive them and to like them. The child's passage from a quasi-musical appreciation of verses into an appreciation of these same verses as language, and a gradual growing understanding of what they mean, may come about through this response. Thus the child is already endowed with an ability to respond to the patterned-sound end of the spectrum. At the pragmatic end, there may also be exploitation of innate mechanisms. Locke (1993: 49–55) argues that a disposition to eye contact and facial recognition is neurologically 'hard-wired', while the universal predilection for turn-taking is an inevitable consequence of a similarly instinctive need for carer and baby to elicit speech sounds from each other, with the result that one falls silent when the other speaks, and conversely starts to vocalize when the other is silent. Tickling rhymes are a pleasant way to maintain this contact. The child, in this view, already has an entry to both the sound patterns and the outcome of oral communication; the task is then to join them together. As we have seen in our analysis of 'This Little Pig', rhythms map on to linguistic structures in ways which, while they do not entirely explain how the child moves from one to the other, do show how verse may facilitate this process. Rhythm and interaction provide a pathway to language through existing gateways.

Early linguistic play

Let us now turn our attention to the reception of verses by children who are beginning to use and understand the structure and lexis of their language (say three-year-olds), and ask what they make of the verses to which they are exposed. In this, we may at times be considering the same verses that were used at an earlier stage, but on the assumption that, although the verse remains the same, the child's understanding of it has deepened and extended. Let us also stay for the time being with traditional nursery rhymes in English, since despite alarmist worries that children's culture is being eroded by the impact of new technologies and lifestyle, there is as yet no evidence that knowledge or use of them is in decline.[20] In addition, when new rhymes are produced, the most successful often imitate the traditional formulae. Though dealing with rhymes in English, I am assuming, as argued above, that the characteristic uses of both sound and meaning are in important aspects widespread if not universal in diverse languages and cultures.

Again, we must be careful not to confuse the adult perception of a rhyme in our speculation about what it is 'like' for the child. From an adult point of view, in addition to their rhymes and four-beat rhythms, the stories told in the traditional nursery rhymes have two very striking attributes. The first is that characters appear and incidents happen without either introduction, explanation, or consequence. The rhymes are like fragments of stories, sometimes even single sentences, unconnected to either a real or even a fictional world.

Diddle diddle dumpling my son John
Went to bed with his trousers on
One shoe off, and the other shoe on,
Diddle diddle dumpling my son John.

And that is all! But 'Who is John?' or 'Who are you?' or 'Why did he do this?', and 'So what?' are not questions which seem to trouble either the adult relayers of these rhymes, or the children who receive them. Yet such isolated, disconnected events and characters appearing without introduction are far from uncommon.

Hickory dickory dock,
The mouse ran up the clock,
The clock struck one, the mouse ran down,
Hickory dickory dock.

Lucy Locket lost her pocket,
Kitty Fisher found it,
There was not a penny in it,
But a ribbon round it.[21]

The second striking feature of English nursery rhymes, from the modern point of view, is that they often take place in a vanished rural world of black sheep and wool bags, shepherd boys and milkmaids, in which the children are busy haymaking, gathering nuts, and pig stealing, and in which a plum is a treat, fiddle music is entertainment, cats fall down wells, and naughty children are whipped.[22] It is a world very far removed from the experience of the majority of modern English-speaking children, and has been so for some considerable time. Even those rhymes with an urban setting, with their church bells and street cries, are as alien to the modern city as the hay fields of the rural ones.[23] These distinctive historical settings bring further obstacles to understanding, compounding those already posed by the fragmentary nature of the incidents. There is a good deal of obscure and archaic vocabulary: 'tuffet', 'curds and whey', 'hay cock', 'hot cross buns', 'pease pudding', 'fleece', 'ware',[24] as well as, even more confusingly, 'false-friend' words whose modern sense the child may already know, but in the past denoted something slightly different. How can you lose a 'pocket'? Why do you 'take off' 'the kettle'? And what is 'a sixpence'?[25] Significantly, children do not always ask for definitions or explanations (and if they do adults may not always be able to give them); yet this does not seem to spoil the pleasure and the worth of the rhymes.

The gap between the child's tolerance of the detached and unexplained meanings of nursery rhymes, and the adult's addiction to more solid and precise explanations, may explain the adult tendency to give credence to spurious historical explanations. Thus 'Ring-a-ring o' roses' is widely believed to be about the bubonic plague, with sneezing (Atishoo!) and a round red sore (the 'ring o' roses') being symptoms, and carrying 'a pocketful of posies' a preventative precaution. Similarly 'Oranges and Lemons' is believed to follow the churches in the same order that condemned criminals were led around London before they were hanged. In actuality, neither interpretation has any historical foundation, and both might be classed as 'urban myths' (Healey and Glanvill 1992). The plague interpretation of 'Ring-a-ring o' roses' owes its currency to an unfounded article in the *Radio Times*[26] rather than to any scholarly source (Opie and Opie 1985: 56, 221). Even where the rhyme does have a serious origin (as in the case of 'The Grand Old Duke of York', which was originally a political lampoon[27]) this does not matter to the child. Yet whatever the origin of a rhyme may or may not be, the important point is that such origins are of as little relevance to the function of the rhymes now as the etymology of a word is to its current meaning. They may lend an extra dimension, but the pleasure of the rhyme does not depend on it.

Why should this be? If the sense of the rhymes is not clear, if indeed they do not make much sense, what is their appeal, and what is the child experiencing when reciting or listening to them? There are, I think, two possible answers to this puzzle, depending on the child's stage of development. The first is that the child accepts the rhyme, or bits of it, as rhythmic sound without meaning. It does not need to make sense, either in whole or in part. From time to time some section may echo the language the child is beginning to use and understand for more sensible matters, but for the moment the rhyme is like music which only occasionally merges into language, as though one were listening to a general buzz of talk which only occasionally becomes clear. (It is rather like the adult language learner's experience of listening to conversation in the language they are in the process of learning.) In this interpretation, even after the child has begun to use speech to make sense, he or she still retains the capacity to revert to using it as mere sound, as older children do in gibberish verses. Even adults sometimes make use of speech sounds in this way, for example in scat singing in jazz, using such formulations as 'shooba dooba doo'.

A second possible answer is that the children *do* perceive the rhyme as meaningful language, but invest the words they do not understand with their own idiosyncratic interpretations, whether at the word level (visualizing 'a tuffet') or at the narrative level (imagining what sort of person Miss Muffett is, and her life before her encounter with the spider). It may be that the child moves gradually from one kind of understanding to another, and perhaps it is only when all the music has yielded to language that the fragmentary and unsatisfactory nature of the 'stories' becomes clear, the mystery of the verses vanishes, the child loses interest in them, and moves on to other things.

Rhymes and literacy

As we have seen, behind the pleasure which children take in rhymes may lie a more serious role in the acquisition of spoken language. In the early stages, rhymes draw attention to linguistic structures; at a later stage they also provide a kind of pleasurable half-way house between language as sound and language as the vehicle of relatively precise meaning. It has also been suggested that rhythm and rhyme may—at least for children acquiring English[28]—aid the entry into written language, by helping in the learning of alphabetic literacy (Cazden 1976: 605; Goswami 1995; Riley 1996: 28). In part, this is because of a general sensitivity to word and syllable segmentation and parallels which rhythm (by separating syllables) and rhyme (by separating phoneme sequences) help to create. In learning to write in English (in which there is a particularly irregular relation between phonology and graphology) there may be a more specific relation between aptitude for rhyming and for reading. Thus problems caused by the very considerable variation in pronunciation of letters and letter sequences can be considerably reduced by acquaintance with families of word endings, or 'rimes',[29] and the spelling sequences which sometimes reflect the spoken 'rhyme'. (The rhyme between '*Heat*' and '*Beat*', for example, is reflected in their identical rime (*-eat*).) Goswami, arguing the case for the relevance of rhyme to learning to read in English, makes the following observation:

> . . . the 17,602 words in the Carroll, Davis, and Richman (1971) word frequency corpus for children are made up of only 824 different rimes, 616 of which recur in word 'families'. In an early analysis of the 500 most frequently used words in primary reading books, it was shown that knowledge of only 37 rimes was sufficient to read all of them. This gives us a clue about the importance of rhyme for reading development in English. A focus on rhyme can significantly reduce the difficulty of the learning task for beginning readers, as the correspondence between the spelling sequences that represent rhymes and their sounds in spoken words is far more consistent than the correspondence between single alphabet letters and individual phonemes.
>
> (Goswami 1995: 67)

Studies of the relationship between the ability to recognize and produce spoken rhymes in children just beginning school and their later success in reading have shown a clear correlation between the two (Bradley and Bryant 1983), and development of sensitivity to rhyme has also proved effective in the teaching of dyslexics (Lovett *et al.*: 1990). Ability with rhyme and rhythm, then, apparently an oral and aural skill, turns out to be an aid to, even a precondition, of literacy. The language development of the child in a literate society cannot be neatly divided into the acquisition of speech followed by the learning of reading and writing, as though they were two quite separate stages. Even before the initial encounter with writing the child is being primed for literacy; and verse may be part of that priming. Approaches to first language acquisition which, in the tradition of linguistics, regard spoken language as primary and reading and writing as only secondary (de Saussure [1915] 1983:15; Bloomfield [1933] 1935:21) tend to overlook this significant role of verse.

The functions of verse: answered and unanswered questions

The traditional nursery rhymes, then, seem to have a number of functions which may partly account for their wide appeal. They bring adult carer and children into contact, even before the child can understand what is being said, thus satisfying an innate need for spoken interaction (Locke 1993:7–8, 217–56), by exploiting an apparently equally innate response to rhythm (Turner 1992). They help the child to identify significant linguistic units, and effect the phonemic, syllabic, lexical and grammatical segmentation which is a prerequisite of language acquisition. By foregrounding formal patterning, it may be that they enable the child to learn aspects of language consecutively rather than simultaneously. The rhymes, it could be argued, draw attention to the formal level first, and then bring meaning into focus by association with it, almost as a kind of after-effect.

In general, verse may help the child to gain control over difficult new language and ideas. The regular rhythm and predictable rhymes may act as a kind of repository for the unknown words and fleeting images whose vagueness allows greater freedom to imaginative and idiosyncratic interpretations. The very regularity and predictability of the verse creates a necessary counterbalance to the extreme unpredictability—and consequently the slipperiness in memory—of the language and the meanings which it carries.

The role of verse in developing both spoken and written language, however, cannot account entirely for its popularity and ubiquity. Both children and adults continue to take an unreasonable pleasure in verse, long after they have mastered a language's phonemic, syllabic, grammatical, and orthographic systems. One possible explanation is that verse is the remnant of a mnemonic device, now partly superseded by literacy, whose usefulness during the longer part of human history has led to a profound liking for it in our species. For just as the words of a song may be called to mind by humming the tune, thus allowing us to pass over any gaps in memory, so the same feat of recall may be accomplished through verse. Yet although the functions of verse may be partly to do with acquisition, and its attractiveness a remnant of its prehistoric usefulness, this is not to say that it is to be accounted for in this way entirely. The question remains of why we, modern adults, still like it so much. We shall return to this central question in later chapters. For now, let us turn to another salient feature of the language which children receive—one which also remains dominant in adult discourse: repetition.

Repetition

Repetition permeates the child's language environment, whether it be at the micro level of the repeated beat of stress-time verse (for rhythm is, by definition, based upon repetition) or at the macro level of the entire discourse (watching the same video, or repeating the same rhyme or joke *ad nauseam*). Between these two poles, there is repetition at every linguistic and discoursal level: of phonemes, of syllables, of grammatical structures, of events within a story, and of elements of stories within a given genre (Propp [1928] 1968).

In very general terms, the dominant focus of repetition moves through the levels of language as the child grows older: from rhythm, to sound, to grammar, to meaning (though this is not to say, of course, that at later ages we lose our attraction to any of these levels). As we have seen, it is rhyme and rhythm which are foregrounded in verses for very young children. Interest in riddles, on the other hand, which focuses attention upon ambiguity and obscurity of meaning, peaks at about the age of eight (Sutton-Smith 1979). Between these two ages, many stories (let us say for 4–5 year-olds) are distinguished by sequences in which there is marked repetition of grammatical structures with only minimal lexical substitutions.

What big	eyes	you've got grandma.	All the better to	see	you with.
What big	ears	you've got grandma.	All the better to	hear	you with.
What big	paws	you've got grandma.	All the better to	stroke	you with.
What big	teeth	you've got grandma.	All the better to	eat	you with.

or

Somebody has been eating my porridge, said Father	Bear in a great,	gruff, growling	voice.
Somebody has been eating my porridge, said Mother	Bear in a mellow,	middle-sized	voice.
Somebody has been eating my porridge, said Baby	Bear in a squeaky,	little	voice.

Such sequences (uncannily similar to the substitution tables used as exercises in structural language teaching) entail both the repetition of rhythm, on the one hand, and the repetition of fictional events on the other. They create rhythm because the repeated elements maintain the same stress patterns; they create a repetition of events because the repeated elements inevitably share meaning as well as structure.

Like the 16-beat verse, they also occur cross-culturally and cross-linguistically, both in enduring traditional stories and in modern writing. This, for example, is a Fulani rhyme from West Africa:

| If a jackal | bothers you, show him a | hyena, |
| If a hyena | bothers you, show him a | lion, |

If a lion	bothers you, show him an	elephant,
If an elephant	bothers you, show him a	hunter,
If a hunter	bothers you, show him a	snake,
If a snake	bothers you, show him a	stick,
If a stick	bothers you, show it a	fire,
If a fire	bothers you, show it a	river,
If a river	bothers you, show it a	wind,
If a wind	bothers you, show it	God.

(Traditional Fulani, translated and cited by Bisong 1995)

And this is the conclusion of a traditional Russian folk tale about a giant turnip which will not easily come out of the earth.[30]

The mouse	grabbed	the cat
The cat	grabbed	Zhuchka the dog
Zhuchka the dog	grabbed	the granddaughter
The granddaughter	grabbed	Grandma
Grandma	grabbed	Grandad

They all pulled and pulled
and the turnip came out of the earth.

Children seem to enjoy such repeated and predictable structures. They do not find them tedious.

Yet repetition at any level is almost always only partial. Beats repeat, but the syllables between them, and thus the speed of delivery, vary. A rhymed word is partly like, but partly unlike, its partner. As in the examples above, many repetitions of word sequences contain slight variations, which from the child's point of view, may aid the perception of abstract linguistic categories. Even where repetition is exact, the self-same sequences of words take on new meanings in new circumstances, or in the light of what has been done or said before.[31] In *Snow White*, for example, when the Wicked Queen interrogates her magic mirror for the second time, she asks the same question ('Who is the fairest of them all?') and receives the same answer ('Snow White'), but the significance has changed radically, because on the second occasion she believes her rival to be dead. Even when an entire text is repeated, it is not exactly the same as on the previous rendering. This is not only because no two live performances can ever be the same. Even in the repetition of recorded language on video or cassette, new details are noticed, new words emerge clearly, characters appear in a different light, and so on.

Repetition has both a personal dimension, as texts are repeated by or for one individual, and an interpersonal one, as they pass from one individual to another. It has both a diachronic dimension, as texts are handed on from one generation to the next, and a synchronic one, as texts spread through a society, between one society and another, or from one language to another. As texts are repeated along all of these dimensions, the degree to which they

change also varies. Sometimes the change is radical, as when an orally transmitted traditional tale is committed to paper, or a literary tale reconstituted
as a cartoon video. Yet even where both words and medium remain the same,
changes of context will ensure that the same *text* is interpreted significantly
differently—that is as different *discourses*—by different listeners (Widdowson
1979: 98).

In the child's life verbatim repetition is by no means exclusive to language
play. It is also a characteristic of highly functional events in the child's life,
such as eating breakfast, going to bed, or getting ready for school. Yet in such
cases it is partly motivated, too, by the rhythm of non-linguistic events, such
as the recurrence of a need to eat in the morning, and so on—rather as the
rhythm of skipping rhymes is motivated by the beat of the rope, or as the
rhythm of verse seems to mirror the necessary rhythms of our bodies. In
other words, where repetition is linked to some accompanying non-linguistic
activity, this fact may provide some partial explanation of it; repetition is
harder to explain in apparently non-functional texts such as stories and
verses, where it seems to exist for its own sake.

The wider role of repetition

As in the case of rhythm and rhyme, it is true that parallelisms at other
linguistic levels have a clear potential to aid language acquisition, and that
their existence can be explained in this way. Grammatical parallelism isolates
units, and shows the repeated structure operating with different components
and with increasing complexity. The very act of repetition also allows greater
time for processing, and creates a generally more secure and relaxed (because
it is more predictable) atmosphere which may aid receptivity. Lexical
substitution in grammatically parallel structures both segments and draws
attention to individual words, while also illustrating their occurrence in
common collocations and colligations. It allows words to be learnt by the
child within a linguistic and discourse context. It also provides an opportunity
for re-exposure (both within the story and as the story is repeated) which is
neither forced nor uninteresting.

Yet we should beware of ever dismissing repetition, any more than rhythm,
as *only* an aid to language acquisition. Though particularly salient in the
playful language of children, it is by no means peculiar to it, and we need also
to account for its continuing presence in the most widely distributed and
highly valued adult discourses. Prayers, liturgies, ceremonies, songs, advertisements, jokes, poems, films, and stories are repeated verbatim; typically they
also contain internal repetition in rhythm, phonological and grammatical
parallelisms, and recurring sections. It may be that the parallelism in these
genres creates an emotionally reassuring association with childhood; but
again this is not necessarily a sufficient explanation for the pleasure which
they give us.

The shift towards meaning

Although in children's verses the linguist or literary critic may see and analyse patterns of rhythm, repetition, and grammatical parallelism, children themselves as they grow older are increasingly likely to see these verses as telling stories, creating images, and/or (in the case of gibberish rhymes) as a means of social interaction—as part of a game, or a joke, an expression of affection or anger, or a demonstration of skill. In this, even more than adults, they display an automatic tendency to focus their attention away from form, and towards semantic reference and pragmatic force. Yet despite this preferential attention to meaning, there is a very particular relationship between the patterning of form, and the creation of imaginary worlds. As with verse, though the phenomenon is particularly evident in children, it is by no means peculiar to them. It is to this relationship between play with language forms and the creation of fictions, and to the role which imaginary worlds play in the lives of both children and adults, that we turn in the next chapter.

Notes

1 For example, in *The CHILDES database of children's language* (McWhinney 1996), which collates data from a large number of researchers, almost all transcriptions are of conversational dialogues between children and adults, or among children.
2 A person silently listening is involved in communication and interaction, even if their responses are not externalized. The monologue to which they are listening, moreover, is likely to be structured interactively, attempting to predict their knowledge, perception, and processing (Widdowson 1978:25–6).
3 Nelson (1989:13) notes with some surprise the dearth of linguistics studies of child monologues between Weir's 1962 collection and her own.
4 The point that salient or repeated texts may need some kind of extra weighting in a corpus has been made by corpus linguists themselves (Francis 1979; Stubbs 1996:11).
5 This is not to say that there is no empirical evidence of any kind to support a selection of texts for consideration, and in this chapter—as throughout the book—I use instances of texts which are widely distributed and known, frequently repeated, and much admired. In this, I have assumed that, even in the modern commercial world of high-pressure marketing, there is some relation between the distribution, knowledge, and popularity of texts, and their importance in the lives of their receivers; that best-selling texts are not just foisted upon the population, but have some bearing upon the likes and dislikes of the people who use them.

6 Some speakers of this rhyme (including myself) say 'piggy' instead of 'pig'. I have preferred 'pig', since it is the version given in many citations and anthologies (for example, Burling 1966; Opie and Opie 1955).

7 For a commentary on studies of the development of phonological discrimination in preverbal children see Locke 1993 : 168–72.

8 The last syllable, selecting the child to be excluded from the circle, falls—one might say iconically—outside the regular scheme.

9 In this it resembles the most famous gibberish rhyme in the English language, Lewis Carroll's Jabberwocky, which while lexically innovative with open class words (brillig, slithy, toves, etc.), uses existing closed class words (and, the, did, in, etc.), and conforms both to the grammar of English and the phonology.

10 Quoted in Jakobson 1960.

11 The term also applies to verse based on patterns of syllable length. Both the term 'foot' (Latin pes; Greek πους) and the names of various types of feet are borrowed from Classical Latin and Greek. As in traditional English grammar, categories not wholly suitable to English have been imposed by classical scholars. Ironically (considering the contrast between foot and stress verse) the use of the Greek word for foot in scansion referred to the tapping of the foot on the floor in time to the beat (SOED).

12 Alternatively, as with many instances of such verses, it is possible to say 'Round and Round the Garden' more slowly in 2/4 time, with half the number of stresses, making it an 8- rather than 16-beat verse. In the 4/4 reading, there is a melodramatic and portentous slowing down on the successive beats of the third line, followed by a scope for acceleration in the fourth line, as the extra syllables are squashed up to keep the rhythm. In the 2/2 reading, the unstressed syllables of the last line are even faster, iconically capturing the surprise movement away from the hand.

13 From the poem 'Messing About' ('Fooling Around') in Under the Bed by Michael Rosen.

14 'This little pig' is 16 beats if one ignores the last line, where the rhythm collapses; 'Round and round the garden' is 16 beats if one chooses—as I have—the faster beat. Even if the reader is not convinced by these examples, any collection of traditional English nursery rhymes will confirm the frequency of the 16-beat form.

15 The word 'line' may seem to be a description applicable only to writing, but there is a spoken equivalent of the line-break in simple verse forms, which is indicated by a pause and drawing of breath.

16 We should not be surprised that a stress verse reading is the most suitable for the English nursery rhymes because—like them—it has a long history in English. It was the metre used in alliterative Anglo-Saxon poetry, and in many ballads and other folk forms; it is still used in many forms of popular verse today, such as the limerick. In modern times it has been revived and elaborated as 'sprung rhythm' in the poetry of Gerard

Manley Hopkins (Hobsbaum 1996 : 53–70).

17 Since the death of Janet Ahlberg, Allen Ahlberg has continued to publish on his own. He is one of the 16 authors (for both children and adults) with over one million loans a year from public libraries.

18 Even when the Ahlbergs' writing is set out in prose, it often lends itself to reading in this style. In an alliteratively titled series of books (which includes in Mr Tick the Teacher, the UK's single best-selling children's title) frequent use is made of this form.

> Mr Creep the Crook was a bad man. Mrs Creep the Crook was a bad woman. Miss Creep and Master Creep were bad children, and 'Growler Creep' was a bad dog.

19 This rhyme, which I first heard in my primary school in the mid-1950s, was recently recited to me by a six-year-old boy. So it has survived, at least for a while, the introduction of metric measurement to Britain.

20 As shown by high sales of nursery rhyme collections (Source: Booktrack). A similar point is made by the Opies about children's own lore in their introduction to The Lore and Language of Schoolchildren (Opie and Opie 1959).

21 The original verison of 'Lucy Locket' (first published in 1777) had an additional stanza, now usually omitted as unsuitable, beginning 'Dolly Bushel let a fart' (Opie and Opie 1997b).

22 From 'Baa Baa Black Sheep', 'Little Boy Blue', 'Where Are You Going To My Pretty Maid?', 'Lavender's Blue', 'Nuts in May', 'Tom Tom The Piper's Son', 'Little Jack Horner', 'Old King Cole', 'Ding Dong Bell', 'Jack and Jill'. The penultimate stanza of 'Jack and Jill', describing how Jill was whipped by her mother 'for laughing at Jack's disaster', is now usually omitted from anthologies. It can be found in Opie and Opie 1955 : 42.

23 From 'Oranges and Lemons'; for a number of 'street song' nursery rhymes see Opie and Opie 1955: 72–3.

24 From 'Little Miss Muffet', 'Hot Cross Buns', 'Pease Pudding Hot', 'Mary Had a Little Lamb', 'Simple Simon'.

25 From 'Lucy Locket', 'Polly Put the Kettle On', 'Sing a Song of Sixpence'.

26 7 June 1973.

27 On the vanity and indecisiveness of Frederick Duke of York (1763–1827), second son of George III.

28 Research to date on other languages using alphabetic writing (German, Italian, Swedish) does not suggest that awareness of rhyme in pre-school children predicts later reading ability in these languages in the way that it does for English (Goswami 1997).

29 The 'rime' of a word is the part which follows the initial consonant cluster, or 'onset'. If there is no initial consonant cluster, then the 'rime' is the whole word. Words are thus divided into onset and rime as follows:

w-ool, f-ull; st-ar, are; C-ole, s-oul, h-e, thr-ee. Clearly, there is a very close relationship between rime and rhyme, although it is not a one-to-one relationship, as the rhyme may employ only part of the rime, as in a rhyme like 'wishing' and 'wanting', the rhyme of 'lane' and 'dame' in 'Baa Baa Black Sheep', or the rhyme of 'hippopotamus' with 'firm to us' in

> The broad backed hippopotamus
> Rests on his belly in the mud;
> Although he seems so firm to us
> He is merely flesh and blood.
> (From T. S. Eliot, The Hippopotamus)

30 The original Russian and Fulani have the equivalent grammatical parallelism.
31 In adult literature, perhaps, the epitome of such a change is the repeated 'And Brutus is an honourable man', in Mark Antony's funeral oration for Caesar in Shakespeare's *Julius Caesar*, III. ii. 79–111.

2 The meanings of language play: imaginary worlds

Shame on you, Comrade Chukovsky, for filling the heads of our children with all kinds of nonsense, such as that trees grow shoes. (...) Why do you distort realistic facts? Children need socially useful information and not fantastic stories about white bears who cry cock-a-doodle-doo.
(Letter written to the children's author Kornei Chukovsky, quoted in Chukovsky [1928] 1963)

It is significant that in many public libraries more space is devoted to 'fiction' rather than to 'fact'. There is surely a deep biological reason for the importance of fiction: that it states and considers alternative possible realities—allowing escape from the prison of current facts. (Gregory [1974] 1977)

Adults and children alike devote a large amount of time and thought to imaginary characters, situations, and events. We do this in a multitude of forms. There is children's play and adult fantasy. There are fictional narratives created entirely through language, such as novels, and short stories; there are fictional narratives which mix language with images, sounds, and music, such as film, opera, theatre, and television drama; and fictional narratives which involve no language at all, such as mime or ballet. There are the static images of some paintings and photographs which depict imaginary situations and events. There is acting, dressing up, and disguise. There are false beliefs and hallucinations (considered imaginary by some and real by others). Indeed, if we were to make our catalogue complete, we might include wishes and lies, and all hypothetical thinking and speculation: every thought and utterance about what might be or might have been, rather than what is.

The extent of this devotion of resources to the imaginary is only partly measurable. In the case of novels and television dramas, there are sales and audience statistics. We know, for example, that in Britain, well over 24 million fictional books are sold each year,[1] and that each week over 18 million people (one third of the population) watch the soap opera *EastEnders*.[2] Yet even in cases of public distribution and observable behaviour, quantification is not always straightforward. There are many books and programmes which occupy an intermediate area between fact and fiction.[3] In the case of more private or internalized imaginary worlds, such as those of children's play or adult fantasy, any exact measurement of the time devoted to them is impossible. Here it is not only that there are too many borderline cases, but that the frequently private nature of these activities creates too many obstacles to observation. There is certainly no way of quantifying lies and hypothetical speculations. The impossibility of precise statistics need not deter us, however. Both intuition and experience testify to the extent of all these modes of thought and behaviour. Children very conspicuously and spontaneously devote a great deal of time to make-believe and stories (whether of their own creation or in those presented to them), but adults by no means lose this inclination, and gravitate towards their own kinds of imaginary world—in the shape of fiction and fantasy—almost whenever they have time. One might speculate that, had adults the same amount of free time as children, they might spend as much time as children in this pursuit.

It would not be appropriate to deal with all aspects of imagination here. Yet we do need to consider language play in the context of imaginative thought in general, and in particular the relationship between the manipulation of linguistic forms and the generation of hypothetical realities. This chapter focuses on the imaginary worlds which are created largely or entirely through language, and may in some sense be regarded as entertainment. I shall refer to these as fictions (whether they are verse or prose, spoken, or written) and consider them all to be a species of language play, in the sense that many of them are enjoyable and popular, but apparently unnecessary to the day-to-day business of survival. As I hope will become apparent as the chapter proceeds, there are many other ways in which fiction can validly be regarded as a type of play—although, if we are to compare it with games, our experience may in many ways be more like that of an onlooker than a participant (Britton 1977).

As so often in the study of language play, there is a fuzzy boundary between verbal and non-verbal activity, and between those activities which we regard as essential and those we regard as extraneous to our survival. A further complication is that, while fictions are playful in the sense of being both superfluous and entertaining, many are also taken very seriously; some are deeply depressing or upsetting; some are considered among the greatest human achievements, and the best provide insights into the human condition which have generally proved far more durable than records of facts (such as historical chronicles) or attempts to capture the nature of reality (such as scientific descriptions and theories).

Fiction is certainly a major use of adult language—both quantitatively, in terms of the amount of time devoted to it, and qualitatively in terms of the importance attached to it. At present, the major source of adult fiction is watching television. In the industrialized world, this is now the greatest use of time after sleeping and working. In Britain, for example, almost 100% of the population watch television regularly, and the average daily viewing time (with some considerable variation among social groups) is between three and four hours (Argyle 1996: 36). Although a good deal of television time is taken up with news, discussions, and documentaries, an even larger and by far more popular part is taken up with fictional stories such as films and situation comedies, and the single most popular genre of TV programme is the soap opera (*ibid.*: 37). Yet television is by no means the only source of fiction, and it has not supplanted the demand for fiction in print and at the cinema. Almost the entire output of the film industry, by far the most profitable part of the book industry,[4] and a large number of computer games and Internet sites, are fiction. It is no exaggeration to say that all the major media are devoted to fiction.

Such an obsession demands explanation, and it is the aim of this chapter—I hope not over-ambitiously—to move towards one. In general, I shall do this by considering fictions which operate through language only, though at the end of this chapter I shall briefly consider some aspects of the relation of language and the moving image in fictions for children on film and television. The task is not helped by a general academic blindness to the issue. Strangely, considering the immense allocation of language and thought to fiction, psychology and linguistics have comparatively little to say on the matter, and fiction is certainly not central to their concerns. The few psychologists and linguists who have addressed the issue confirm this neglect. Gregory ([1974] 1977) expressed the view that it is the external physical world which is structured by real events, while the mind is largely occupied with hypothetical ones. He advocated a new paradigm for psychology as 'a science of fiction' in which it would

> consider behaviour as being largely controlled by fiction. (. . .) This would make psychology something of an unnatural science; but this may be its true relation to physics.
> (Gregory [1974] 1977)

In psychology 25 years later, however, there is no sign of this radical suggestion gaining ground.[5] In linguistics (especially stylistics) and in literary criticism and media studies, although there is no shortage of works *about* fiction, the question of *why* it exists is rarely posed.[6] For serious speculation on this question, it is to two different and apparently opposite sources that we need to turn. The first is to writers of fiction themselves—and later in this chapter we shall look more closely at the views of two writers in more detail. A second source, perhaps surprisingly, is evolutionary theory, where a realization of the immense role played by fiction in human life is leading evolutionary theorists to take a serious (if sometimes somewhat naive) interest, rather than dismissing it as 'mere aesthetics' and therefore the academic property of the arts (Pinker [1997] 1998: 538–45). In response, some aestheticians, linguists, and literary theorists have used insights from evolutionary theory both to address the question of the function of fiction and to hazard answers (Dissanayake 1988; Carroll 1995; Dunbar 1996). In retrospect, this development seems hardly surprising. Given that an obsession with fiction is so characteristic of our species, it may in future seem extraordinary that psychologists, biologists, and evolutionary theorists ever ignored an explanation of its origin and function as a major challenge for their disciplines.

Ironically, some of the reasons for this neglect of fiction in the so-called human sciences may be ideological rather than scientific. The concentration of linguistics and psychology upon language used for practical and transactional activity may be inspired more by the work ethic, and the notion that science should deal with useful facts rather than frivolous fictions, than by observation of what humans actually use language for, or which aspects of that use are most important to them. (That fiction is a fact of mental life, and that there can be facts about it even though it is not factual itself, seems to have been overlooked.) In addition, perhaps, adults wish to emphasize the differences between their own behaviour and that of children, rather than the similarities.

The result is a fragmentation of the study of imaginative behaviour which obscures both its extent and its identity. Fiction is cordoned off in 'the arts'; child make-believe has been the domain of psychology. Linguistics shows interest in these areas only indirectly, in stylistic analysis of literature and in studies of child language. At a time when the dominant paradigms see language either as an abstract system divorced from meaning, in the case of Chomskyan formalism, or, in the case of Hallidayan functionalism, as a social semiotic, it is perhaps inevitable that the internalized use of language as a means of hypothetical thought and self-regulation receives short shrift.

Relatives of fiction

Before directly addressing the issue of the function of fiction, and its relation to linguistic form, let us briefly look at two other types of imaginative activity which bear a very close relationship to it: make-believe and fantasy. By gaining some insight into what they share with fiction, on the one hand, and how they differ from it on the other—and in particular how they do or do not depend on language—we may be better placed to consider the particular place of fiction in language play.

Make-believe

By make-believe, I mean the acting-out of an imaginary world by behaving as a character in it, and often by dressing up as one, too. As such, it is largely the property of children, although it also features in adult activities such as charades, fancy-dress balls, and carnivals. Adult dramatic improvisation, and perhaps even dramatic performance and ritual, might also be put under this heading. Make-believe is very likely to involve language, as children suggest to each other what form the imaginary world might take, negotiate who is to do what, and then speak to each other in character. Even children playing alone employ language in their make-believes,[7] although as they grow older and more self-conscious they may be less inclined to do so, leading us to regard the disappearance of solitary make-believe as one indication of childhood's end. For children, there is a substantial overlap between fiction and make-believe, although while the former persists into adulthood, the latter disappears.

Fantasy

By fantasy I mean imaginary events which are created in the mind but not shared with others. To the extent that adult fantasy may be verbal—involving imaginary conversations, or even being realized in words—it should come under the heading of language play. I shall treat it as an adult phenomenon, on the grounds that in children it is likely to merge into make-believe. Indeed, to a degree it could be regarded as a substitution for make-believe, without the external manifestations, and involving more adult topics. It also bears an interesting relation to fiction, and for the adult story-teller, it might even be a prelude to creation.

A key difference between fantasy, on the one hand, and make-believe and fiction, on the other, is that fantasy, almost by definition, is not social, and for this reason is less likely to be structured or articulated in a way which is clear to a second party. (In the play of very young children there is a similar lack of accommodation to others.) Although it is universal among adults, and indeed takes up a good deal of our time, it is also a source of embarrassment. Its nature changes as soon as it is made public, for a shared fantasy is in some sense no longer a fantasy, and becomes, by being shared, a fiction or a game. On the other hand, it may not always be as internalized as we should like to believe. There are times when adults, thinking themselves to be alone or unobserved, can be heard to speak, or at least seen to mouth the words of their fantasy conversations. We have all, perhaps, had embarrassing experiences in this respect.

Though dismissed, denied, and disguised, fantasy is certainly taken seriously by psychologists, and of course psychoanalysts, though—significantly— more for the insight it offers into mental illness than for its role in normal life. As studies suggest that the majority of 'normal' fantasy is predominantly of imaginary sexual encounters, imaginary successes (such as winning the lottery), or imagined conflictual conversations in which the fantasizer gains victory over his or her opponents (Klinger 1971; Singer 1975: 55–6), it is worth noting that internally they act out competitive scenarios similar to those externalized in many games.

The relation of make-believe and fantasy to fiction

One way of conceiving how fiction is related to make-believe and fantasy, on the one hand, and to reality itself, on the other, is to regard it as, in the words of James Britton (1977), 'a third area' between the two. If the child and the adult are instinctively impelled to detach themselves from reality in make-believe and fantasy, then fiction forms a bridge between them:

> The essential purpose of activity in this area for the individual will be to relate for himself inner necessity with the demands of the external world.

This bridging is aided by the fact that, while in both make-believe and fantasy we are participants, in fiction we are—as it were—spectators at the game rather than players (Harding 1977). In this sense, assuming that it can be educational, fiction instantiates a sophisticated extension of a peculiarly human ability, termed 'meta-play' by Reynolds (1972), which is to learn by watching the play of other individuals, rather than by playing ourselves. Contrary to much current educational thinking, especially in language teaching theory, vicarious experience and passive observation may be more conducive to certain types of learning than active participation, allowing the benefits of greater detachment, objectivity, and reflection, free from the pressure of having to take local moment-by-moment decisions—hence the great popularity of both spectator sports and fiction.

The functions of imaginary worlds

Traditionally, the question of what function these imaginative flights might perform—assuming that there is one—has been most frequently asked about the games and make-believe of children, as though the role of imagination in childhood was quite different from that in adulthood. What I am trying to suggest here, however, is that while there may be some functions of imaginative activity which are peculiar to children, there are others which continue throughout life. Indeed, if we accept the view that children's make-believe transmutes into adult fantasy (Klinger 1971), and consider that fiction appeals to all ages, then there may be less difference than commonly supposed (other than the time and social status accorded to them) between the imaginative behaviour of adults and children. Where explanations are offered of the role of fiction for children, we should consider (unless there is good reason not to) that they may apply to adults too.

If we were to confine ourselves to children, however, the central question about fiction could be posed as follows. Why do not children, when there is time to spare, simply do nothing, or use the time to find out about the actual world, rather than watching or reading stories about animals who talk, witches who weave spells, carpets which fly through the air, or—in more 'realist' fiction—people and situations which, though plausible, do not exist?

As members of the most intelligent species, children have a lot to learn. They also have a lot of free time, and a good deal of surplus energy, since their basic needs are taken care of by others. At first glance, it does not seem to make sense that at this crucial stage of life we humans should devote so much of our time and energy to learning 'fictional facts', such as what happened on Grey Rabbit's birthday, rather than actual ones about, say, the life cycle and behaviour of real rabbits. If, as evolutionary theorists argue, human behaviour reflects the needs of hunter-gatherer societies, then, as far as rabbits are concerned, it would be more useful to learn how to catch them and cook them—or in the case of the modern child, where to find them on the supermarket shelves.

The same question may be asked of adult behaviour, though to a lesser extent and with qualification. Adults may still benefit from the learning of new facts, though their need to do this—at least in times of social stability—is likely to be less pressing. They have less free time and energy, having expended both in meeting the pressures of survival, and for this very reason may need fiction as a source of escapism, relaxation, and wish-fulfilment.

Service and creativity explanations

I want to suggest that, as a starting-point for both children and adults, we might posit two types of explanation of the human need for fiction.

The first type, which I shall call 'service explanations', identifies fiction as a disguised form of more straightforwardly functional and educational uses of language. It explains fiction away, as it were, by saying that although language is being used to refer to states of affairs which do not exist, this enables the recipient to find out more—albeit indirectly—about the actual world. Such explanations are examples of what the influential play theorist Johan Huizinga ([1944] 1949) refers to—critically—as the idea 'that play must serve something which is *not* play, that it must have some kind of biological purpose'.

The second type, which I shall call 'creativity explanations', is larger and more ambitious. It sees fiction not as an aid to other functions, but as the origin and condition of distinctly human modes of thought, enabling such activities as science, art, and religion. Widdowson (1992a: 77) suggests a similar function for literature when he writes of it as 'recreation' in a sense derived from the word's etymology: re-creation. Creativity explanations bear out Huizinga's notion of play 'as a concept [which] cannot be reduced to any other mental category'. In them, fiction is no longer regarded as the servant of our ability to carry out everyday operations—operations which, though more complex, are similar to those carried out by animals—nor as a subordinate activity to be indulged when other 'necessary' ones are over. It is seen as *the* central human linguistic and psychological activity from which others stem.

The two types of explanation are not mutually exclusive. The acceptance of one does not imply the rejection of the other. A piece of fiction may allow both service and creativity explanations. There is also, paradoxically, a way in which, by its very uselessness, fiction which performs no immediate service is particularly useful, for by freeing the mind from obligation and constraint, it refreshes, rearranges, and provides the free play of ideas on which innovative thinking depends (Cook 1994a).

Service explanation 1: an aid to language acquisition

The view that fiction aids first language acquisition is certainly a service explanation. If the role of early rhymes and stories is to first draw children's attention to, and then reinforce, linguistic units and structures, as argued in Chapter 1, it is clear that fiction, being relatively unconstrained by the limits imposed by an actual world, allows its inventor greater freedom to manipulate these linguistic units and structures in ways which draw attention to their formal characteristics. Rhythms, rhymes, puns, and parallelisms are all more easily composed if one is allowed to choose words which not only do not refer to the actual world, but do not even have to be plausible in it:

> My dinosaur
> was getting thinner
> and so I brought him
> home for dinner.
>
> He ate as fast
> as he was able:
> he ate the food,
> he ate the table.
>
> He ate the fridge,
> he ate the chair,
> he ate my favourite
> teddy bear.
>
> He is a very
> naughty pet.
> He even ate
> the TV set.[8]
> (Thomson: 1993)

With or without parallelisms of form, good fiction serves to expand vocabulary, and this is traditionally invoked as one of the main reasons for wide reading in childhood.

Service explanation 2: a social education

Another service explanation of fiction, which it shares with games, is that it provides an education in interpersonal relations. It is rather obviously true that while specific characters do not actually exist, they do enter into the same kind of relationships and face the same kind of problems as real people in the actual world. For this reason, children can learn a great deal about social relationships and conflicts, even when the society they are reading about is inhabited by witches and wizards, or by talking animals or toys. They may even learn more readily *because* the settings are so extraordinary, in the same way that the skills needed for survival in adult life—such as throwing, chasing, fighting, teamwork, and calculating the intentions and abilities of others in order to outwit them—are perhaps best learnt in a game where they are broken down into manageable components and can be perfected without damaging consequences. The argument that we sometimes learn best as onlookers rather than participants also applies. In this interpretation, the love of fiction may have been environmentally selected in the process of evolution for the same reasons as the love of gossip (Carroll 1995; Dunbar 1996). Humans, living in large communities, need to co-operate extensively with strangers, but are also in competition with them for resources. Consequently, we need to hone our skills in dealing with novel social situations, to assess whose intentions are honourable, who is to be trusted, and how the malicious are to be outwitted. In addition, both fiction and gossip may develop our ability to empathize. Survival and procreation may depend upon the possession of these skills.

Service explanation 3: group solidarity

Yet another service explanation of fiction is the observation that the act of sharing a story creates affiliations and group solidarity by establishing and reinforcing relationships between storyteller and listener (Bernstein 1960). Those who know the same stories become an interpretative community, in the sense defined by Fish ([1976] 1980); they have a common pool of knowledge for allusion and discussion, which helps them to include members and to exclude outsiders.[9] In this view, it is the storytelling which matters rather than the stories themselves—in fact, the content of the stories could be anything, provided they are peculiar to the group. However, while this view may be true, and explain the *existence* of stories, it does not help towards an explanation of why the content of the stories should be as it is, or indeed why they are fictional rather than factual. In keeping with our progress from the private to the public world, we shall return to the issue of the larger macro-social functions of fiction in creating group identity in the next chapter. Let us for the moment, however, pursue its more private function in micro-social interpersonal relationships, through the views of two writers who, being both eminent literary historians and successful writers of fiction, were well-placed to assess its appeal in a wider perspective.

A creativity explanation

The Russian historian and children's writer Chukovsky ([1928] 1963) suggests that the very bizarreness of events in children's stories may enable them to gain a greater grip on reality. This is in part a service explanation, but it also creates a bridge towards a larger claim, and one which for us has the important characteristic of linking the function of fiction with the playful manipulation of linguistic form.

Chukovsky observes that in traditional children's stories it is the norm, rather than the exception, for events to be impossible in the actual world. As an example he cites the methods of transport used in Russian folk tales and rhymes. Characters ride on all sorts of impossible steeds—hens, cats, beavers, goats, frying pans—but never horses. 'It was only yesterday', comments Chukovsky, 'that [the child] assimilated the important fact that the horse exists for transportation, yet today they knowingly ascribe this function to every unlikely creature.' Indeed, even when a horse *is* available in one tale, it cannot perform its usual function, but must defer to something else:

> I harnessed the horse
> But the horse did not budge;
> I harnessed the gnat
> And the gnat sped away
> To the barn.

In stories, reversals occur at the level of events. In a different way, in children's 'lore', they may occur in semantic contradictions within clauses:

> The blind man gazes
> The deaf man listens
> The cripple runs a race
> The mute cries help

They may even occur at phrase level:

> One and a half milks of jug
> The peasant grabbed the dog and beat the stick
> The dough is kneading the woman

Chukovsky's examples are from Russian, but the occurrence of similar reversals, at all these levels, in other languages, suggests a more universal appeal. The strange steeds are reminiscent of the flying carpets of *The Arabian Nights*, Father Christmas's flying reindeer, witches' broomsticks, or the peach ridden by Momotaro in a Japanese folk tale. Opie and Opie (1959: 24–6) catalogue phrase-level semantic contradiction for humorous effect in English children's lore. They dub this phenomenon 'tangle talk', and trace the origins of some examples as far back as the 14th century. So although the language is English, and the realia belong to one era or place, there is nothing culturally specific about the technique:

> One midsummer's night in winter
> The snow was raining fast,
> A bare-footed girl with clogs on
> Stood sitting on the grass.
> (Opie and Opie 1959: 24)

or

> Ladles and Jellyspoons
> I stand upon this speech to make a platform,
> The train I arrived on has not yet come,
> So I took a bus and walked.
> I come before you
> To stand behind you
> And tell you something
> I know nothing about.
> (*ibid.* 1959: 25)

Speculating upon the origin and function of this use of language, Chukovsky recounts the behaviour of his own two-year-old daughter:

> For her, at that time, as for many other children of similar age, it was a source of great emotional and mental activity, although in itself seemingly insignificant, that a rooster cries cock-a-doodle-doo, a dog barks, a cat miaows.

> These simple bits of knowledge were great conquests of her mind. Indelibly and forever did she ascribe to the rooster the 'kukareku', to the cat the 'miaow', to the dog the 'bow-wow', and showing off justifiably her extensive erudition, she demonstrated it incessantly. These facts brought simultaneously clarity, order, and proportion to a world of living creatures as fascinating to her as to every other tot. But, somehow, one day in the twenty-third month of her existence, my daughter came to me, looking mischievous and embarrassed at the same time—as if she were up to some intrigue. I had never before seen such a complex expression on her little face.

> She cried to me even when she was still at some distance from where I sat: 'Daddy, 'oggie—miaow!'—that is, she reported to me the sensational and, to her, obviously incorrect news that a doggie, instead of barking, miaows. And she burst out into somewhat encouraging, somewhat artificial laughter, inviting me, too, to laugh at this invention.

But I was inclined to realism.
'No,' said I, 'the doggie bow-wows.'

'Oggie—miaow!' she repeated, laughing, and at the same time watched my facial expression which, she hoped, would show her how she should regard this erratic invention which seemed to scare her a little. (. . .)

It seemed to me at that point that I understood the reason for the passion that children feel for the incongruous, for the absurd, and for the severing of ties between objects and their regular functions, expressed in folklore. The key to this varied and joyful preoccupation which has so much importance to the mental and spiritual life of the child is play, but play with a special function.
(Chukovsky [1928] 1963)

The capacity for such reversal and distortion of reality is important to the development of interpersonal relationships in two opposite ways: as humour allowing bonding, and as practice in prevarication—for each individual needs to lie and deceive as surely as they need to co-operate. In this sense the reversals described by Chukovsky and the Opies, to which I am assigning a creativity explanation, can also be assigned a service explanation. But these immediate social uses, though important and perhaps the origin of this behaviour, are not necessarily its *only* function. The point of importance to the argument here is that it is also dependent upon language, and is—like language itself—distinctively human. The two-word clause which Chukovsky's daughter uses is the simplest possible: subject + predicator. As an example of the two-word stage in child-language development, it indicates the point at which the child may be said to first deploy grammar, selecting words paradigmatically and combining them syntactically.[10] It shows also that she has acquired the essential ability to *dis*sociate the different levels of language. She sees them as independently operable, and realizes that patterns at the syntactic level (in this case NP + VP) do not have to correspond with semantics or pragmatics. In a similar way, as we have seen, nursery rhymes encourage phonological patterns which can seem independent of sense. Yet no sooner had Chukovsky's daughter mastered these crucial aspects of human language ability, than she used them to create a fantastic fictional reality in which dogs miaow. Without the clause structure NP + VP, such an activity would be impossible. The human capacity for humour, deceit, and the creation of imaginative realities would be severely curtailed, if not made impossible altogether.

This point about the dependence of fictional realities upon linguistic structure is made by another literary scholar and writer of fiction, J. R. R. Tolkien, in a discussion of fairy stories, when he observes how the structure of the noun phrase allows the creation of fantastic realities:

The human mind, endowed with the powers of generalization and abstraction, sees not only *green-grass*, discriminating it from other things (and finding it fair to look upon), but sees that it is *green* as well as being *grass*. But how powerful, how stimulating to the very faculty that produced it, was the invention of the adjective: no spell or incantation in Faërie is more potent. And that is not surprising: such incantations might indeed be said to be only another view of adjectives, a part of speech in a mythical grammar. The mind that thought of *light, heavy, grey, yellow, still, swift*, also conceived of magic that would make heavy things light and able to fly, turn grey lead into yellow gold, and the still rock into swift water. When we can take green from grass, blue from heaven, and red from blood, we have already an enchanter's power . . .
(Tolkien 1964: 25)

A contemporary linguist, of course, might well take issue with some of the formulations used here. One might doubt for example, whether—as seems to be implied—the human mind could have been 'endowed with the powers of generalization and abstraction' before language. Language is, after all, already an abstraction, a second order of reality, making fiction a third (Widdowson 1987, 1994). And one might object that the phrase 'the invention of the adjective' seems to make unwarranted assumptions, both about the sequential appearance of parts of speech, and about human control over language. Nevertheless, an essential point about language is well made. Syntax brings with it the power to generate alternative realities. Conversely, the power to create these alternative realities may be dependent upon syntactic form. Tolkien is describing it here at phrase level, just as Chukovsky, writing about his daughter, had described it at the level of the clause.

Although the primary functions of language are often conceived to be social organization and the accumulation and transmission of factual knowledge, with fiction and formal patterning arising as minor if entertaining by-products, this order of origin and dependency can easily be reversed. It might be that, both ontogenetically and phylogenetically, the first function of language is the creation of imaginative worlds: whether lies, games, fictions or fantasies. From this use could have emerged the capacity for intricate social organization and complex knowledge. But in this case it is these which would have been the by-products rather than the prime movers.

Yet in Tolkien's view this creative capacity of grammar does not automatically create fictions.

Anyone inheriting the fantastic device of human language can say *the green sun*. Many can then imagine or picture it. But that is not enough . . . To make a secondary World inside which the green sun will be credible (. . .) will probably require labour and thought, and will certainly demand a special skill, a kind of elvish craft.
(Tolkien 1964: 45)

Here I wish to part company with Tolkien, and also to rephrase his ideas, or at least adapt them, to more applied linguistic terminology. It may indeed be that 'labour and thought' are required to create imaginative worlds of worth, but there may also be a factor in their creation which requires not the increase of control over language but its abnegation. While the language system clearly allows the generation of an infinity of utterly new sentences in the sense stressed by Chomsky (1957, 1965) and thus of an infinity of imaginary worlds (with green suns, green ideas, barking cats, or what you will), it is also constrained by force of habit. As many linguists have recently observed, a good deal of actual language use is not creative at all, but composed of 'ready-made', 'pre-fabricated' 'chunks' (Pawley and Syder 1983; Sinclair 1991: 109–21). As for our thoughts about *what might be* rather-than *what is*, they too are constrained by what actually happens. For the majority, who lack 'the elvish power' of a Tolkien or a Chukovsky, the ability to create the fantastic is severely circumscribed by the weight of the actual and the plausible. The resource of creativity is available, even immanent in language, although convention often restrains us from exploiting it. In theory, language and thought are ready to create attractive fictions. In reality, they are bound and constrained.

It is here that we return to the role of the manipulation of form and its connection to meaning.

Semantic language play: form and meaning

> I walk along, waving my arms and mumbling almost wordlessly, now shortening my steps so as not to interrupt my mumbling, now mumbling more rapidly in time with my steps. So the rhythm is trimmed and takes shape—and rhythm is the basis of the poetic work, resounding through the whole thing. Gradually individual words begin to ease themselves free of this dull roar . . .
> (Mayakovsky)[11]

In the previous chapter we looked at play with speech sound and linguistic form, speculating on the reasons for its attractiveness to small children and its possible role in language acquisition. The question was left open, however, as to why this delight in the manipulation of form extends beyond childhood, and what its role may be for adults and for older children who have already acquired the grammar and phonology of a first language.

One partial explanation of the function of play with form is that it is particularly fertile in generating imaginary worlds, situations, characters, and events, allowing possibilities to emerge which might otherwise have been eliminated by the force of the habitual. For language which is driven by the patterning of form (for example into rhythm and rhyme) still inevitably generates meanings: ones which are often simultaneously unlikely and attractive.

This can be seen most 'purely', as it were, in nonsense verse, such as Edward Lear's, where the words seem—though deceptively—to be driven very little by considerations of meaning, and rather conspicuously by patterns of form:

The Owl and the Pussy-Cat went to sea
In a beautiful pea-green boat.
They took some honey, and plenty of money,
Wrapped up in a five-pound note.
(From *The Owl and the Pussy-Cat*)

Here, to an extent, objects come into existence in the fictional world because of the demands of formal patterns. It is largely for reasons of rhyme that the characters go by 'boat', take 'honey' and 'money', and use 'a five-pound note'. These words syllabically all fit the metre too. The fiction thus created (to the extent that it is constructed on the basis of sound and abstract structure rather than probability or a previously constructed imagined world) thus seems to incorporate a wild and random element, to be controlled by language itself rather than by reality or the will of the writer. (It is not totally so, of course: for though choice is constrained, there are many other words which both rhyme and scan; at least one word in each pair of rhymes—and not necessarily the first one—can be chosen freely. There are also some semantic constraints: though animals do not use money, it will fit into a boat.)

Grammatical strings, however, no matter how random or disregarding of actual possibility they may be in the writing, inevitably *take on* meaning for the reader (and for the writer as reader of his own creation) and it is this fact which writers such as Lear have exploited so successfully. Although there may be 'a set towards' the message form in the writer (Jakobson 1960), the reader's attention (especially perhaps a child's) may be consciously focused on the meaning. In a similar way, in language teaching textbooks using grammar-translation or graded structures, the bizarre sentences deriving from the writer's focus on a particular grammatical construction, have a potential to become part of a weird imagined world for the student.[12]

Sentences for Translation
1 Excuse me Madam, the young lady whose ring was lost on the beach is at the door.
2 The girl from whom I received this letter will arrive next week.
3 The man to whom you sold the car has left. What, left! And he hasn't paid me for it yet.
4 At dinner we shall eat the fish we caught this morning.[13]

In these examples, each illustrating a defining relative clause, the need to use a particular structure guides and limits what can be said, rather as the rhyme does in *The Owl and the Pussy-Cat*.

Many readers, unlike some writers, are 'set towards' meaning. For this reason, attempts to create stretches of language which conform to linguistic rules but lack meaning seldom achieve their aim, for meaning is imported into them automatically, perhaps through an innate disposition, by the human mind. Probably the most famous failure to create such a meaningless but grammatical string is Chomsky's

> Colorless green ideas sleep furiously.
> (Chomsky 1957: 15)

This sentence, having been constructed to illustrate, as Chomsky says, the fact that 'the notion of "grammatical" cannot be identified with "meaningful" in any semantic sense'[14] (*ibid.*), seems to have captured the imagination of students and subsequently the public so completely, that it is probably the best-known and most often quoted sentence that he (or perhaps any linguist) has produced. (It is, for example, his only comment on language cited in many dictionaries of quotations).[15] One reason for this failure is that such 'meaningless' sentences, however impossible they are to interpret as referring to a real world, can, like *The Owl and the Pussy-Cat*, be interpreted as referring to an imaginary one. (Alternatively, they may be interpreted meta- phorically or metonymically as referring to the actual world, as in a reading in which 'green' means 'environmentalist', 'sleep' means 'remain in the mind but are no longer voiced', and 'furiously' means 'causing mental turmoil'.) It may even be the dissociation of such texts from the actual world, and their incapacity to refer to anything with which we are familiar, which makes them so very memorable, and the images which they inspire so psycho- logically salient. In fact, in Alexander Pope's *Dunciad*, 'ideas' are said to 'sleep', and the phrase 'green thought' (not very different from 'green ideas') does occur in Andrew Marvell's poem, 'The Garden' (Harland 1993: 21):

> Meanwhile the mind, from pleasure less,
> Withdraws into its happiness;
> The mind, that ocean where each kind
> Does straight its own resemblance find;
> Yet it creates, transcending these,
> Far other worlds, and other seas;
> Annihilating all that's made
> To a green thought in a green shade.

Like such poetic uses, Chomsky's sentence remains with us presumably because we *can* visualize corporeal green ideas, just as we *can* visualize an anthropomorphized owl and cat. Language interpretation is constrained neither by reality nor by previous occurrence. 'The mind', as Marvell says, 'creates'.

Many avant-garde artists have pursued to extremes this capacity of language to generate meaning for the reader, despite the fact that it is abandoned partly or wholly as the main criterion for choice by the writer. Thus, when the Dada poet Tristan Tzara created poems by pulling words at random out of a hat (Richter 1965), or the novelist William Burroughs cut and folded the pages he had written to bring half-sentences together in random combinations (Odier 1970), or Marc Saporta published a loose-leaf novel in a box so that readers could shuffle the pages (Burke 1994: 59), they did so in the knowledge and with the intention that readers of the results (including themselves) would nevertheless find meaning in them. Similarly, the genre of the lipogram novel, written on the principle that it must not contain a certain letter of the alphabet, has produced works which are not only as meaningful as any other novel, but have even been consumed by readers who have not noticed the formal principle behind their construction. (Such was the case with the first reviews of Georges Perec's novel *La Disparition*, written without the letter 'e'—a particularly extraordinary feat in French. The letter's absence symbolized the wartime death and disappearance of the author's parents (Bellos 1993). In French, the letter 'e' and the word 'eux' ('them') are pronounced identically.) Even 'poems' generated by computer programs inserting content words into ready-made grammatical frames have been interpreted by human readers as meaningful—though not very good (Boden 1992: 158).[16]

The human mind, then, takes control of language which does not refer to any known or possible state of affairs by understanding it in some non-literal way, as fiction or metaphor. That is not to say, of course, that this necessarily makes the text interesting or worthwhile. Total surrender to the random (as in the case of Tzara) or control by some purely mechanical constraint (as in the case of computer-generated 'poetry') is likely to generate texts which are ultimately rather boring.[17] The introduction of *some limited* random determinants, however, *in combination with* authorial judgement, may help to create richer texts by weakening the constraints of probability and allowing writers to see possibilities which might otherwise have escaped them. We shall return to this exploitation of random factors more fully in Chapter 5.

When choice of words is dictated in whole or part by some formal or random factor, it has the effect of making meanings less predictable, less precise, and apparently out of the author's control. Forms may be more precise, but meanings become less determinate. Although there is no text, even the most factual and mundane, whose meaning is ever fully determinate, in the sense of transmitting to the receiver exactly the ideas intended by the sender, it is reasonable to talk of degrees of indeterminate meaning in texts, and to regard those which display more indeterminacy of meaning as more fertile in their capacity to stimulate variable and interesting interpretation. Yet this fertile indeterminacy may originate not only in the composition of the text—as, for example, in the writer's submission to the constraint of rhyme—nor in the relation of what is written to states of affairs generally recognized as actual or possible (as in Chomsky's 'green ideas' sentence); it may also originate from the reader's own mental state, and in particular from his or her ignorance of conventional meanings. This leads to the disturbing conclusion that some aspects of our response to certain texts are impoverished by an increase in our conventional understanding of the language and its uses, and explains perhaps why we can never recapture our childhood excitement at listening to certain imperfectly understood stories. It may also help to explain why adults are often attracted to language which—for reasons of obscurity, complexity, or archaism—remains indeterminate to them.

Indeterminate meanings: two examples

1 *Little Grey Rabbit*

Let us pursue this idea of indeterminacy further by considering how a passage larded with unfamiliar vocabulary may appear to the child to whom it is being read. Let us take as an example a page from a widely-read children's book, *Little Grey Rabbit's Birthday Party*, by Alison Uttley:

> At four o'clock they sent Grey Rabbit upstairs, while they got ready the tea. They ran down the garden to the beehive for the cake. Hare put a butterfly net over his head, lest he should be stung, but the bees had gone. They lifted up the straw skep, and there was the cake, looking nicer than ever, and around it were many little pots of honey, each as big as a thimble. The pots were made of golden wax and the honey was scented with wild thyme.
> They carried the treasures indoors and placed them on the table. Grey Rabbit came running downstairs.
> 'Oh! Oh!' cried Grey Rabbit. 'What's this?'
> 'It's somebody's birthday cake', said Squirrel.

There will, of course, be considerable variation in understanding, depending on the child's age, general vocabulary, and experience of the world. There will also be variation in how unknown words are tackled, depending on whether the child has a predilection to ask for their meaning, or the reading adult to explain them. We might also suppose that some of the realia in this passage, such as 'beehives', 'skeps', and 'thimbles' were more familiar to children in 1944, when the book was first published, than they are today, when the book has been in print for over 50 years. But let us assume, for our purposes here, a child to whom a large number of words are unknown (maybe 'beehive', 'butterfly net', 'lest', 'straw skep', 'a thimble', 'golden wax', 'scented', 'wild thyme', 'treasures') and let us also assume that these words are passed over without explanation by the adult who is reading the story aloud. The issue on which I wish to speculate is how these words, being unknown, are understood (if at all) by the listening child. It is a question which is not only relevant to children's language. In the next chapter I shall argue that encounters with unknown, opaque language are a central feature not only of children's experience of fiction, but of many pleasurable instances of adult language use as well.

There is a picture on the facing page, and presumably the child may be aided by the accompanying picture (perhaps with the help of a pointing finger) towards some understanding of these phrases. For this passage, referents are depicted for all of the following noun phrases: 'the garden', 'the beehive', 'the cake', 'Hare', 'Squirrel', 'a butterfly net', 'his head', 'the straw skep', and 'little pots of honey'. Yet not every word is or can be illustrated. Referents apprehensible to the senses may present fewer problems than verbs or grammatical words (such as 'lest'). Yet even they present problems. They may be mentioned as absent ('the bees had gone') or as metaphorical comparisons ('as big as a thimble'); they may be too general ('the treasures'), or be present to some other sense than sight ('scented with wild thyme'). Illustration, moreover, though it may help, does not bypass the problem of definition. Even in the most apparently straightforward cases ('a butterfly net') there is room for considerable error. It would be quite reasonable from the illustration, for example, for the child to infer that a butterfly net is something to wear near beehives, rather than to catch butterflies. Even where there is no misleading evidence, only a part of the target denotation may be evident. The size and outline of a thimble may be clear from this text and picture, but not its function or usual context.

A good deal, then, of a child's encounters with unknown words is likely to be marked by imprecise, partial, or idiosyncratic interpretation. Certain attributes (size in the case of 'thimble') become disproportionately salient. In the passive and silent activity of listening to fiction, the extent of this idiosyncratic interpretation is difficult to assess. Elicitation studies of children's word understanding are unlikely to reveal how the word is interpreted in context and at speed. Yet the hypothesis that children do attribute vague and eccentric meanings to unknown words and phrases is corroborated by their active use of vocabulary. Children commonly over- or under-extend certain components of meaning at the expense of others. Examples abound in the literature on child language. Bowerman (1978), for example, reports how her daughter used 'moon' to refer to all crescent-shaped objects, including grapefruit segments and the letter C, but was annoyed to hear 'dog' used for any dog other than her own. The frequent errors reported both in the academic literature and in popular anecdote testify to a high tolerance of the bizarre and illogical (hardly surprising when 'correct' interpretations are often equally outlandish). Errors of word identification and segmentation are particularly liable to originate in genres (such as songs, stories, prayers, and hymns) where there are no clear consequences of misunderstanding to indicate the mistake. One child thought that the Lord's Prayer asks God to 'Lead us not into Penn Station' (Peters 1983: 64), another that the hymn 'Gladly the cross I'd bear' is about 'Gladly, the cross-eyed bear'. When I was a child I sang a hymn asking Jesus—I thought—to 'pity mice in plicity' (not 'my simplicity'), and imagined a 'plicity' to be a kind of cupboard in which mice were trapped. All readers, no doubt, can supply such examples of their own.

2 'La Toilette'

In first language acquisition, there may be advantages in an experience of discourse which allows word meaning to be interpreted with a degree of indeterminacy and idiosyncrasy which would be unacceptable or even dysfunctional in adult transactional encounters, but which allows the child to gradually 'home in' upon more precise and conventional meaning. Yet, as in the case of parallelism and repetition, the existence of discourse which seems particularly likely to allow for such flexibility cannot be explained entirely as an aid to acquisition. The child's tolerance of unknown words is perhaps only different in degree from that of an adult reader, who may also, on encountering unknown words, assign to them a general impressionistic function, especially in fiction and poetry. Widdowson (1992b) makes this point in a discussion of how, in the Hornblower adventure stories, abstruse 18th-century seafaring vocabulary serves to enrich the atmosphere of the tales, even when its precise meaning is unknown to the reader.

It may be that the adult liking for fiction is *in part* due to the freedom of interpretation which it allows, and the absence of negative consequences when one individual's interpretation diverges from those of others.[18] In this sense, in reading fiction, we are able to prolong the child's more passive and less responsible relation to language. The common adult affection for obscure language (for example in religious liturgies and texts) may stem from some cognitive benefit deriving from immersion in words whose significance, by virtue of being vague, is also a stimulus to a sensation of mental freedom and possibility. In adult encounters with literary, religious, or archaic language, there may be active enjoyment of words whose meaning is only imperfectly known, and perhaps some benefit to the mind of not seeking to pin down meaning too precisely. Consider as an example (unless you happen to know what it means) the effect of the word 'slub', and perhaps 'ciborium', in 'La Toilette', by Seamus Heaney (1984):

> The white towelling bathrobe
> ungirdled, the hair still wet,
> first coldness of the underbreast
> like a ciborium in the palm.
>
> Our bodies are the temples
> of the Holy Ghost. Remember?
> And the little, fitted, deep-slit drapes
> on and off the holy vessels

regularly? And the chasuble
so deftly hoisted? But vest yourself
in the word you taught me
and the stuff I love, slub silk.

Could not such vocabulary activate in the adult some of the mystery which
'thimbles' and 'butterfly nets' may have for the child, and in so doing, perform
some function other than a straightforward expansion of vocabulary, though
they may do that too? This is a point to which we shall turn more fully in the
next chapter.

Images and language

There is an important caveat to my claims about the indeterminacy of meaning
in texts for children, which has already been mentioned, but deserves rather
more comment. This is the constraint placed upon the interpretation of
words by pictures. It goes without saying that children's books are generally
more copiously illustrated than adult books (*Little Grey Rabbit's Birthday
Party*, for example, has roughly one picture to every 150 words), and the
elucidation of unknown vocabulary is presumably one of the functions of
the picture–text combination. One might even say that 'good' illustrations to
children's books should, together with intrinsic interest and charm, help to
illustrate unfamiliar language in this way. This will also account for the
gradual withdrawal of illustrations from books as children get older. The
importance of pictures in language development is underlined by the fact
that, far from being a fruit of new technology, they have a history as long as
books for children themselves. Nor are they solely the result of publishers
and writers wishing to make books more pleasurable for children. In the
past, the reason for including them has often been for instruction rather than
seduction (Townsend 1990: 112–24), and they can be found as much in the
dourest schoolbooks and manuals of morals and manners as in fairy tales
and fantasies.

Nevertheless, despite this long history, it is true that, in the 20th century,
this relation between pictures and words in the language experience of
children has changed drastically, not only because of an increased reliance of
books upon pictures, but particularly with the advent of the moving image.
In films, television programmes, and videos, the order of precedence is inverted.
It is words which are forced into the background, and seem to provide
illustration, while the picture—with all the extra and more explicit meaning
made possible by animation—comes to the centre of attention. This might
seem to make a good deal of my argument in this chapter simply out of date.
The modern child's experience of fiction, it could be argued, is as much
through the medium of the moving image, as it is through books and spoken
stories.

This would certainly seem to be borne out by distribution figures. Consider, for example, the case of Walt Disney video cassettes, whose sales reach astronomical proportions. The figures which follow are for Britain, but reflect the success of Disney videos in many countries in the world. In Britain, which in 1995 had a population of just over 6 million children between 3 and 10 (the age group Disney's own research shows to be the main market), the video cassettes of *The Lion King* and *101 Dalmatians* sold 3.5 million and 2.6 million copies respectively, each within two years of their release. *The Jungle Book*, with sales of 4.5 million, is the most successful video release ever in Britain. As many video cassettes are shared by siblings or seen by friends, it seems safe to assume from these figures that each Disney video is seen by almost every child in the country. In addition, it is estimated that each Disney video cassette is viewed on average 35 times.[19] As similar ratios of sales to child populations are found in other English-speaking countries, it is very possible that they are the most widely distributed and well-known texts for children in the English-speaking world.[20]

Such popularity is often viewed with dismay by traditionalists, who see the success of the moving image in general as a threat to the reading habit and the influence of books in children's lives (Townsend 1990: 347–9). The same critics are more specific in the case of Disney, deploring the superficial and sentimental rewriting of the plots of children's classics, and the international homogeneity introduced by large-scale worldwide distribution.[21] In addition, for younger children the replacement of books by video cassettes and television supplants personal interaction with an individual adult storyteller, while for older children they encourage listening passively rather than reading actively. The moving image, unlike the still image, leaves far less to the *ima*gination (the etymological link is not insignificant).

Yet whatever the justice of these evaluations (and I personally agree with all of them), the change does not undermine the claims which I am making, for two reasons. The first is that they bear testimony to the dominance of fiction, even at a time of changing modes of communication. Second, and more remarkably, while it is true that language is pushed into the background, a great deal of the language in videos and on TV programmes is still very playful, in all the ways typical of more traditional genres. The soundtracks of several of these most successful video cassettes incorporate the same kind of play with language as successful written or traditional orally-transmitted texts for children.[22]

In the songs and dialogues of *The Jungle Book*, for example, there is extensive exploitation of linguistic resources and patterning of linguistic form. The famous song sung by Baloo the Bear on his first meeting with Mowgli, for example, exploits contrasting dialects, alternation between song and speech, and the integration of words with music, action, and dance. There are also puns ('bare necessities'), alliterations ('the bees are buzzing'), and intense and complex rhymes ('When you look under the rocks and plants/And take a glance at the fancy ants', 'I mean the bare necessities/That's why a bear can rest at ease'), and tongue twisters:

When you pick a paw-paw
Or prickly pear,
And you prick a raw paw,
Next time beware.
Don't pick the prickly pear by paw
When you pick a pear, try to use the claw.
But you do not need to use the claw
When you pick a pear of the big paw-paw.

(*The Bare Necessities* Words and Music: Terry Gilkyson © 1964 Wonderland Music Company, Inc. International Copyright Secured. All Rights Reserved. Used by permission.)

Depending on the child's age there must be elements of this linguistic finesse which are either unnoticed or misunderstood (all passing too quickly to be explained or commented upon by an adult companion, as they might be in the reading of a book). If the phrases 'bare necessities' or the name 'paw-paw' are unknown, for example, then the puns will be missed; and a child is unlikely to be aware of the social significance of the different dialects. Yet one may also suppose that it is partly this complexity which accounts for children's eagerness to see the scene many times, that there is an awareness of virtuosity even if the details are unknown, and also that repeated exposure gradually reveals more and more detail. In this the experience of language is not dissimilar to that which I have suggested for *Little Grey Rabbit*.

The movement away from the book, and towards the moving image, then (lamentable as it may be in other ways), by no means necessarily entails—so far at least—an end to linguistic virtuosity and verbal display. On the contrary, the survival of many of the features of children's lore and children's literature adds strength to the argument for their universality and importance. If, cynically, their incorporation is commerically inspired, it still testifies to the fact that this is what children want to hear. Even allowing for the appeal of pictures and music, and for the fact that children's taste is to some extent manufactured by the hype and merchandizing which accompanies video releases, it still seems reasonable to say that a good part of the appeal of the genre resides in language, and that this language can be both memorable and attractive for reasons which have nothing new about them. 'Super-cali-fragilistic-expi-ali-docious', the famous nonce (and nonsense) word in the Disney film of *Mary Poppins* is presented in the familiar 4/4 stress-time rhythm, and presumably appeals for the same reason as much older predecessors:

Supercalifragilisticexpialidocious
If you say it loud enough you'll always sound precocious

Supercalifragilisticexpialidocious
Even though the sound of it is something quite atrocious

(*Supercalifragilisticexpialidocious* Words and Music: Richard M.
Sherman/Robert B. Sherman © 1963 Wonderland Music Company, Inc.
International Copyright Secured. All Rights Reserved. Used by
permission.)

Conclusion

This chapter has suggested that one of the functions[23] of the patterning of
linguistic forms (as described in Chapter 1) may be to act as a catalyst in the
creation of imaginary worlds. This partial explanation, however, only replaces
one set of problems—the relation of formal patterning and imaginary worlds—
with another problem: the function of the two together. For this problem I
shall suggest two possible solutions, one cognitive and the other social. A
cognitive function may be to create greater flexibility and adaptability in
unforeseen circumstances. Imaginary worlds allow experimentation with
possible eventualities which the mind, locked in its routines, might otherwise
not have seen. For the moment I shall leave this function to one side, to be
expanded upon later, in Chapter 5. It is to the social functions of both formal
patterning and imaginary worlds that we now turn in Chapter 3.

Notes

1 Source: the publishing organization, Booktrack. This figure is calculated
   by adding the figures for adult fiction for 12 weeks and multiplying by
   4.3. As this does not include the considerable sales of books by newsagents,
   the actual figure is much larger.
2 Figure for April 1996. Source: Broadcasters' Audience Research Board.
3 Among works classed as fiction, there is a spectrum ranging from novels
   which incorporate descriptions of actual historical characters and events
   (such as *War and Peace*), or are closely based on the author's actual
   experience (like *Sons and Lovers*), through those which place fictional
   events in actual settings (like *Bleak House*), those whose characters,
   places, and events are all fictional, but nevertheless plausible (like
   Mansfield Park), right through to those which are utterly fantastic (like
   Peter Pan or *2001*)—and all sorts of degrees and mixtures of these
   categories. For an attempt to draw up a taxonomy of fictions, see Warlow
   1977.
4 Source: Booktrack.
5 Bruner (1986) is a retrospective collection of papers relating to fiction
   and imagination. Yet while it purports to depict the centrality of these
   issues in psychology, it does so by referring to work which would normally
   be considered to belong to other fields, such as literary theory.

6 See, however, Searle 1975b.

7 As documented both in psychology, following Vygotsky [1933] 1976, [1934] 1962, and Piaget [1926] 1959, and in linguistics, see Weir 1962 and Nelson 1989.

8 'My Pet Dinosaur' by Charles Thomson in *Dinosaur Poems*, edited by John Foster and Korky Paul, Oxford University Press 1993. [Originally from *I'm Brilliant*, Collins Books.]

9 A similar notion of 'discourse community' is employed in Swales's definition of genre (1990: 21–32).

10 The notion advanced against this grammatical view of language acquisition that children use ready-made chunks of language which are only later broken down and analysed (Peters 1983; Pawley and Syder 1983), while borne out by many child utterances at this stage, is rather conspicuously *not* supported by the large number of children's idiosyncratic and unique combinations.

11 Quoted in Kristeva [1974] 1980.

12 For a discussion of the relationship between textbook sentences and lines of poetry, see Widdowson 1984: 160–75.

13 Sentences for translation focusing on the relative pronoun in Speight, *Teach Yourself Italian*. 1962. London: Teach Yourself Books.

14 In later writing, Chomsky (1965: 11) uses the term 'acceptable' rather than 'meaningful', in contrast to 'grammatical', to describe such cases.

15 *The Oxford Dictionary of Quotations*, 1996, for example, gives three quotations from Chomsky. One is about politics, one about intellectual enquiry in general. The 'green ideas' sentence is the only one about language. The same three quotations appear in several other popular dictionaries.

16 One collection of computer-generated 'poetry' is *RACTER 1985*, discussed in Dunbar (1996: 80).

17 This is not to say that the act of production is not of interest. Tzara's action, and the fact that computers can be programmed to simulate poetry, are both interesting as performance, and as a stimulus to thought about the production of poetic text. Yet once this is appreciated, new texts produced by these two methods are unlikely to sustain interest in themselves.

18 Reader-response criticism (see Eco 1979; Freund 1987) has explored how this aspect of literary experience occurs, but not why it is sought out and valued.

19 Sales figures and estimate of viewing times supplied by Disney's UK distributor.

20 If one takes into account translations, they may be the most widely-known texts for children in the world.

21 For a scathing literary attack on the values of Disney, see the closing pages of E. L. Doctorow's novel, *The Book of Daniel* (1972: 292–8).

22 Disturbingly, however, later films (*The Lion King, Pocahontas, The Hunchback of Notre Dame*) tend to rely more upon animation and non-verbal suspense and sentiment, and less upon language.

23 Another function suggested by Newman (1986) and Turner (1992) may be neurological. Rhythm and other linguistic patterns may stimulate integration of the activities of the left and right hemispheres of the brain.

3 The uses of language play: competition and collaboration

So far we have considered, and defined, language play in terms of its linguistic forms and the meanings—particularly imaginary meanings—which it can produce. As far as its social contexts and functions are concerned, the argument has focused mainly upon instances of language play which are personal and private. This is not without reason, for it is to intimate environments that language play may—at least at first glance—seem most appropriate. Rhymes, stories, and television programmes are associated with the home, and with a use of language in interaction with one person or a few other people. The author and the TV presenter, though actually communicating with many people, create the illusory effect of intimate interaction. But we have also alluded in passing to the resemblance of these private uses of language to those in the most public places and events: sporting contests, places of worship, ceremonies, courtrooms, newspapers, performances of song and drama. In this chapter, we shall turn our attention away from the role of language play in more intimate interactions and towards its use in more public contexts, but we shall also consider the reasons for, and the significance of, the overlap between the two. In particular, we shall consider how certain types of play with language, which once carried great institutional weight, are now relegated to the domain of the childish, trivial, and weakly humorous—and speculate on why this may be.

The similarity between public and private discourse resides not only in a frequent focus upon fiction and the patterning of forms, but also often in subject-matter. For it is in both that we find the most direct reference to the emotional impact of birth, death, illness, sex, family life, social identity, and religious belief. We are less likely to find either language patterning or intimate subject-matter so prominent in those intermediate situations which are neither particularly public nor private, in the civil but unemotional daily intercourse of work. This is not to say that intimacy does not occur. As many relationships formed at work become close, there is an intertwining of affective and transactional behaviour. Yet at work neither language patterning nor discussion of life's larger problems are perceived as central to what is being done—though they may occur incidentally.

It is not the case, however, that certain genres of language play occur in the most private spheres, and others in the most public. It is often the same texts which have a double life. Thus although we may experience fictional books and programmes privately, they are also—as the words 'published' and 'broadcast' make clear—very widely disseminated. When we step outside our homes, they are known to strangers and acquaintances and can provide a useful common source of reference. This is part of a general tendency. The vehicles of adult language play tend to occur in both types of setting, rather as children's play is divided between the public environment of the playground, and the intimate environment of the home. Prayers are recited at the bedside and in the cathedral; stories are read silently or acted out on stage and cinema screen; jokes are exchanged with close friends or told to large audiences by professional comedians; songs are broadcast widely, but also repeated in solitude; advertisements are seen on roadside hoardings and on TV in the privacy of the home. Graffiti (another use of language particularly dedicated to play) are written secretly in public places, and often concern subject-matter which is very intimate (such as sex) or very public (such as politics) (Blume 1985; Cook 1996). All of these genres speak to us of experiences which we recognize as common, but yet seem intensely personal.

Bulge theory

This convergence is not limited to play. Wolfson (1988) has commented on a general tendency for language use to be similar in interactions where relationships are intimate and equal, and those where the power of one interactant over the other is very clearly defined. Thus we find that many linguistic forms—taboo words or the imperative in English, for example—may be used with impunity to intimates, as well as in situations of open aggression and undisguised power. Utterances like 'You're a bastard' or 'Make me a cup of tea' can indicate friendship, on the one hand, or aggression or authority on the other. Languages with a so-called T/V distinction between familiar and polite pronouns (*tu* and *vous* in French, for example) provide another illustration. The *tu* form is used both to subordinates and intimates (including God), the *vous* form to everybody else.[1] It is not only language but also physical behaviour which is often similar in these apparently opposite relationships. A good deal of the paralanguage of intimacy—unwavering eye-contact, significant silences, touching, proximity—is also involved in aggression. The person who looks into your eyes from a close distance may be about to kiss you or hit you (see Figure 3.1 opposite).

   Wolfson's observation is that in modern urban societies relationships of intimacy, clear authority, and naked aggression are the exception: two tapering ends of an onion. Most interactions take place within what she refers to as 'the Bulge',[2] the day-to-day unemotional transactional encounters of modern urban existence. Playful language fits the theory: it is often at the centre of attention when it is at one of the two tapering ends rather than in the middle. It is at these opposite extremes that relationships, whether of power

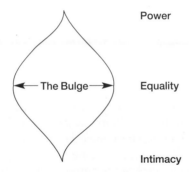

Figure 3.1: A bulge-theory view of social relations

or solidarity, are firmly established prior to, and extra to, most spoken interactions. Above and below the bulge, language is not being used to create the relationship. It can therefore be used more freely for other purposes, including play.

Competition and collaboration: an analogy with ball games

The similarity of language use in these two different types of relationship reflects the opposed functions of language in bringing people together and forcing them apart, distinguishing between those who are 'in' and those who are 'out'. In different instances of language play, there may be a greater focus on one or the other. (In the recitation of nursery rhymes, for example, the social focus is clearly upon developing a bond.) Yet it may also be that the acts of inclusion and exclusion are reciprocal: the existence of one always entails the other, rather as 'lending' by one person always entails 'borrowing' by another. Certainly, language play in the public arena often simultaneously establishes the solidarity of some participants by demonstrating their rejection of others.

There is a useful analogy to be drawn here between these social effects of language play and those of ball games. Socially, the acts of speaking and of playing ball can be seen as different ways of doing very similar things, and the analogy is worth pursuing, both as a way of understanding the social use of language play, and of developing the notion of linguistic interaction being in general 'game-like'.[3]

Like language play, ball games seem to be universal in human societies (Blanchard 1995:100–4, 150) and to be used both collaboratively and competitively. Tylor, one of the pioneers of anthropology, described them as follows:

Beyond mere tossing and catching, the simplest kind of ball-play is where a ring of players send the ball from hand to hand. This gentle pastime has its well-marked place in history. (. . .) The passion for ball play begins not with this friendly graceful delivery of the ball into the next hand, but when

two hostile players or parties are striving each to take or send it away from each other.
(Tylor 1879: 66 quoted in Blanchard 1995: 10)

Like turns in conversation, the ball passes from one person to another. When it is thrown with the intention of making it easy to catch (as it might be between parents and their small children), then the game, like a friendly conversation, creates or represents a feeling of group identity and collaboration. It is this use of the ball which explains its etymological connection, in several European languages, to words for communal dancing and singing, for historically, in many societies, the three occurred together. As Tylor explains:

> The ball-dance is now scarcely to be found but as an out-of-the-way relic of old custom; yet it has left curious traces in European languages, where the ball (Low Latin *balla*) has given its name to the dance it went with (Italian *ballare*, *ballo*, French *bal*, English *ball*), and even to the song that accompanied the dance (Italian *ballata*, French *ballade*, English *ballad*). (*ibid.*)

It is when the ball is thrown competitively, however, with the intention of making it difficult for the opponent to catch, and to 'get them out', that it becomes, as in a verbal argument, an instrument of competition. (Significantly we refer to such arguments as slanging *matches*, and talk of those involved *scoring points* against each other.) In team sports, the ball is used in both ways at once, collaboratively with those in one team, and antagonistically with those in the other. In single-combat games (tennis singles, for example) the ball is used competitively by two opponents, but a communal identity is created among two groups of spectators through the act of cheering on their champions.

This chapter focuses upon the social use of language as a ball: both as an instrument of competition, and as a means of expressing shared beliefs and identities. We shall look in turn at aspects of contests (which force people apart), at rituals (which bring them together), and between the two at humour (which does both).

Verbal duelling

In anthropological linguistics and sociolinguistics, a good deal of attention has been given to a form of language play, often described as 'verbal duelling', in which words are used like the ball in a contest between two opponents who are being cheered on by their respective supporters. Like sporting contests, verbal duels may be a prelude to violence—as in the rampages of football fans, the pre-fight exchanges between boxers, or the exchanges of insults and boasts before combat (Shippey 1993). Yet, whatever their consequences, and however bitterly fought, competitive ball games and verbal duels both depend upon a degree of co-operation between the two sides. Both accept shared conventions, and their violence is limited or symbolic.

'Verbal duelling' is particularly common between males. It manifests itself in the exchange of clever and intricate insults and boasts, in storytelling competitions, or the setting of verbal puzzles such as riddles. In a classic paper, for example, Gossen (1976) documents the elaborate contests in the indigenous Chamulan community in southern Mexico, in which, to the applause and appreciation of onlookers, pairs of unmarried youths trade brief, witty insults in exchanges which can go for as many as 250 turns. In Gossen's explanation, these contests provide both an outlet for aggression and create a sense of solidarity in a society whose strict sexual morality results in enforced celibacy for many young men, followed by late marriage and economic dependence on in-laws. The rules of the contest are that each utterance must echo its predecessor phonologically, while simultaneously being as offensive as possible, usually by including some insult to the opponent's sexual capability or inclinations (see Figure 3.2 overleaf).

This coincidence of form, meaning, and function characterizes verbal duelling in many different societies, whether the instances are simple or complex. Sherzer (1992), for example, gives the following extract from an exchange of insults between adolescent African-Americans:

A Your momma drink pee.
B Your father eat shit.
(*ibid.*)

Here the retort repeats the rhythm of the first insult, parallels it grammatically, and sets up the lexical oppositions *momma/father*, *drink/eat*, *pee/shit*. The events are fictitious; the effect insulting. The exchange is a move in a contest and provides entertainment for the onlookers (even if it is hardly a masterpiece of creativity).

Verbal duelling has been thoroughly studied and (unlike some of my other categories of language play) consistently named as 'play' in linguistics. However, it is usually described by those who study it as an aspect of the language behaviour of societies and social groups other than their own.[4] Other well-known descriptions, for example, concern the ritualized boasting and abuse of teenage Afro-American gangs known as 'the dozens' (Abrahams 1962; Labov 1974), of Turkish boys (Dundes, Leach, and Ozkök 1970), and Anglo-Saxon warriors (Shippey 1993). This brings to the fore a perpetual problem in the analysis of play. Western academic studies are happy to label aspects of other people's behaviour as 'play', but unwilling to see behaviour from their own social environment in the same light, despite very evident similarities. (There is a related reluctance to compare children's make-believe with adult drama; or competitive games with serious conflicts.) In this, it seems that commentators are influenced more by the low status accorded to play in a utilitarian industrial culture than by any spirit of objective enquiry. Thus,

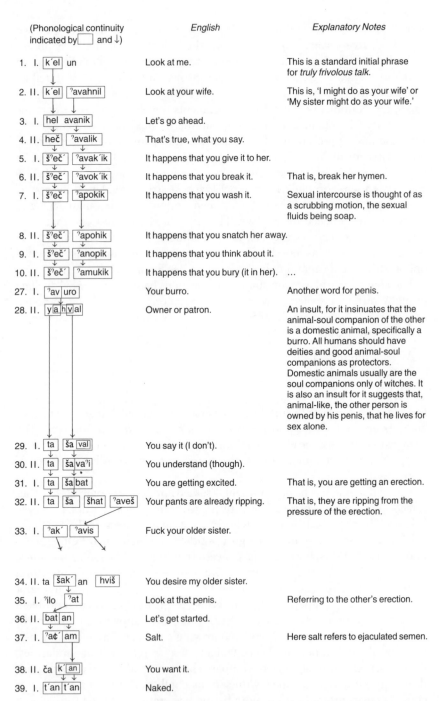

(Phonological continuity indicated by ☐ and ↓)

English

Explanatory Notes

1. I. ⟨kʼel⟩ un — Look at me. — This is a standard initial phrase for *truly frivolous talk*.

2. II. ⟨kʼel⟩ ⟨ʔavahnil⟩ — Look at your wife. — This is, 'I might do as your wife' or 'My sister might do as your wife.'

3. I. ⟨hel avanik⟩ — Let's go ahead.

4. II. ⟨heč⟩ ⟨ʔavalik⟩ — That's true, what you say.

5. I. ⟨šʼečʼ⟩ ⟨ʔavakʼik⟩ — It happens that you give it to her.

6. II. ⟨šʼečʼ⟩ ⟨ʔavokʼik⟩ — It happens that you break it. — That is, break her hymen.

7. I. ⟨šʼečʼ⟩ ⟨ʔapokik⟩ — It happens that you wash it. — Sexual intercourse is thought of as a scrubbing motion, the sexual fluids being soap.

8. II. ⟨šʼečʼ⟩ ⟨ʔapohik⟩ — It happens that you snatch her away.

9. I. ⟨šʼečʼ⟩ ⟨ʔanopik⟩ — It happens that you think about it.

10. II. ⟨šʼečʼ⟩ ⟨ʔamukik⟩ — It happens that you bury (it in her). ...

27. I. ⟨ʔav⟩ uro — Your burro. — Another word for penis.

28. II. ⟨y a h v al⟩ — Owner or patron. — An insult, for it insinuates that the animal-soul companion of the other is a domestic animal, specifically a burro. All humans should have deities and good animal-soul companions as protectors. Domestic animals usually are the soul companions only of witches. It is also an insult for it suggests that, animal-like, the other person is owned by his penis, that he lives for sex alone.

29. I. ta ⟨ša⟩ ⟨val⟩ — You say it (I don't).

30. II. ta ⟨ša⟩va'i — You understand (though).

31. I. ta ⟨ša⟩bat — You are getting excited. — That is, you are getting an erection.

32. II. ta ⟨ša⟩ ⟨šhat⟩ ⟨ʔaveš⟩ — Your pants are already ripping. — That is, they are ripping from the pressure of the erection.

33. I. ⟨ʔakʼ⟩ ⟨ʔavis⟩ — Fuck your older sister.

34. II. ta ⟨šakʼ⟩ an ⟨hviš⟩ — You desire my older sister.

35. I. ʔilo ⟨ʔat⟩ — Look at that penis. — Referring to the other's erection.

36. II. ⟨bat an⟩ — Let's get started.

37. I. ⟨ʔaȼʼ am⟩ — Salt. — Here salt refers to ejaculated semen.

38. II. ča ⟨kʼ an⟩ — You want it.

39. I. ⟨tʼan tʼan⟩ — Naked.

Figure 3.2: Extract from a transcript of verbal dueling in Chamula
(Gossen 1976:131–2)

while they describe as 'play' the ritualized boasting of teenage gangs, the chants of football fans (Argyle 1996:234), or the ritual exchanges of native American tribes (Schwartzman 1978:283–301), they have not extended the term to such activities in their own societies as party politics, the marketing campaigns of rival firms, advocacy in law, or clashes in academic conferences and journals, despite the fact that these modern Western activities often have many of the features of the 'exotic' verbal duelling described in the literature.

The angry exchanges between the leaders of the two main British political parties across the floor of the House of Commons are a case in point. The conflict is highly stylized, as the leaders, with their cheering or jeering supporters behind them, attempt to 'out-talk' each other, strutting, posturing, insulting, and joking. As in other verbal duels, there are prescribed limits, and no physical violence.[5] The following exchange between the former British Prime Minister John Major and the then Leader of the Opposition, Tony Blair, is typical.

> **Tony Blair:** Isn't it extraordinary that the Prime Minister of our country can't even urge his party to support his own position. Weak, weak, weak!
>
> **John Major:** Whenever the Right Honourable Gentleman gets abusive, we know he's losing.
>
> (Prime Minister's question time, The House of Commons, London 30 January 1997)

To an outsider anthropologist, this might seem unambiguously a case of verbal duelling, language play in ritualized symbolic conflict. The antics are not seen as play within the context of contemporary British society, however, as this would attach to them the word's belittling connotations as something trivial, unimportant, and not serious—although the verbal duelling of 'the dozens' is presumably as serious to the gang members as national politics is to politicians. Here we may fruitfully make use of the 'etic'/'emic' distinction (suggested by Pike (1954–60), by analogy with the distinction between phon*etics* and phon*emics*), in which 'etic' categories are those identified by criteria formulated outside the group being studied, and 'emic' categories are those significant to insiders. In these terms, 'play' as an 'etic' category is clearly not coterminous with 'play' as an 'emic' category. In an 'etic' sense, Blair and Major were playing, though they do not regard this behaviour as such themselves. In a society which derogates 'play', the 'etic' category is inevitably far bigger than the 'emic' one, for insiders eliminate activities from the category of 'play' as soon as they begin to take them seriously.

Evolutionary explanations

At first glance, the phenomenon of verbal duelling seems to lend itself perfectly to an explanation from the standpoint of evolutionary psychology— a discipline (to be examined in more detail in Chapter 4) which accounts for present-day human psychology in terms of the natural selection of advantageous behaviour in hunter-gatherer societies (Tooby and Cosmides 1992). Such an explanation of verbal duelling might then be extended to language play as a whole. The argument might run as follows. Language is used in the duel because it is one of the key human attributes. Skill with language demonstrates mental agility and social panache, both qualities which are desirable in a mate. The male victors of verbal duels are more likely to attract females to breed with them, and thus to pass on these qualities. When the two opponents confront each other, there is little in the way of information that needs to be exchanged. They and the onlookers know who they are and why they are fighting. For the contest to take place, however, something has to be said, preferably something which demonstrates the inventiveness and the quick-wittedness of the contestants. Play is the answer, and the result is imaginative fictional inventions, or skilful language patterning (similar to that in literature and poetry). Indeed, storytelling competitions and song contests can be regarded as a form of verbal duelling. Thus an evolutionary psychological approach to language play might postulate that it originated in verbal duels between males competing for mates, but subsequently took on a life of its own.

Wolfson's bulge theory can also be extended to support this view, for it is only in modern urban democratic societies that 'bulge relationships', and consequently 'bulge language', have come to take up the greater part of our lives. In hunter-gatherer bands (supposedly, for evolutionary psychology, the only social organization to have influenced the evolution of innate characteristics), relationships were presumably almost all at the tapering ends of Wolfson's onion: associations of autocratic power and submissive obedience, of intimacy or—in the face of other bands—aggression. These are the relationships in which we find language play, and they are still (as gossip, fiction, and news stories testify) the areas of life which we find most interesting. It is in exchanges of power and intimacy, where relationships are already established and there is little information to exchange, that we find those repetitious, superfluous, and factually uninformative uses of language which characterize language play.

There are many species of animals where conflict between males in competition for females may be symbolic rather than actual (Colman 1982: 238; Ridley 1994:125–65). Birds like the black grouse, for example, come to a special mating ground, or 'lek' (a word which derives from the Swedish for 'play') where the males parade their plumage and the females choose between them (Ridley *ibid.*: 136). Such 'play' also creates '*dis*play' (the echo is no coincidence), a word which Darwin (1872) used to describe the stylized gestures of animals which communicate, for example, such basic attitudes as dominance, appeasement, and fear, and which he explicitly likened, in an equation of animal and human behaviour, to the portrayal of the same attitudes by actors. Though the origin of display is in conflict with others, elements of the behaviour may persist when the animal is alone, perhaps as a reflex action, or as a way for the animal to represent its identity to itself. Display is thus symptomatic, even in animals, of the capacity for symbolic representation, of making one thing stand for another, which is essential to both language and play. In humans, skill with words is often worn and used like plumage in birds: the best story or speech, the meanest insult, the hardest riddle, the biggest boast—the brightest and biggest tail.

One possible, if ultimately incomplete explanation of this, is to posit a causal chain in which we humans, like many other animals, channel an innate disposition to compete into symbolic conflicts, and that for this purpose, instead of splendid antlers or tails, we have developed language. A symbolic contest needs realization through some activity, and in human life this can be done through language play and games of skill. In evolutionary theory, the so-called sexual selection (Darwin 1871) of apparently useless or even dangerously cumbersome features such as the peacock's tail is often explained as indirectly indicating qualities which are desirable in a mate (Tooby and Cosmides 1992:246).[6] The bird which can maintain such a long and awkward tail, it is supposed, clearly has energy to spare. In humans, verbal dexterity may have something of this superfluous quality; but it is also, as witnessed by numerous legendary characters from Odysseus to Brer Rabbit, an index of intelligence, making it as appropriate a display for the species as, say, aerial acrobatics are for some birds. One of the attributes humans select for when choosing a mate, it has been suggested, is playfulness—hence the frequent requirement of 'a good sense of humour' in lonely-hearts advertisements (Dunbar 1996:202–3), and the association of the playful with the erotic is revealed by words and phrases such as 'playmate', 'playboy', 'foreplay', and 'playing with yourself' (Sigmund 1995:209–11).

In these ways, verbal duelling can provide evolutionary psychology with a link between the behaviour of humans and the behaviour of animals, allowing language play to be traced back to pre-human origins, despite the fact that animals do not have language. It could even be extended into a hypothesis about the origin of language itself. There are, however, a number of limitations to this rather straightforward and highly speculative evolutionary explanation, whether of language in general or of language play in particular. Though one of the main functions of language may have been, and indeed still is, its agonistic use, it does not follow that its other playful functions, such as the creation of poetry or fiction, or its more practical functions, such as conveying information and forming social networks, should have come into existence solely for this purpose. It could equally be that, just as the peacock's tail developed from feathers evolved for more mundane purposes, so language play built upon features of language already developed for other uses. Phylogenetically, as ontogenetically, each function may have developed in tandem and been mutually reinforcing.

Moreover, even if the evolutionary origin of language were *partly* in its playful agonistic use, that does not necessarily mean that contest is the major function of language play today. Though language play may have arisen in contest, this use gives rise to various epiphenomena, with functions of their own, which outgrow and supersede their origin. From the insult, the joke, and the riddle may have arisen imaginary worlds which, developed into full-fledged fictions, allow their creators to explore hypothetical circumstances and events, thus increasing the key human attribute of flexibility in dealing with unforeseen eventualities. Language play, even if first developed in conflict, may have changed the nature of language itself, making it capable of far more than mere lekking. Thus while it would be foolish to deny that there is an agonistic role for language play, and even that this might be its origin, we need to look much further for a full explanation of its importance and function.

In the next chapter, we shall return in more detail to the adequacy of evolutionary explanations of language play and the degree to which its origins can be traced to verbal duelling. For the moment, it is worth remarking that the forms which language takes as a means of creating group solidarity and expressing aggression far transcend in complexity the demands of the lek. Striking examples of such apparently superfluous complexity are to be found in the instances of language play examined in the remainder of this chapter: play languages, jokes, riddles, puns, and religious and magical rituals.

Play languages

Play languages are defined by Sherzer (1992) as 'linguistic codes derived by a small set of rules from a language in common use in a particular speech community'. Often they are based upon some relatively straightforward principle, such as the reordering of syllables. (This simplicity, however, does not make them easy either to produce or to understand.) Like verbal duelling, they are found in diverse communities throughout the world, and thus seem to have developed independently. Sherzer (*ibid.*) gives the following examples:

Pig Latin
Give it to me = Ivgay itay ootay iymay

French
Parler à l'envers (Verlen or Larpen in French)
Passe-moi la bouteille = Sap mois la toubeille

These are European examples, and may have a common origin. The universal appeal of such procedures, however, is evident in the occurrence of this same principle[7] of inversion in play languages throughout the world. In Cuna[7] (an indigenous language in Colombia) it is used in a play language in which the final syllable becomes the first (Price and Price 1976):

osi (pineapple) sio
ope (to bathe) peo
takke (to see) ketak

Although some play languages are used for fun (Stewart 1979), they can also have a more serious social function in creating group identity, and are often used by an underclass for purposes of secrecy and for protection against the majority (Price and Price 1976; Sherzer 1976; Halliday 1978). They are thus, like the boasts of verbal duelling, both an act of solidarity and exclusion. Yet they also create a sense of enjoyment which persists even when their value in conflict or for secrecy no longer exists. What starts life as a thieves' argot may end up as a game or a joke. The attractions of play languages, like those of many other aspects of language play, can only partly be explained by social utility.

Humorous language play: aggression and resistance

In verbal duelling the same ritual insult which the speaker uses to cause offence to his opponent, simultaneously raises laughter, and augments the sense of solidarity among his supporters. It also asserts a claim for a position, very often one of leadership, within the group. In one view, joking and laughter are always aspects of aggression. Indeed, pessimistically, there are those who have suggested that laughing *with* somebody almost always entails laughing *at* somebody else (Rapp 1951; Morreal 1983),[8] and the suggestion is that verbal humour originated in, and is always entwined with, assertions of superiority. This view has a long history. Thomas Hobbes, in 1650, observed that

> The passion of laughter is nothing else but sudden glory arising from sudden conception of some eminency in ourselves, by comparison with the infirmity of others, or with our own formerly: for men laugh at the follies of themselves past, when they come suddenly to remembrance, except they bring with them any present dishonour.
> (*Human Nature* 1650, quoted in Raskin 1985:36)

And it persists in 20th-century theories of humour too. According to Fry (1963):

> Laughter is then variously explained as resulting from feelings of superiority in attack and again as compensatory reaction to feelings of inferiority in battle.

Such explanations, though they may not be complete, are certainly not to be discounted. There are many aspects of humour and laughter which are intimately concerned with contests. The subject-matter of jokes is often about areas of competition, such as sexual seduction, ethnicity, and politics, and the act of telling a joke is frequently one in which the hearer's powers of interpretation are tested. This is particularly true in riddles—which act like a challenge to the recipient to find a solution—but it is also true of jokes in general. By 'getting the joke', the recipient displays both ingenuity and access to shared knowledge and values, including those which are conspiratorial or taboo. Among children and teenagers, for example, understanding sexual allusion is taken to indicate experience and maturity. Laughing (or not laughing) at a racist joke may indicate whether (or not) prejudices are shared.

This use of humour to establish solidarity need not always be to assert superiority or drive home a victory, however. A good deal of humour— perhaps the best—is so-called 'losers' humour': a means of rebellion, a resistance to tyranny, and a compensation for defeat. To this category belongs the whole wealth of jokes about oppressive and corrupt regimes, self-satisfied hypocrisy, and the arrogance of those in power—the fun of the joke being augmented by the illegality and danger in either telling it or laughing at it.[9] To put it another way: humour and dissidence are in sympathy, while humour and conformity to establishment values are often at odds.

Yet if verbal humour is used in aggression and resistance, it is equally a means of reconciliation. For example, the angry duelling exchange between Tony Blair and John Major quoted on page 67 was halted and defused by a humorous intervention from the Speaker of the House of Commons, Betty Boothroyd:

> Order, order! I think there are a lot of members of this house who have got a good deal of pre-electional tension.

This intervention raised laughter from both sides, momentarily uniting them in the joke. At the risk of unnecessary explanation—ever present in any analysis of humour—Boothroyd uses 'pre-electional tension' to suggest the phrase 'pre-menstrual tension', often invoked by men to explain emotional and unreasonable outbursts by women. Reversing sexual stereotypes, she uses it to criticize and explain the petulant behaviour of the two men, by attributing it to the imminent general election.

Where an insult seems to be the paradigm means of using language to force people apart, then, humour seems intuitively to be its mirror image: a way of bringing them together. While agonistic play seems to be concerned with pomposity and posturing, separateness and self-importance, humour often deflates that arrogance, and emphasizes what the speaker and the listener have in common. The relationship of the two, however, is not always so simple. Abuse may be humorous; humour may be abusive. A joke can bring some people together in the very act of repudiating a common enemy. So even if not mutually implicated, the two opposite purposes are closely related.

Not surprisingly then, jokes and insults often make similar uses of language (and as such are another example of bulge theory). Both may use taboo words and address taboo topics, for example. An interesting permutation of this close connection are so-called 'joking relationships'[10] in which people relate through banter and mockery, expressing their affection through utterances which if taken literally would be rude. When used by subordinates to those in power, such jesting momentarily reverses the ordinary hierarchies of their social network (Douglas 1968). Joking relationships are thus clearly an example of play, as defined by Fry (1963:125):

> Play . . . is behaviour which depends on the mutual recognition (through metacommunication, internal or external) that that behaviour does not mean the same thing as does that behaviour (fighting, etc.) which play represents.

Joking, then, is to insulting, as competitive play is to fighting: the use of the same or very similar behaviour for the opposite effect. As we shall see below, it is an inversion which seems to have a particular and dangerous attraction for humans. But it also demands ingenuity, since it requires great skill to remain on the borderline, without being perceived as having strayed across into aggression.

Humorous language play: possible explanations

Accepting this view of humour as performing these social functions of aggression, rebellion, reconciliation, or solidarity, however, is not to say that it is entirely accounted for in this way. Raskin (1992) points to the existence of two other traditions in humour theory: a psychoanalytical approach, in which humour is viewed as the outcome of release; and a cognitive explanation, in which humour seems to result from the perception of incongruity. To these might be added a third, somatic explanation. In medical science there has been a growing view of humour as having beneficial therapeutic or prophylactic effects on health (Jacobson 1997).

1 Release theory

Freud (1905) saw linguistic humour as a psychological mechanism bringing repressed desires into consciousness, and as 'an outlet for mental, nervous, and psychic energy after strain, struggle or tension' (Raskin 1992). As such, humour, like other forms of play, may help self-regulation. If we view joy as the emotional consequence of release, then this feeling in itself may, as Darwin claimed, lead to laughter:

> Joy, when intense, leads to various purposeless movements—to dancing about, clapping the hands, stamping etc., and to loud laughter.
> (Darwin 1872:207)

It is the physical consequences of laughter which may have the positive effects on health referred to above. There is, however, a certain circularity in release theory. While this feeling of joy can be accounted for as the outcome of 'release', or even of victory in contest, it cannot always be so easily explained away. While release may lead via humour to relaxation, and an improvement in mood and health, the reverse is also true: that a good mood makes humour more likely. Even Freud (1905) had to acknowledge that the 'most favourable' condition for verbal humour to be appreciated is 'a generally cheerful mood in which one is inclined to laugh', thus making this mood both the cause and the effect.

2 Incongruity theory

Many theorists of humour have advanced the view that humour is created by the perception of incongruity: when phenomena seem to be contradictory, or when a new stimulus is inconsistent with past experience. Incongruity, of course, is by no means limited to language. It may be visual—as in clowning, silent film, or captionless cartoons—or it may be musical, or in some other mode. It also seems to pre-date language in child development. Infants as young as four months respond with laughter to 'violations of expectations', and this laughter at incongruity leads to 'arousal boosts (i.e. moderate increases in arousal level)' which are then followed by 'arousal jags (sharp decreases in arousal after previously high levels)' (Pien and Rothbart, cited in McGhee and Chapman 1980:2). The laughter accompanying these rapid changes leads in turn, in all age groups, to the production of pleasurable endogenous opiates in the brain (Dunbar 1996:182): a rewarding reaction which, presumably, has been environmentally selected in our species for a reason. The human response to incongruity in verbal humour, in other words, seems to be built upon some general innate liking for incongruity in general. The question then arises—to be confronted in a later chapter—as to why human beings should have developed so positive a reaction to contradiction and the violation of expectation.

3 Raskin's theory of script incongruity

In his book *Semantic Mechanisms of Humour*, Victor Raskin (1985) applied incongruity theory to verbal humour. He takes as his material for analysis 'set piece' jokes: the kind which can be repeated in many different situations, rather than those spontaneous jokes which arise from, and are only funny in, one particular context. Defining 'semantics' as an area which is not sharply distinguished from pragmatics, but constantly merges into it (and is thus eternally problematic) Raskin seeks to define how, in his examples, incongruity is inherent in certain textual features in such a way that—at least for many speakers of the language in many situations—the joke will be perceived as funny. To do this, he adopts the notion of the schema as developed in several related disciplines in the 1970s and 1980s.

Schemata are organized 'packages' of encyclopaedic knowledge about typical instances and likely sequences of events which the mind uses to predict outcomes and to fill in missing details. Schema theory suggests that people understand new experiences by activating relevant schemata in their minds (Schank and Abelson 1977; Schank 1982). Elements which are not specifically mentioned may be expected to be present by default in the absence of any information to the contrary. In many situations, schematic processing allows people to interpret new experiences quickly and economically, making intelligent guesses as to what is likely to happen, even before they have explicit evidence. Thus, if I tell you that 'I went to a restaurant last night', you are likely to assume (without being told) that I sat on a chair, ordered a meal, paid, and left. If you later discover that I sat on the floor, cooked the meal myself, robbed the till at gunpoint, or stayed all night, you will adjust your understanding accordingly. Schemata vary according to cultural norms and individual experience: whether restaurants are expected to serve alcohol, whether they are routine or special places to eat. Despite these differences, however, in many cases it is reasonable to assume that schemata are shared. The mutual understanding and appreciation of a particular text may establish that speaker and listener share the same assumptions. In fact, one view of joke-telling would be to attribute it to exactly this function.[11]

Raskin (1985)—who uses the related term 'script'[12] rather than 'schema'— adopts the view that words and sequences of words in a text act as 'triggers' in activating particular scripts for text processing. The script should therefore be considered (despite the obvious scope for individual variation and difference) as part of the semantics of words: 'a large chunk of (. . .) information surrounding the word or evoked by it' (*op. cit.*: 81). His claim is that, whereas in 'normal' non-humorous communication the activation of incongruous scripts is avoided (or, if it happens accidentally, quickly clarified), in verbal humour such script ambiguity is both courted and much appreciated. It is, in fact, the origin of the joke, and the cause of the laughter.

To demonstrate his ideas, Raskin (*op. cit.*: 117–27) analyses the following anecdote in some detail, and with some show of formality:

> 'Is the doctor at home?' the patient asked in his bronchial whisper. 'No', the doctor's young and pretty wife whispered in reply. 'Come right in.'

As a joke, the story has some obvious shortcomings. As Raskin himself comments, it is rather dated, particularly by its allusion to the practice of calling on a doctor at home. As an example for analysis, however, it does have a number of advantages:

It is not an obvious pun nor an allusion and is therefore of a medium degree of complexity within the set of simple jokes. It is not terribly funny nor terribly unfunny. It is not too short nor too long. None of its parameters, in other words, is extreme, atypical, or extraordinary in any sense. (*op. cit.*: 117)

In Raskin's view, the story activates two different and incompatible scripts: the one to do with visits to the doctor, the other with marital infidelity. The key to this humorous clash is in specific words which can trigger either script. Thus the 'Visiting the Doctor Script' is triggered by the words 'doctor', 'patient', 'bronchial whisper', and neither the presence of a 'wife', nor the question 'Is the doctor at home?' are incompatible with interpretation via this script. The word 'whisper', however, may also trigger a script for conspiracy, and more specifically, in the context of a man asking a woman in a whisper if her husband is out, marital infidelity. The word 'wife', which is compatible with the 'Visiting the Doctor Script', now takes on a new dimension, emphasized by the words 'young and pretty' which, while relevant to the 'Infidelity Script', are not at all relevant to the 'Visiting the Doctor Script'. The joke is that the script obviously activated in the wife's mind by the whisper is different from that being followed by the patient, and also at first by the hearer of the joke. She has understood 'the doctor' as a synonym for 'your husband', and interpreted the whisper as one occasioned by conspiracy rather than bronchitis: a fact which, amusingly, suggests that opportunities for infidelity are uppermost in her mind. Perhaps, too, the gratuitous mention of 'young and pretty' suggests a change in script for the patient. There are, as it were, two stories activated at once, the first one suddenly shifting to the next.

| 'Is the doctor at home?' | the patient | asked | in his bronchial whisper. |
| 'Is your husband at home?' | the man | whispered. | |

| 'No', the doctor's wife | | replied. |
| 'No', the doctor's young and pretty wife | | whispered in reply. |

'Come back later.'
'Come right in.'

In this explanation, two phrases—'bronchial whisper' and 'young and pretty wife'—are crucial to the incongruity which makes the joke funny. The theory thus acknowledges the importance of wording in humour, though not to an extent which would exclude paraphrase or translation. One could say, for example, 'attractive wife' or 'in a low voice' without losing the point. In other words, the joke does not depend upon *exact* wording. This illustrates two important points about the way in which scriptal ambiguity differs from the linguistic ambiguity which occurs in sentences such as

Flying planes can be dangerous.
She cannot bear children.

The first point is that such sentences, if used in context, are unlikely to be perceived as ambiguous at all. Secondly, their ambiguity is so tied to exact wording that it cannot be paraphrased or translated. Scriptal ambiguity, on the other hand, like that in the joke about the doctor's wife, is likely to cause a double-take in processing. It is also much more readily translated into another language.

Here we might appeal to a useful distinction drawn by the philosopher Henri Bergson ([1899] 1956) 'between the comic expressed and the comic created by language'. It is the former rather than the latter which is the domain of 'scriptal ambiguity'. 'The comic created by language', on the other hand, resides in jokes dependent upon exact wording, like puns—to which we shall return shortly.

Shortcomings of the scriptal ambiguity view

There are a number of ways in which schema theory as a methodology for text analysis can be criticized. Script assignation seems rather arbitrary, and analysis *post hoc* rather than predictive. Nevertheless, applied to this anecdote, the approach seems to work adequately as an explanation. As a general theory of verbal humour, however, there are a number of problems. One is that there is no attempt at explaining *why* script incongruity in general might be funny, or why certain incongruities are funny rather than others. In the above analysis, for example, the alternative combination:

> ('Is your husband at home?' the man whispered. 'No', the doctor's wife whispered in reply. 'Come back later.')

is equally incongruous, but not at all funny. The point missed by Raskin, perhaps, is that it is not the cognitive fact of scriptal ambiguity *per se* which makes this joke potentially funny, but the social implications of this particular incongruity alluding to sexuality.

A second problem is that the theory offers no explanation of the occurrence of script incongruity with effects other than humour, especially in literature. There is no reason, for example, why the opening sentence of J. M. Barrie's *Peter Pan*

All children, except one, grow up.

cannot be analysed in terms of script incongruity, too. Here, it might be said, an Inevitability of Ageing Script is disrupted by an Eternal Youth Script, and by implication the world of banal facts is disrupted by that of fantasy and magic.[13] Yet the effect, though aesthetically pleasing, is in no way humorous. And lest this example from a fantasy for children be thought too light, it is not difficult to find such literary incongruities of much greater weight: whether at sentence level ('none of woman born shall harm Macbeth'), or on a more global and more discoursal level in, say, the clash between the philanthropic altruistic intentions of Raskolnikov in *Crime and Punishment* and the murder which he actually commits,[14] or between the imperative to action and the disposition to contemplation in *Hamlet*.

There is perhaps, behind this failure to account for a significant shared ground between humorous and non-humorous discourses, a particularly modern desire to keep certain types of linguistic activity firmly under control, and to deny them the potential social and psychological power which they have exercised in other ages and places. Raskin, like many other contemporary analysts of verbal humour (Nash 1985; Chiaro 1992), treats the joke as a clearly-defined entity, distinct from other more serious discourses. His set-piece jokes have clear beginnings and endings; their exclusive purpose is to be funny. 'Serious' communication halts while they are being told, and resumes when they have finished. The boundaries are clear.

Riddles

As with many other aspects of language play, this attitude towards humorous language illustrates the inclination of modern Western society (including academic analyses) to relegate playful behaviour to a separate and less important domain: that of the childish, the trivial, and—indeed—the 'funny'. The riddle and the pun are two outstanding examples of this relegation. While both are generally regarded in modern society as 'humour', often of a particularly infantile and feeble kind, they have in other times and places exerted more weighty social influence in ritual, art, religion, and magic (Hasan-Rokem and Shulman 1996; Redfern 1984; Ulmer 1988; Culler 1988). Thus it is a far cry from the children's riddles reported by Opie and Opie (1959), such as

> What goes up when the rain comes down?
> An umbrella.

> Why did the bull rush?
> Because it saw the cow slip.

to the role played by the riddles of the Ancient Greek oracles in myth and drama, on which life and death depend:

> There is a creature that moves upon the earth
> On two feet, on four, and on three.
> Sophocles: *Oedipus The King* (1978:102)

The decline in status of the riddle is reflected in the fact that this particular one—the question posed to Oedipus by the sphinx—was versified and used

as a joke by Scottish schoolchildren, unconscious of its origin, in the 1950s.
(Opie and Opie 1959:76)

> Walks on four feet
> On two feet, on three,
> The more feet it walks on
> The weaker it be.
> (The answer is a person: crawling, walking unaided, and then walking in
> old age with a stick.)

In many diverse societies riddles play or have played a central part in the
rituals and processes of transformation. Thus Hasan-Rokem and Shulman
(1996) report how, among the Gonds in central India, men gather at the
borders of their village when one of their number is dying, and recite riddles
to the beating of a drum. Handelman (1996:49) lists studies—in societies as
far apart as Africa, the Caribbean, and South-East Asia—of the use of riddles
in marriages, funerals, wakes, religious worship, and the choice of a king. In
addition, as Kaivola-Bregenhøj (1996) observes, riddles are in many societies
a part of courtship, education, greeting, narratives, and songs.

In addition to these more serious uses in traditional societies, riddles have
also been a mainstay of adult entertainment. Kaivola-Bregenhøj (*ibid.*)
describes how in farming communities in rural Finland, even well into the
20th century, people would gather to exchange riddles, with precedence
being given to the older members and any visitors, as being likely to have the
greatest repertoires. Many of these refer vividly to the realia of a pre-
industrial agricultural lifestyle:

What is the ox's eye on the wall?	A knot.
Take it away it increases, put it back it decreases.	Light when covering and opening the barn window.
Something goes down laughing and comes up crying.	A bucket.[15]

Others refer to realia still familiar in urban society:

A doorless shed full of food.	An egg.
A red rafter with lots of white chickens.	Gums and teeth.

Some, from both these categories, to the embarrassment of the guesser, flaunt
sexual suggestiveness:

A hairy thing lies on a thigh, looking to see when it can get in a hole.	A spindle.
Hangs in the daytime, put in a hole at night.	A coat hook.

Those who persistently failed to guess the riddles would be banished from
the room in disgrace to the fantasy land of Hymylä, described as 'a topsy-

turvey world in which all the customs and practices of our world are reversed' (*ibid.*). There they might be dressed in a crazy fashion, with their coat inside out, and asked to stir porridge with an axe or chop wood with a ladle, until released by 'the mistress of Hymylä', one of their tormentors, who told them the answers to the riddles they had been unable to guess. Though amusing to the majority, this banishment was also a serious disgrace, with an element of fear (Handelman 1996).

Why is the riddle so powerful in so many societies? It is ideally suited to competition, and to the establishing of both social inclusion and exclusion. Like metaphors, and formal and scriptal ambiguities, it conflates two worlds. By setting up one frame of reference and then replacing it with another it seems to symbolize transitions. By first decontextualizing phrases and then providing them with a context, it expresses in miniature the power of language both to obscure and to illuminate, to refer to both the fantastic and the mundane. These facts may explain its appeal, but not its decline. It may be that in modern life, the riddle, to be taken seriously, has had to change its name. The modern 'lateral thinking problem', for example, (de Bono 1970) can be viewed as a modern riddle, disguised as a mental test. It is a moot point whether the essence of the riddle may have survived in such reincarnations. Is its spirit still with us, for example, despite changes of form and use, in such modern practices as the setting of tests in education, or the creation of deliberate obfuscation in—for example—literature and advertising?

Puns

Closely related to the riddle, often employed in it, and similarly devalued in modern life, is the pun. Raskin omits it, deliberately and specifically, abandoning in doing so the 'objective' scientific stance which he adopts towards his subject-matter elsewhere. His reasons are as follows:

> It is the easy availability of puns which makes them a cheap and somewhat despicable type of humour for many individuals and social groups.
> (Raskin 1985:141)

This vehemence is significant. For the pun displays two characteristics which are quite antithetical to modern attitudes to language. First, it is the extreme case of a use of language in which exact wording is essential. It is the paradigm case of Bergson's 'comic created by language', and rests upon the use of formal semantic ambiguities (of the flying-planes-can-be-dangerous kind) discounted in Raskin's theory. Second, the pun seems to create an inversion, in which language itself seems to dictate meaning, rather than the other way round. To say why these two characteristics of the pun are antithetical to modern attitudes to language will require a closer analysis of the pun, and of its decline in status.

In the contemporary science-dominated world, punning is kept at arm's length; people frequently apologize for punning (by saying 'no pun intended') and the ritual response to puns is a groan, even when their wit is also simultaneously enjoyed or admired. 'Europeans . . .' writes Ahl '. . . are trained to admire irony but to disapprove of puns' (Ahl: 1988:21). Puns are regarded as childish trivia, unsuitable for serious subjects or discourses, and in a sense all puns, even good puns, are bad puns. While other forms of word play that force incongruous juxtapositions of semantically separate concepts (rhyme, alliteration, metaphor, irony) receive serious and respectful attention in literary criticism, punning is largely ignored or scathingly dismissed. (I feel some hesitation myself at including such a long section on puns in this chapter.)

This opposition to, if not fear of, puns has a long and respectable history. Aristotle saw them as a danger to philosophy (Ulmer 1988); Dr Johnson regarded them as 'the fatal Cleopatra' which spoilt Shakespeare's plays (Redfern 1984); the literary critic William Empson described them as not 'manly' (Ahl 1988). Yet this rationalist disquiet and disapproval, the downgrading of puns to the realm of childish play, is in no way a universal or historically consistent phenomenon. The oracles of the ancient world used puns as prophecy:

Domi ne stes/Domine stes = Do not stay at home/Lord, stay.

was the ambiguous answer of the oracle at Delphi to a general who sought advice on whether to stay or go (Crystal 1987:63). Classical Roman poetry is often structurally dependent upon puns (and anagrams, which are their visual equivalent) (Ahl 1988).[16] In the Bible, the verse which provides the authority for the Catholic belief in the apostolic succession, Christ's charge to Peter

Thou art Peter, and upon this rock I shall build my church.
(Matthew 16:18)

is a pun in the original Greek, where the Greek name (πέτρος) 'also means "rock"'.[17] Yet it is hardly a light or culturally unimportant utterance.

Although literary puns have often been treated by critics as slips of taste (or even of the pen) this view has not been shared by many of the 'best' writers. Shakespeare was a dedicated punster, not only for comic but also for tragic purpose, though this is often obscured by etymological change, and needs explication by glossaries and notes. An example is Hamlet's cry:

'Is thy union here?'
(Hamlet V ii:340)

when he realizes that his mother has drunk the wine laced with a poisoned pearl (*union* was another word for pearl in Elizabethan English) by the man she has joined in the *union* of marriage, thus bringing about her *union* with death. Here a pun compresses meanings and emotions in a powerful and poignant manner. The pearl was an established symbol for the soul[18] and Gertrude's life is slipping away as the pearl dissolves in the wine, just as her virtue (in Hamlet's view) was destroyed by her intoxication with Claudius, who was himself addicted to wine.

In modern times, puns have resurfaced with a vengeance in high literature and art, visually as well as verbally in surrealist poetry and painting, and most notably in James Joyce's *Finnegans Wake*, a book which, having started with a title which itself contains several puns (le fin = the end, Fiann = an Irish folk hero; egan = again[19]; wake = funeral/wake up) continues in the same vein for over six hundred pages. In the 20th century, puns have also gained respectability from their importance in psychoanalysis and the philosophy of deconstruction (Ulmer 1988), a change supported by growing awareness of the different attitude towards punning not only in earlier periods of European culture but also in other cultures (they are regarded for example as a 'navigator of thought' in Zen Buddhism (Redfern 1984:146)). Though held in low esteem, the pun is still omnipresent in popular culture, in the tabloid press, in advertisements, placards, shop signs, graffiti, and in comedy.

Why are puns so controversial and why do they arouse such widely differing responses: of pleasure and a sense of profundity on the one hand, of contempt and derision on the other? Perhaps some insight may be gained by examining particular instances more thoroughly and contrasting a modern light-hearted use of a pun with more serious uses in the past. In *Puns*, Redfern (1984) gives (without further comment) the following example:

> A man always bought his wife her favourite flowers, anemones, for her birthday. One year, he arrived at the flower shop late, and, as they had run out of anemones, he bought her some greenery. When she received the bouquet she commented: 'With fronds like these, who needs anemones?'

This is a classic punning joke, using the slightest phonemic substitution and addition to yield virtual homophony. It is also a story in which the pun is the point itself, rather than some additional embellishment or decoration. If, therefore, the reader does not like puns, or does not like this particular pun, then he or she will not like the whole story, for there is nothing else there: the pun does not emerge from a fictional world: the fictional world is constructed in order to create the pun. If we reconstruct the creation of this story, it is very likely to have proceeded backwards, beginning with the set utterance 'With friends like these, who needs enemies', proceeding to the spoof substitutions, and then creating the man, his wife, and her birthday in order to lead to this conclusion. Why are her favourite flowers anemones rather than tulips? Why has the flower shop run out of them? Why does it have only greenery instead of, say, daffodils? The answer to all these questions is clearly: to enable the punch-line to take the form it does. This illustrates both the nature of the pun and its disruptive anarchic power. For not only does the composition of the story run backwards, but the whole functioning of language is thrown into reverse.

Perhaps this inversion is the source both of the power of the pun, and the horror and loathing which it inspires in commentators. The orthodox modern view, reflecting both popular wisdom and the standard outlook of a rationalist scientist world view, is that language serves to represent the world. Within a language, signifiers ('anemones', 'friends') have an arbitrary but socially conventional and shared relationship to concepts (de Saussure [1915] 1983:67–9)[20] which in turn represent both the external and internal world. This enables language to perform, in a fairly orderly way, its main functions of conveying information (its ideational function) and establishing social relationships (its interpersonal function) (Halliday 1973:22–46). The code is there to serve a purpose, not to take on a life of its own. There are however, within the code, confusions, crossovers, and coincidences. Homonyms[21] —the stuff of puns—are obvious instances, although in 'normal' communication they do not pose a problem as the sense intended is usually clear from the context. If it is not (as pointed out by Raskin in his discussion of formally ambiguous sentences) clarification is made by the sender or sought by the receiver of the message, all in an orderly manner. In the story above, however, this is overturned. Confusion and meaningless coincidence is not only *not* avoided but deliberately sought out and created. Signifiers appear not to *represent* events and people but, through a chance association, to *create* them. Rather than conveying any information about the world, language says something useless about itself. Though the story may be used inter-personally to create phatic communion when there is nothing else to say, this does not explain why a punning story should be used to do this rather than something else.

In the case of the fronds and anemones, all this may seem rather trivial. Some people like such stories and some do not, and in contemporary society, where puns are used only recreationally, it does not much matter which sort of person one is. Though punning may have the *potential* to overturn the rational empiricist view of language, it is not through stories such as this one. When we turn, however, to other examples—Christ's words to Peter, or Hamlet's to Claudius—the issue is less easily dismissed. If both the choice and the qualities of the apostle, and consequently the basis of an institution as powerful as the papacy, seem to emerge from a chance and apparently meaningless coincidence; if the themes and images of one of the greatest works of literature can be so focused in four words, then puns seem to be of quite a different order.

In the pun, the relation of language and reality seems inverted. By virtue of exact wording, a linguistic form which appears to represent one reality suddenly rebounds upon itself and creates another. Where there was 'no pun intended', it can even appear to do this independently. As such, the pun is a miniature of language play functioning creatively, apparently forcing its users to surrender to chance coincidences in the language, as though to powers beyond their control. In its ability to invert and to subvert, the pun can seem a remnant of a different cosmology in which language creates new realities. It preserves (if only metaphorically) some trace of the uses of language in magic; and it is this association which perhaps accounts for the vehemence of the reaction against puns in rational philosophy and empirical science.

Inversion through play

To the modern mind, this long disquisition upon the pun may appear to be a digression leading us away from the more obviously social uses of language play as symbolic aggression, or as an index of solidarity. The inversion of the relationship between language and meaning in pun production may seem to be a cognitive rather than a social phenomenon. Yet this separation of the two realms, and the related view of play language as a private matter, may itself be symptomatic of changes in attitude to language play.

There is, in the pun, the power to invert the established order (in this case the relation of language and reality) by means of the exploitation of arbitrary features within the language code. Inversion of this kind is, as we have seen in earlier chapters, a common feature of language play, and indeed of play in general. In children's 'tangle talk', in the improbable events that emerge from rhyme, in the bizarre reversals of reality in folk tales, in the topsy-turvy land of Hymylä, we can perceive very clearly the ability of language 'to turn the world upside down'—if not the actual world, at least the inner world of the imagination—an ability which while clearly and immediately evident in children's language use, is still present, in more complex and more powerful ways, in adult literature. In a similar way, the play of words in adult humour has both the capacity (as revealed in Raskin's analysis) to substitute rapidly one interpretative schema for another, and more generally to convert the serious into the lighthearted, to disrupt work and study, and to deflate, and thus subtract from, the arrogance of the powerful. Something of this disruptive and unruly quality remains in contemporary discourse in the puns of tabloid headlines and of graffiti, taking and overturning the establishment view about a serious subject. On the day when the boxer Mike Tyson, by biting off his opponent's ear lobe, 'brought the world championship into disrepute', in the words of the serious press, *The Sun*'s headline was 'WORLD CHOMP'. In a similar way, graffiti, especially those appended to public notices or other graffiti, often ridicule by exploiting the linguistic ambiguity of phrases referring to the most serious emotions and institutions:

AVE MARIA—Don't mind if I do.
ELVIS LIVES—And they've buried the poor bugger.

This pleasurable power to invert the established order is not only a feature of language play, but of play in general. In sporting contests, players who may be unequal in other contexts meet on equal terms. Social attributes, such as wealth or status, which may form the basis of hierarchical relations outside the game, are replaced by others such as skill with words, or coordination of body, hand, and eye. As victory in some games can earn both wealth and status, it may even establish a new hierarchy in 'real' life. Something akin to such reversal is present even in the animal world, where the actual physical superiority (being able to win in a fight) is replaced by the symbolic superiority of singing loudest or having the brightest tail. In games of chance, the usual human desire to exert control over events is deliberately, and sometimes completely, relinquished. In dressing up, one person becomes another. While in some games of vertigo, such as acrobatics, or the fairground helter-skelter, the world is—quite literally—turned upside down.

In the modern world, this power of play to overturn the established order persists, but is marginalized or carefully controlled. It is placed in the domain of the child, or, in adult life, either deemed to be serious (political verbal duelling), treated with disdain by the establishment (tabloid and graffiti puns), or accepted but carefully cordoned off (a game or comedy show). As revealed by sacred and literary riddling and punning, however, this exclusion of disruptive language play from social events of high status, is by no means the norm in all societies. There have been earlier periods of European history in which the integration of the playful and the serious has been so pervasive, and to the modern mind so surprising, that it should give us pause for thought about the degree to which the nature and function of play are indeed universal. In his analysis of medieval carnival, the Russian philosopher Bakhtin ([1940] 1968) describes how the values of the ascendant ideology of the Catholic Church were on certain feast days temporarily, and institutionally, suspended. In illustration he cites (Bakhtin [1934] 1981) the wide circulation of bawdy parodies of the Lord's Prayer, and gives this (rather mild) example:

> Pater noster, tu n'ies pas foulz
> Quar tu t'ies mis en grand repos
> Qui es montes haut in celis
> *(Our Father, thou art not daft;*
> *For thou hast given thyself a good rest,*
> *Who hast ascended into Heaven.)*

In these spoof prayers it is significantly play with language—in particular the macaronic mixing of vernacular with Latin—which effects the parody: this mixture, as Bakhtin points out, symbolically overturning the usual and historical hierarchical relation between the languages involved.

What is surprising from a modern point of view is that this apparent rebellion was not something which took place illicitly, but institutionally. These bawdy prayers were recited on carnival days in the same churches, and even by the same priests, whose authority—from a modern point of view— they seem to overthrow. Apparently, however, this did not detract from the sincerity of serious worship on other days. This stark contrast between attitudes in our own and earlier times might lead us to conclude that, whatever the truth of universalist evolutionary arguments about language play (to which we shall turn in Chapter 4), there is clearly significant cultural and historical variation in its social status and function.

Play-like language in magic and religion

Perhaps the most startling and extreme social use of the apparent powers of language to invert existing states of affairs is in magic. Here it is not the ascendancy of one social class over another which is challenged but the very subordination of humanity to the power of natural forces. Magic can be defined as the belief that certain practices, including the recitation of certain sequences of words, have the power to control and influence both people and the natural world, either directly or through the invocation of supernatural spirits and forces.[22] Magical beliefs and practices are universal (Brown 1991: 69; Glucklich 1997). In many societies, they are major social institutions. Commonly, magic is believed to cure and heal, harm enemies and help friends, and harness natural forces. In addition, it is regarded as emanating from a gifted or special individual. With considerable similarity across disparate cultures, magical linguistic formulae are marked by a number of characteristics which, significantly, might nowadays be more readily associated with play. They must be performed with meticulous exactitude; they often make no sense to their users; they gain power through repetition; they lay particular store on the power of names (Glucklich 1997:203–20).[23]

Though few people in modern society would subscribe to the actual power of such linguistic practices to change the material world, it is clear that language use with these features (which are also typical of language play) is present, and exerts considerable psychological power, in many contemporary activities of great social significance, particularly organized religion. Whether magic is distinguished from religion, or whether the two are seen as opposite extremes of a continuum is largely a matter of belief: clearly there are both similarities and important differences. Obvious similarities are that both acknowledge the supernatural, and both make use of ritual. There are many religious practices, for example, in which the exact repetition of liturgies by members of a priesthood is regarded as essential for proper observance. (So much so, that when attempts are made to introduce change—as in the replacement of the Latin Mass or the Anglican *Book of Common Prayer*—there is strong and emotional opposition.) A difference between magic and religion, on the other hand, is that while the former claims to control the environment and supernatural forces, religion tends more to acknowledge human helplessness and the need for divine assistance (Malinowski 1948:3).

Those unsympathetic to religion can account for these similarities with the argument that religion descends directly from magic.[24] Yet the social importance attached to exact wording, obscure meaning, repetition, the power of names, and the rights of certain individuals to use certain forms of words, extends far beyond the domain of either, suggesting perhaps a more general social function for these features of language use than the practice or observance of beliefs. They remain significant elements in many secular popular events, ceremonies, and legal proceedings. For example, the chants of sports fans urging their team to victory retain some characteristics of incantation for success. Modern societies still exercise legal restraints upon the use of blasphemous and obscene language, taboo words, the use of names, and direct quotations.[25] In the class of speech acts known as 'declarations' (Austin 1962)—acts such as swearing an oath, naming a child, declaring war, sentencing a criminal—important social events come into existence, but only, by convention, if a certain form of words is uttered, in the right circumstances, by the right person. The act creates itself; there is no external reality to which it refers.

It is not only in public discourse that language still retains some of the features and functions of magic. Exact forms of words, and the acts of naming and repeating, may assume enormous importance in intimate relationships too—in arguments, promises, and declarations of love. In Chapter 2, for example, we have seen how rhymes—often as vague in meaning to their users as spells and liturgies are to their believers—may act to create and sustain relationships. Although forms of words may not control physical forces, they can certainly change the course of the social and psychological world.

Two attitudes to language

At the risk of simplification, it seems possible to identify two general and opposed attitudes to language, whose relative influence differs both historically and culturally. In the first view, significance is held to emerge from words themselves, to create, for example, magical acts, fictional worlds, or access to divine revelation, and the power of language to create such significance is held to reside in individuals of particular power or exceptional talent. In the second view, the power of language is considered to be its ability to refer to reality (to which it is therefore subordinate), to hold truths which are independent both of particular forms of words and of particular speakers. The former effect of language is apparent not only in magic and ritualistic religion, but also in poetry, fiction, and many playful uses of language; the latter is more evident in the discourses of technology and business.

These ways of engaging with language can be conceived as the opposite ends of a spectrum. At one end is a focus upon the forms of language divorced from their conventional meanings; at the other is a focus upon meanings in which forms are viewed as mere vehicles—with a host of intermediate positions between the two. In the former view linguistic forms have an intrinsic value, whether or not they are also assigned meanings; in the latter, forms are viewed as dispensable, and it is meanings which are held to exist independently.[26]

Sound, form, rituals	Meanings, interpretations, beliefs
Performance, incantation	Reading, understanding
Dependence on individuals	Objective independent truth

Figure 3.3: Opposing emphases in language use

This distinction, however, exists not only *between* spiritual and literary discourses on the one hand, and more factual, transactional ones on the other; it is found *within* conceptions of religion and literature as well. In our discussion of humour I have referred to Bergson's distinction 'between the comic expressed and the comic created by language'. This distinction might here be usefully extended. Religious truth and literariness are held, to varying degrees, to be expressed or created by language.

Exact wording in religion

In some religious practices, for example, proper conduct of the faith is dependent upon exact repetition of ritual entrusted to a priesthood. In others, liturgy and ritual are less significant, and the power of the priesthood is lessened or dispensed with altogether. What counts is the objective meaning which religious texts convey or inspire: the existence and nature of God, and the sincerity and virtue of believers. I shall refer to these, respectively, as 'ritualistic' and 'non-ritualistic' religious practice. Among ritualistic approaches, there are some where the form of words in texts and liturgies is paramount, and others where the importance attached to forms of words is associated with an equal emphasis upon understanding. At the extreme end of our spectrum are practices, found across faiths, where understanding the sacred words is deemed unimportant. Within Buddhism, for example, there are sects for whom the sound of words assumes a power independent of their meaning. A Nichiren Shoshu Buddhist should say the words 'nam-nyoho-renge-kyo' every day, whether or not he or she knows its meanings ('I devote my life to universal laws of cause and effect'). Similarly, in Hinduism, the sacred verbal formulae of Vedic mantras are repeated hundreds or even thousands of times on important occasions such as bathing in the Ganges (Glucklich 1997:204).[27] In Islamic countries where Arabic is not the native language, there are many Muslims who learn to recite long sections of the Koran without understanding what they are saying. Similarly, in many Jewish communities of the diaspora, Hebrew is recited at bar mitzvahs and other rituals by people who only have a limited understanding of the language (Glinert 1993).

Perhaps the most extraordinary and extreme focus upon the forms of religious wording, however, and disregard of literal meanings is to be found in the Judaic and Christian Kabbalistic interpretation of scripture. Here, in an operation reminiscent of word games with acrostics and anagrams, the words of the scriptures are treated (despite their evident conventional meanings in Hebrew and Greek) as a puzzle containing hidden meanings, to be discovered by interpretations of names as puns, by reversals and shuffling of letters, and by arithmetical calculations in which the letters are assigned numerical values (Eco [1995] 1997:25–34, 117–43; Steiner 1975:60–5). No aspect of the text, however apparently trivial, is to be ignored. Dan (1993) describes how according to one Kabbalist Hasidic scholar, Rabbi Eleazer:

> When one is studying a biblical verse, one should interpret it taking into account the following: the shape of the letters of the alphabet, the external image they present; the shape of the decorations with which they are adorned; the shape and sound of the musical signs which accompany the syllables; the shape and sound of the vocalisation marks which are added to every syllable; the fact that some letters are written in a larger or smaller fashion than the rest; the fact that some letters may be pronounced differently than they are written; the number of times each letter is mentioned, and the number of letters which are absent from this biblical section; the number of holy names and other terms; the many possible permutations of every group of letters; the numerical value of the letters; the combinations of first and last letters, and all the other methodological 'gates of wisdom'. (*ibid.*:22)

Kabbalistic reading, in other words, is focused upon meaning, but on meaning of an esoteric nature, which being encrypted in particular linguistic forms, is indissolubly linked to every detail of them. In effect, it treats the scriptures as a word game devised by God. Significantly, its practice has traditionally been regarded in Jewish culture as dangerous and closely related to magical power. In this context, exact wording takes on extraordinary importance. 'The omission or the addition of one letter' says the Talmud, 'might mean the destruction of the whole world' (quoted by Steiner 1975:61).

In religious practice, belief in the importance of exact wording is mirrored in attitudes to the paraphrase and translation of scriptures. Where the original wording matters, it follows that the original language (Arabic, Ge'ez,[28] Greek, Hebrew, Sanskrit, Tibetan) must be used.[29] Consequently, it must be learnt by the faithful for whom it is not a first language. Religion thus remains internationally a widespread reason for foreign language learning, if only to the extent demanded by particular practices. In ritualistic practice, this may entail only knowing how to pronounce the language for recitation, while in non-ritualistic practice it may involve the ability to read and understand the holy texts.

Religious ritual preserves some of the attitudes of an oral culture in which language is always performed in context and associated with actions. Insistence on original wording can also reflect a fear of the loss of knowledge through change. Many non-ritualistic practices, on the other hand are closely associated with widespread literacy. Literacy frees the believer from dependence upon custodians of the holy word; reading allows the time needed for careful interpretation; translation implies that the message is somehow 'the same' in different languages. Thus the less hierarchical social structures associated with the end of a theocracy, the belief in a textual meaning beyond the words, the divorce of language from a given context and performer, were all made possible by printing and translation. On the other hand, it is also true that the written text, away from the absence of the distractions of ritual action, encourages the attachment of greater importance to wording—and this is indeed what happened in many non-ritualistic sects.

It is worth noting that there is a dichotomy in literary uses of language rather similar to that in religious practice. Like religious ritual, literature has retained high social status, despite its frequently playful nature. It, too, has been uncoupled from any necessary link to recitation and performance, by the wider availability of books and the practice of silent reading. The rise of the novel is inextricably linked to the new circumstances of production and consumption brought about by printing (Watt [1957] 1963). Poetry and drama are now frequently experienced in silence and isolation rather than in public performance, the act of reading lessening at once the effects of sound, but also increasing the individual's capacity to focus upon meaning and interpretation.[30]

In literary theory there is a related dichotomy in the contrast between those approaches (such as formalism and stylistics) which view literary meaning as dependent upon specific wording, and others (such as Marxist and some schools of psychoanalytic criticism) which see the value of a literary work in the actualities (albeit fictional actualities) to which those words refer. Literature, in this latter view, provides insights into psychology and society, and these insights, though presented in one form of words, might still be paraphrased or translated into another (Cook 1994a:125–56).

Conclusion

Play, ritual, and art—as many writers have observed—are difficult to separate from each other in any principled way; and many theorists have suggested play to be the origin of the other two (Spencer 1898; Dissanayake 1988).[31] In this spirit of treating the three as related, this chapter has approached very different uses of language—duelling, trivial jokes, play languages, riddles, puns, magical and religious ritual, and literature—as though they are not only comparable in form, but also fulfil the same social functions. While in modern society they differ greatly in social status, this has not always been so in the past. To some readers it may seem objectionable to link the serious discourses of literature and religion with the trivia of humour and abuse, or the discredited practices of magic. Yet such an objection only underlines the extent of the change. The persistence of playful and ritualistic uses of language, even when the social functions or beliefs which motivated them have disappeared, suggests a present need which goes beyond a historical or evolutionary explanation of them as remnants from the past. The persistence of playful language may be due to its power not only in the interpersonal, aesthetic, and spiritual spheres, but also in scientific understanding, innovative thinking, and the survival and adaptability of individuals, societies, and the species. If this is so, then the common opposition drawn between a rational and transactional use of language on the one hand, and an apparently mystical and playful one on the other, may be unfortunate, misleading, and even dangerous. It is to the issue of the functions of play and playful language that we turn in the next section.

Notes

1 These are generalizations, and disregard differences between the use of such pronoun distinctions in different languages. Use of these pronouns may be symmetrical (both parties using the same form of address) or asymmetrical, with the more powerful party using the T form and the less powerful the V form (Brown and Gilman 1960). In French, as in many other languages with a similar distinction, there is a growing tendency for symmetrical use of the *tu* form to be more widely used.

2 The phrase originally derives from the bulge of the line on a graph which plots the occurrence of certain types of interaction against differential power.

3 For a description of the close relation between children's ball games and language games, see Opie and Opie 1997a.

4 All the studies of play languages and verbal duelling cited in a survey by Schwartzman (1978:283–301) deal either with children or with non-Western societies.

5 By tradition, each speaker from the front benches must remain behind a line on the floor, to ensure that he (and nowadays she) cannot cross swords with their opposite number.

6 It may also arise for more arbitrary reasons. Gould (1985:43) writes that: 'Darwin proposes—and I suspect he was largely right—that different standards of beauty arise for capricious reasons among the various and formerly isolated groups that people the far corners of our earth. These differences—a twist of the nose here, slimmer legs there, a curl in the hair somewhere else—are then accumulated and intensified by sexual selection, since those individuals accidentally endowed with favored features are more sought, and therefore more successful in reproduction.'

7 Also known as Kuna.

8 Though others, more optimistically, have suggested that even the most belligerent jokes help to deflect, deflate, and modify aggression (H. Jacobson 1997).

9 Raskin (1985) claims that such jokes flower in periods when repression is still present, but less severe than formerly. Thus, in his experience, Soviet jokes (which form the bulk of his examples) were more evident in the partial 'thaw' initiated by Krushchev, than under Stalin.

10 As in the case of verbal duelling, studies of joking relationships are mostly of 'exotic' societies, though such relationships are equally common in contemporary urban culture (Bricker 1976).

11 This paragraph is from Cook 1997. For further and more detailed discussion of schemata see Cook 1994a, Chapters 1 and 3.

12 Schank and Abelson (1977:41) define scripts as structures 'that describe appropriate sequences of events in a particular context . . . a predetermined, stereotyped sequence of actions that defines a well-known situation'. Raskin uses the term rather more generally as a synonym for schema.

13 The structure of the sentence in which the bald statement 'All children grow up' is interrupted by the parenthetic proviso 'except one' seems iconically to capture this disruption.

14 For further discussion see my book *Discourse and Literature* (Cook 1994a).

15 This is in fact an English riddle cited by Kaivola-Bregenhøj as similar to the Finnish ones.

16 Another visual equivalent of the pun is concrete poetry in which the shape of the verse creates a picture of the subject matter, as in *Easter Wings* by George Herbert, 'The Mouse's Tail' in *Alice in Wonderland*, and Guillaume Apollinaire's *Calligrammes*.

17 The pun also exists in Aramaic, the language which Jesus spoke. The Aramaic word for rock, *kefa*, (Hellenized as *cephas*) actually occurs in the Greek text of John 1:42. (Philip Pike, Reading University, personal communication.) The pun also survives in French, where both Peter and rock are 'pierre'.

18 See, for example, *Pearl*, by the Gawain poet.

19 The puns on 'end' and 'again' may refer to the fact that the closing words of *Finnegans Wake* can be read as the first half of the sentence with which it begins.

20 Saussure himself had an interest in anagrams (Starobinski 1971).

21 As well as complete homonyms (e.g. 'bank' as a place to keep money, and 'bank' as the side of a river) puns also make use of homographs (words which are written identically but pronounced differently, such as 'st.' (the abbreviation for 'saint' or 'street'), and homophones (words which are written differently but pronounced identically, such as 'heard' and 'herd').

22 For a refutation of this view see Glucklich 1997:156, 221–2, and *passim*.

23 Malinowski, with rationalist fervour, scathingly suggests that this provides an easy let-out: when the magic does not work, it is because there must have been an error in the spell.

24 In another view, magic derives from religion (Bouquet 1962:48f).

25 In the case of company and brand name logos, even the use of the forms of the letters needs permission (see Cook 1992:57, 78, 84).

26 A parallel to this dichotomy of religious attitudes can be found in modern linguistics, in the current dispute over whether the mind represents meaning in language itself (linguese) or in some other internal non-linguistic symbolic system of its own (mentalese).

27 Tantric mantras are also used for secular purposes: 'For instance, someone desperate for wealth may find a quiet isolated spot and recite the following formula 21,000 times: *Oṁ hrīṁ klīṁ śrīṁ namaḥ*. The words mean nothing in literal translation, except the last one, which means *obeisance*' (Glucklich 1997:205).

28 A liturgical and literary language used in Ethiopia.

29 An interesting development of this belief is when the exact wording of a translation assumes the same sacred status as the original, as illustrated in the case of the Latin Vulgate and the Authorized Version of the Bible.

30 The mystery and ambiguity of both liturgical and poetic discourse can be diminished by the time available for reading, although arguably there are prose styles whose studied opaqueness combats this by introducing new and peculiarly orthographic types of obscurity.

31 The boundaries between the three are uncertain, making it possible to describe instances of linguistic play and poetry, or linguistic play and ritual, along continua rather than discrete categories. This fact, incidentally, allows a gradual progression from the light to the serious which can be helpful in the teaching of difficult poetry (Bisong 1995; Widdowson 1992a).

PART TWO

Theories and explanations

4 The nature of play: evolutionary and cultural perspectives

In the first part of this book, we have examined how play permeates language at the three levels of linguistic form, semantic meaning, and pragmatic use. Such ubiquity demands some explanation, and it is the purpose of this second part to place the topic within a broader conceptual framework. There are two ways of theorizing language play: one is to regard it as an aspect of *play in general*; the other is to seek out distinct qualities in *language play in particular*. This chapter will take the first of these paths, considering theories of play in general.

In recent years, explanations of human behaviour—including play—have been clouded by a bitter debate between two opposed schools of thought. Both have something to add to our understanding of play, and in this chapter we shall draw upon both, while discounting extreme positions which claim a monopoly on insight and deny any validity to the other. The first—an evolutionary perspective—is interested in behaviour which is characteristic of the human species, and therefore, when considering play, examines only those elements which are universal, and the ways in which they are like or unlike animal play. The second—a cultural perspective—is interested in behaviour as an expression of cultural differences, and therefore, when considering play, examines historical and social variation, focusing upon human play as qualitatively different from that of animals. As we are treating play as central to human life, and as one emphasis or the other is implicit in much of contemporary academic debate about the nature of humanity, let us look briefly at the premises of these two approaches in general, before employing each in turn for its relevance to play.

Relativist and universalist views

For the greater part of this century, the prevailing wisdom in the 'human sciences' has favoured—implicitly or explicitly—a relativist view of the human mind and behaviour, as being determined more by cultural than by biological forces.[1] Cultures have been seen as taking on a disembodied life of their own, displaying characteristics different from and more powerful than those of either the human species or of the individual humans who compose them. A culture, in this view, cannot be understood by reducing it to its individual members and then studying their separate natures, on the assumption that all significant human characteristics, being genetically transmitted, will be found within each individual organism. Nor can mental and cultural phenomena be understood by reference to the workings of the body or the brain. Such 'reductionism' is seen as suitable only for the natural sciences, and the term has often been used pejoratively to criticize those bent on exporting it into the humanities. The emphasis in this approach, then, is constructivist, believing that language and culture largely determine the 'reality' in which we live, by moulding the mind into a variety of shapes. Even science, which purports to describe reality, is considered in some post-structuralist writing to be as determined as any other discourse by culturally specific and historically variable ideology (Foucault [1969] 1977).

In recent decades, this relativist view of human behaviour has been challenged by a new 'evolutionary psychology' which regards both human mind and behaviour as largely delimited by genetic inheritance, interacting with environmental factors. This genetic inheritance is seen as the product of selective adaptation to the prehistoric environment in which people lived as hunter-gatherers for by far the longest (and in evolutionary terms the only significant) period of their history: for the 4 million years or so of hominid evolution, as opposed to the 12,000 or so years since the appearance of agriculture. As a result of this adaptation, it is claimed, there are species-specific characteristics (a universal human nature), shared by all individuals and consequently by all societies. Distinctive features of the species, such as language,[2] high intelligence, and complex social organization, have developed for the same reasons that other distinctive features have been naturally selected in other animals. Humans, though superficially different from other animals (as all species are by definition different from each other) are also similar to them at a deeper level, in that human nature has been determined in essentially the same way as the nature of other animals. Dolphins dive, scorpions sting, storks migrate, and zebras gallop, just as people everywhere talk, dance, sing songs, play games, tell stories, and engage in a whole host of other activities. One evolutionary anthropologist (Brown 1991:130–41) has gone so far as to make a list of those human activities which, being found in all societies, can in his view be regarded as innate characteristics of the species, and constitute what he describes as the culture of the 'Universal People'.

In the 1980s and 1990s the movement has gathered momentum as biologists and geneticists, encouraged by new evidence in their favour, and no longer tainted in the public mind by the association of 'social Darwinism' with the eugenics movement, have ventured back into discussion of such areas as politics, culture, and religion.[3] In doing this they explicitly counter-attack the post-structuralist view which attempts to position science as but one among many culturally-determined 'discursive practices' constructing reality (Foucault [1969] 1977). We might characterize it as a battle in which, with gathering momentum, the two sides increasingly attempt to encroach upon each other's territory: relativists try to capture science, scientists to appropriate the study of culture. This latter intention is already honoured by evolutionary explanations of aesthetics (Dissanayake 1988), anthropology (Brown 1991), literary theory (Carroll 1995), social psychology (Barkow, Tooby, and Cosmides 1992; Pinker [1997] 1998), and sexual psychology (Ridley 1994; Diamond 1997).

The new evolutionary psychology has been vociferous in its opposition to the view of human behaviour as culturally constructed and determined, disparagingly referring to it as 'the standard social science model', and setting out its own credo as a mirror image of the relativist position (Brown 1991: 9–37; Tooby and Cosmides 1992:24–40; Pinker 1994:405–11). Evolutionary psychology is realist, believing in an objective reality to which language refers, and of which science gains increasing understanding. It is materialist, believing that mind, language, consciousness, and culture can be explained as deriving from physical processes, and in particular the biochemical processes in the human brain. No duality of mind and brain is accepted: any inability to account for mental processes in terms of neuronal activity is believed to result from incomplete knowledge (Dennett 1991). It is reductionist, believing that human phenomena are to be understood by isolating their components, and it is neo-Darwinist, believing that human life is an interaction of environmental features with genetically determined species-specific adaptations, including, as well as specialized bodily organs, specialized 'modules of mind'. In the view of evolutionary psychology, humans are essentially the same the world over and throughout history. Our brains have developed through natural selection to do the things we need to do—or at least the things, such as spear throwing, and gathering and collecting, which we needed to do during the evolutionarily significant part of our development. Consequently, it is argued, the mind is not a general malleable intelligence, but highly modular, pre-programmed to have certain specialized faculties which unfold in a predictable and internally determined manner as our organism develops, just as flight develops in birds, or—on the more physical side of our own lives—the ability to walk appears, or our reproductive organs develop at puberty.

Such a view may provide important insights into play, though we must also bear in mind those aspects which it cannot capture. Some features of play may be determined by evolved cognitive modules. This would explain why many of those skills which evolved during the hunter-gatherer phase of hominid life, though we do not necessarily all *need* them today, often survive in our games and leisure activities, such as, for example, hunting and collecting, dog-handling, pet-keeping, and accurate throwing. It might also explain why certain leisure activities are more popular with women while others are more popular with men, the difference reflecting the division of activity among hunter-gatherers. If so, evolutionary psychology offers an explanation not only of play in general, but also of very specific forms of play. In its view, the nature of play, including perhaps that of language play, will be universal, and its origins prehistoric. It will confer some evolutionary advantage, explaining both its prevalence and its pleasures. On the other hand, evolutionary psychology cannot explain some of the more delicate variations in play between cultures—why some games catch on in some societies and not others—nor why some modern forms of play do not bear out evolutionary predictions. The actual preferences of the two sexes for leisure activities in contemporary Britain, for example, do not all bear out the evolutionist claim about sex roles in hunter-gatherer societies. Collecting as a hobby is more popular among men (Argyle 1996:43–50).

This characterization of the relativist/universalist debate is brief and simplified—yet it is in such stark terms that it is often presented. The conflict of opinions is overblown, a melodrama which brings perhaps excitement to academic debate, but which really—other than in the most ludicrous claims or false evidence—is not about two irreconcilable explanations, but about a question of degree. Few biologists, anthropologists, or linguists would be foolish enough to deny that there is *both* a biologically and a culturally-determined aspect to our behaviour, although in their zeal for one or the other (and perhaps driven by some innate agonistic disposition to contests and trials of strength!) they do often treat the issue as a battle to be won, and do consequently simplify issues unnecessarily. When looked at more soberly, it is clear that the issue is the balance and relationship between biological, cultural, and individual factors, both in human life in general and in the two aspects of it which are of concern to us in this book: language play and language learning. A relativist view, however extreme, must logically contain a basis for comparison, and if we say (for the sake of argument) that 'a language determines thought patterns' or that 'sexuality varies from culture to culture' we acknowledge implicitly that language, thought, culture, and sexuality are universal. Conversely, universalist claims do not imply that human behaviour is as predictable as that of non-organic matter, or even of other species, but only that there are powerful universal constraints underlying it. Yet as in all such academic battles, there is capital to be made out of dogmatism. In these circumstances, there is a real danger that one extremism may simply be replaced by another, that moderate and more reasonable points of view may be misrepresented and ignored, that—to put it more colloquially—the baby (either one!) may be thrown out with the academic bathwater.

In the remainder of this chapter I shall take the view that there is something to be gained from both sides. Much of the research discussed predates recent explicit formulations of the two positions, but is implicitly either universalist or relativist in stance, and is the kind of work on which the two camps now draw. First, we shall consider some insights which have arisen from seeing human play as a form of evolved behaviour similar to that of animals, fulfilling functions for the individual which are essentially the same in all times and places. Second, we shall turn to insights which have arisen from seeing it as different from animal play, fulfilling functions for society, and consequently a culturally-variable phenomenon.

Insights from animal play: identification and extent

Whatever the degree of similarity between human and animal play, the way in which they are identified and observed must be quite different. In human life, whether behaviour counts as play is very much a question of attitude and subjective perception, so that the same action—tripping somebody up, for example, hiding from them, or deliberately misleading them—can be construed either as play or non-play depending on the attitude of the participants. In fact it is very often this attitude which *makes* something play rather than anything intrinsic to the behaviour *per se*. People are playing when they say and believe that they are playing. A good deal of child discourse around play, for example, negotiates these attitudinal entries and exits in and out of play: 'Let's play', 'Let's pretend', 'Let's stop for a minute', 'I'm only playing', 'That's not allowed', and so on.[4]

One obvious obstacle to the study of animal play, however, is that, if the distinction between play and non-play were similarly a question of attitude, there would be little one could do to discover it. Animals cannot comment on what they are doing; they cannot be interviewed by ethnographers, and obviously enough, therefore, all conclusions must be confined to the observation of behaviour. On the other hand, animals themselves may incorporate more non-verbal signals of playfulness into their activities (Taylor-Parker 1984). The dog who leaps with wagging tail or the cat who cuffs with retracted claws are two well-known examples. In the so-called rough-and-tumble play of fighting and chasing common to many young animals, and apparently universal among human children, there are behavioural cues, such as restraint of force and the absence of signs of injury and distress, which reliably indicate that the activity is playful and not serious (Boulton and Smith 1992).

Overt signals such as these lead observers to believe that animal play

> can be reliably recognized and scored by independent observers, a fact which is sometimes used to argue for animal play being a real phenomenon.
> (Burghardt 1984)

and even fairly tightly defined as

> all motor activity performed post-natally that appears to be purposeless, in which motor patterns from other contexts may often be used in modified forms and altered temporal sequencing.
> (*ibid.*)

Observed and defined in these ways, 'play' has been recorded in all orders of mammals and in a more limited form in birds, though not in the cold-blooded vertebrates (fish, amphibians, and reptiles) or invertebrates. There are, moreover, substantial similarities between play in different species, so much so that—as the sociologist Goffman has observed—there is even play *between* species, as when, for example, a person and a dog play together: 'a fact not to be dwelt on when we sustain our usual self-congratulatory versions of the difference between us and them' (1974:41).

There are, however, substantial differences between species in the extent and nature of play. Most notably, the more intelligent the species, the more it plays, and the more intricate are its games. Humans bear out this general biological truth, and it is no coincidence that we are both the most intelligent and also the most playful species (Taylor-Parker 1984). One feature of human play which distinguishes it from that of animals then, is its quantity. Human infancy, in particular, is not only distinguished by being longer than that of animals, but also by its extraordinary playfulness, almost as though this unusually extended period exists *in order* to play:

> For a series of years, we find life virtually controlled by play. Before systematic education begins, the child's whole existence, except the time devoted to sleeping and eating, is occupied with play, which thus becomes the single, absorbing aim of his life.
> (Groos 1901:369)

By some definitions of 'play', to be examined later in this chapter, this absorbing preoccupation is not only evident in human infancy. It continues throughout childhood, youth, and adulthood.

On these facts then, animal ethologists agree: play is a real and recognizable phenomenon found in many species, with intelligent species playing most of all. It is in the wake of these facts and assumptions that the speculation begins—and some inevitable differences of opinion. There seems to be implicit agreement that although play 'appears to be purposeless', this actually masks some deeper cause: the apparent purposelessness is only in the short term; in the longer term it must have some evolutionary advantage. There are a host of theories as to what the longer-term functions of play might be. Some of these may also apply to human play, though that is not necessarily to say that they account for it entirely. For our purposes, we shall need to assess which features and suggested functions of animal play are relevant to language play, and to what degree. We also need to make a decision. Is play always, as evolutionary psychology would have it, to be accounted for as serving some other activity related to survival, or may it be an end in itself?

Insights from animal play: social functions

In animals and humans alike, play increases contact between 'littermates' (Martin 1984) and may thus lead to increased co-operative efficiency (Fagen 1984). Individuals who are used to co-operating in play, judging each other's capacities, reaction times, and attitudes, are better able to collaborate in more urgent situations and practical acts: fleeing predators, hunting, building shelters, and so on. In addition, the constant interaction of siblings may effect the familiarity (as opposed to actual consanguinity) which it is now believed creates—both in humans and other mammals—the psychological barrier to incest in adult life (Brown 1991:118–30).[5]

The social function of play, however, like the social function of language among humans, is not only co-operative. It is also used to exclude from the group, to establish hierarchies, to overpower and outwit, breaking relationships as well as forming or maintaining them. Members of the same species are in competition with each other as well as with other species (Weiner 1994), and frequent play may, like communication in general, enhance the capacity for selfish manipulation of other members of the community (Dawkins and Krebs 1978). Skills learnt in playing may be easily transferred to fighting and deception. Rough and competitive play may also allow a controlled outlet for an instinct to hurt others which in humans could be described as sadism (McGinn 1997).

Humans, then, like many animals, play socially. But we play more than they do, and in ways which are both more complex and more rule-governed. The key to this difference and this development is language, which has enabled us to make the rules of sports and games complex in ways which would have been quite impossible without it. Indeed, language and games have a particular affinity. Both demand turn-taking and restraint; both enable enhanced co-operation; both are of potential mutual benefit. Both are also vehicles of deceit and manipulation.

As animals lack language, and generally use their bodies rather than voices in play, it might seem at first glance that observation of their play will be of little relevance to an understanding of language play. Yet there are aspects of human language play in which talk (or just vocalization) may serve the same social functions as bodily movement and contact do among animals. The constant playful activity of young mammals makes them both easier to monitor and more easily prevented from wandering away (Müller-Schwartze 1978). In a similar way, the 'playful' babbling of the human baby and the constant stream of egocentric speech from the toddler may have evolved to ensure contact between mother and infant, while allowing the mother to divert her gaze and her hands to other activities (Locke 1993:108). Nor is it only in the forests and long-grassed savannahs of prehistory that infant vocalization serves this purpose: even in the modern world, a sudden silence from an out-of-sight child is still a warning signal to an adult! Similarly, among adults, playful talk and gossip may regulate and maintain relationships in the same way as physical grooming does among other primates (Morris 1967), perhaps having a positive effect on health by satisfying a need for recognition (Berne 1968:15). What chimpanzees do with their hands, human beings may do, to a lot more of their fellows, by speaking. As Dunbar (1996) suggests, arguing very much from the standpoint of evolutionary psychology, language may even have evolved primarily for this purpose, allowing humans to build and maintain larger social networks than their primate 'cousins'. It is interesting to speculate whether the universal human fondness for congregating to hear songs and stories—or, in the modern family, to watch television (Argyle 1996:186)—is not another instance of language serving this function of group creation.

Animal rough-and-tumble play, which enhances the individual's ability to hunt, fight, and flee, also leads indirectly to co-operation (Boulton and Smith 1992). This is not necessarily the result of altruism, however. It may be motivated by each individual's interest in maximizing the benefits of play for themselves. For the game to continue, no victory can—by definition—be final. This leads in turn to self-restraint on the part of those who would win in actual contests, since it is in their interests, just as much as those of the weaker members of the community, to adjust their skills to suit their playmates, in order to prolong their own play. This motivation also leads to role reversals which give each individual practice in a variety of parts: as chaser and chased, victor and vanquished, leader and led. In these respects, the competitive play of children and animals may seem to be rather alike. Yet while with animals such constraints and reversals may be impulsive and arbitrary, in human competitive games, even among quite small children, they are formalized by rules and conventions which can be explicitly stated by the players, and are culturally transmitted, so that in versions of the ubiquitous children's game of 'tig', for example, there are clear rules about what can happen (*ibid.*).

Co-operation in games may be further motivated by the principle of 'social exchange' (Cosmides and Tooby 1989). This, while it is of relevance to gregarious animals in general, has assumed much greater importance in human societies. The hypothesis is that humans play fair by each other (both in the literal and metaphorical senses), not necessarily for reasons of altruism, but because if they do not their fellows may be unwilling to collaborate with them again, and in addition may spread the news of their unreliability. Dunbar (1996), extending his theory that language enables larger social networks, even proposes that such gossip about reliability and unreliability was, in human prehistory, one of language's earliest and most seminal functions. As the size of human societies increased—so the argument goes—it became more likely that an individual would need to collaborate with others known only by hearsay. At the same time, the principle of social exchange was strengthened by the greater likelihood of needing to collaborate with others more than once. In modern urban societies, although the likelihood of a second meeting is often negligible, the general tendency to be fair and civil to strangers can still be attributed to this evolved mechanism of self-interest. In the view of evolutionary psychology, it is not that we have lost our ruthlessness, but that we simply have not lived long enough in an urban environment to have adapted to it.

Alternatively, our civility may derive from a genuine altruism, a disinterested sense of justice, and comity (kindly and considerate behaviour towards others) motivated by the general desire to maintain harmony and well-being (Aston 1988, 1993).[6] If so, this attribute is perhaps uniquely human. Why, for example, do we apologize when we dial a wrong telephone number, when there is no benefit to ourselves? Out of a misplaced self-interest inherited via our hunter-gatherer ancestors, with its origins in the behaviour of even more remote pre-hominid apes, or out of courtesy and concern, and a wish to avoid conflict?

The universality of altruism, and of moral codes which advocate it (however imperfectly followed), pose a serious problem for evolutionary psychology. Their existence seems to contradict the individual selfishness logically inherent in Darwinism. Dawkins (1976) has tried to explain away the problem via the concept of 'kin selection', arguing that individuals act in the interests of their genes rather than of their own organism, and thus at times put the interests of their relatives before their own. 'Social exchange' is another attempt to provide a solution, suggesting as it does that apparent altruism may in fact be in our own interest. Yet there remains, as we all know, a constant internal conflict in the human mind between the interests of self and other—which provides the stuff of literature, moral education, and religion. Danielson (1992), a moral philosopher with an interest in computers, has attempted to investigate the degree to which altruistic morality is rational through a series of elaborate computer games simulating moral dilemmas. Interestingly, and significantly, he has been unable, as he himself admits, either to formulate rules for predicting—or to demonstrate any logic in—actual human behaviour when faced with choices between altruism and selfishness. Yet however inconclusive the outcome, games are a fitting means for investigation. With their constant demand for the assessment of others, their elaborate etiquette and intricate rules, and their strange mix of competition and collaboration, they both reflect and enhance the behaviour necessary to balance altruism and selfishness, and to allow both communal harmony and individual advancement. Games are both a dramatization and symbolic representation of the conflict between the demands of self and other, and a training for coping with it—perhaps a better one in practical terms than religion or philosophy.

Insights from animal play: internal functions

In addition to its *inter*-personal social functions, it is also possible that play, both animal and human, may have *intra*-personal functions, both psychological and somatic, which allow individuals to regulate and maintain desirable internal states.[7] A widely accepted theory of this type is that play in infancy uses up 'surplus energy' (Spencer 1898), and burns off 'behavioural fat' (Müller-Schwartze 1978), an effect which has the added advantage of leaving youngsters exhausted and thus, as already mentioned, less likely to wander off into danger. Moreover (as every parent knows) there are benefits for adults if this play exhaustion leads to the young sleeping longer and more soundly.

Another theory of this type, developed as an explanation of human play but also possibly applicable to other intelligent animals, is that the pleasure of play derives from a balance of challenges and skills, which leads to an intense state of self-absorption and self-awareness (Csikszentmihalyi 1975). Play serves to alleviate boredom by raising the level of physical and mental activity, while at the same time reducing anxiety by setting challenges which are attainable. The result is what Csikszentmihalyi describes as 'flow': an agreeable sensation which serves to regulate levels of activity and mood (Csikszentmihalyi 1975, 1997). The state is summed up in these words of a rock-climber:

> When I stop to think about it I realize that an important part of the state of mind is enjoyment. I get so involved in what I am doing, I almost forget about time. When I experience this state of mind, I really feel free from boredom and worry. I feel like I am being challenged or that I am very much in control of my action and my world. I feel like I am growing and using my best talents and skills; I am master of my situation.
> (Allison and Duncan 1988, quoted in Argyle 1996:165)

This theory also explains why activities which are play for some individuals are sources of terror or boredom for others (why I, for example, would find rock-climbing intensely frightening, or why a set of grammar exercises found tedious by some students are found exciting by others). Differences arise not only from varying levels of skill, but also from different individual predilections for risk-taking (Russell 1993:5). The notion of flow also reinforces the notion that play is an internally-defined experience rather than a type of external behaviour.

Insights from animal play: play as learning

In addition to these functions, play—both animal and human—also provides training and practice in the manipulation of the environment, and allows the young to practise necessary activities without serious consequences (Bruner

1976). This explanation is as widespread as it is obvious. Young animals and children alike are seen to play out the activities which will be important to them as adults: antelopes leap and dodge (Byers 1984), cats pounce and worry (Caro 1981), and children create play worlds in which they are mummies and daddies and various kinds of worker. To do this they use language playfully, as inevitably as kittens use their paws. The many human games which involve accurate aiming and throwing,[8] and which are particularly popular among males, are perhaps residual evidence of the importance of throwing among hunter-gatherers over a long period of hominid prehistory. (There is evidence that the ability to throw accurately, like the ability to acquire language, depends on evolved specialized and innate cognitive structures in the brain (Calvin 1993:230).) Playing games, moreover, allows us to break down difficult skills into manageable components, to be reassembled into a working whole at a later stage. This can perhaps increase efficiency and also make the task, in parts, less daunting than the whole, a point which is expressed very vividly by Fagen (1984) in an analogy between learning through play and walking down a precipitous path:

> At least in humans, a landscape is, in large part, what we think about it. The trail that led down to the beach from an Alaskan cabin where I once lived is an example. Most of this 'trail' was vertical, a descent via fixed rope down a steep cliff. Formidable though it appeared when viewed as a whole from above or from below, the trail was easy when viewed one step at a time in the mind's eye during actual travel. Each move was technically trivial, although the whole was fairly spectacular.
> (*ibid.*: 168)

The apparent obviousness of the preparatory role of play, both for animals and humans, may blind us to an important difference between two types of preparation. This is the distinction between play whose function is to promote *particular* skills (leaping and pouncing, spear-throwing, knowing multiplication tables, or whatever) and play whose function is to promote an increase in *general* flexibility and adaptability, including especially the generation of new ideas. It concerns, in other words, the degree to which play functions as 'training' or as 'education' (Widdowson 1983:16–20). Here we encounter a possible qualitative difference between animal and human play. It may be that human play, in addition to the function of specific training which it shares with animal play, also performs an educational role by increasing *general* flexibility, thereby allowing humans to develop, both as individuals and societies, a greater understanding of their environment, and more creative responses to it.

Animal and human play

The social, internal, and learning explanations of play advanced above are broadly applicable to animals and humans alike, and can be explained from the perspective of evolutionary psychology, which acknowledges differences among species, but sees them as emerging in essentially similar ways. In this view, humans *are* different, but only in the same sorts of ways as each species differs from another, and our behaviour—including play and language—is to be understood by looking at its evolutionary origins. For this reason we should expect to find similarities of behaviour, and an insight into our own, by examining the play of those species to which we are most closely 'related': the other apes and, to a lesser extent, intelligent sociable mammals in general. Differences are ones of emphasis and quantity rather than of essence. With our more intricate and competitive societies, we are more preoccupied with social exchange, and consequently have developed elaborate games with more formalized rules. Similarly, with our particular reliance upon intelligent flexible responses to new circumstances, we have developed forms of play providing education as well as training. In turn, these emphases have been made possible by the development of language—a uniquely human attribute. Presumably, language and intricate games developed in tandem, each enhancing and promoting the other. Perhaps the need for complex language arises from the need for complex games. There are all sorts of speculations which could be made.

A good deal of the mainstream psychology literature on play subscribes implicitly to such a continuity theory of animal and human play, assuming that insights into one are also insights into the other (Aldiss 1975; Bruner *et al.* 1976; Smith 1984; Boulton and Smith 1992). It deals with the kind of explanations which we have examined above. In addition, as play among animals tends to be largely the prerogative of youth, it often focuses, primarily or even exclusively, upon childhood play. Indeed, it is often assumed without comment in the psychology literature that play *means* essentially children's play.[9] Where adult play is considered, it is presented as merely a continuation of childhood activity, a faint and atavistic infantile echo (which undoubtedly it may on occasion be). It is this perception of adult play which has led to its comparative neglect in psychology.

Cultural approaches

An alternative to these standard psychological ideas is to posit a sharp discontinuity between the role of play in animals and certain aspects of play among adult humans. Studies based on this premise, while not denying the animal element in human play (particularly among children) are more likely to comment upon aspects of adult behaviour which—while they may have their origins in our evolutionary forbears or our own childhoods—have developed in ways which are now quite distinctive, and need to be examined by quite different criteria.

This perception of play as primarily or exclusively a childhood phenomenon may reflect the tendency of a society which suppresses or marginalizes play to deny the play-like nature of many of its activities. Lines are hard to draw. Play is a particularly difficult term to define, and it is thus relatively easy to re-classify a playful activity as something else. Especially problematic is the distinction between serious activities which share some of the forms of play, and play itself. There are a number of studies which tend to class activities as 'games' or as 'play' which for most people seem very far removed from their usual notions of these terms. Thus we find writers treating as 'games' such activities as electioneering (Colman 1982:195–234), nuclear arms races (Brams 1975:30–9), or the domestic lives of alcoholics (Berne 1968:73–81). Here there is clearly a danger of forcing together activities which are essentially different from each other, or whose relationship to play is metaphorical rather than actual, and imposing upon the players of games an analysis and evaluation which is not their own. Theories which represent life-destroying activities as games are clearly relentlessly 'etic' rather than 'emic', and they juggle with definitions in ways which can be challenged as arbitrary and sophistic. Yet they can also serve to highlight similarities between apparently disparate activities, thus providing valuable insights into both.

Though we may balk—as insiders—at the analysis of some of our most serious activities as play, we might consider whether we apply the same reservations when considering animals and children. All description of animal play must be, by definition, 'etic' (see p. 67). Perhaps too, when we describe children's make-believe as 'play', and mean by this term something trivial and inconsequential, we are also applying an 'etic' category. Sometimes children's play is manifestly very serious to the children themselves, just as adult sports, conflicts, and social rituals are to us. It is true that when adults and children speak together of 'play', they manage successfully to refer to the same activities, and thus communicate on a practical level in utterances such as 'Can I go and play now?', or 'Stop playing now, it's bedtime.' This superficial success, however, may mask a deep difference. For what the adult perceives as trivial and consequently labels 'play', the child may consider serious. Conversely, as many novelists have realized when portraying adult concerns through a child's eyes, adult enterprises can also seem quite trivial to children. It is a question of perspective. There is nothing new in the observation that play is relative:

> We lacked neither memory nor intelligence, because by your will, O Lord, we had as much as were sufficient for our years. But we enjoyed playing games and were punished for them by men who played games themselves. However, grown-up games are known as 'business', and even though boys' games are much the same, they are punished for them by their elders.
> Saint Augustine's *Confessions*, AD 398 (quoted in Brumfit 1991:18)

Homo Ludens and the play of culture: the theories of Johan Huizinga

An interesting 'etic' approach to adult play, which makes no appeal to biology, and which insists on describing serious activities as elaborations of play, is that of the Dutch historian and philosopher Huizinga, who sees play as the origin of civilization and culture (Huizinga:[1944] 1949). The title of his book, *Homo Ludens*, captures his view concisely, defining our species—in contrast to 'Homo Sapiens' (Man the Knower), or 'Homo Faber' (Man the Maker)—as 'Man the Player'. The subtitle,[10] 'a study of the play-element of culture', encapsulates a second point equally neatly: that play-elements are integral to, and are indeed the origin of, the most serious of human activities, including law, warfare,[11] courtship, religion, art, education, and philosophy. Huizinga sees culture as something which emerges from play, rather than the other way round. 'Civilization', he writes, 'arises and unfolds in play.'

Huizinga acknowledges that there are elements of continuity running from animal through children's to adult human play, but declares his focus of interest to be adult play, which he regards as qualitatively different. Central to his theory, for example, is the notion (easily acceptable to modern evolutionists)[12] of play as agonistic: contests arise from an innate universal disposition to competition between members of the same species. Yet Huizinga is also keen to emphasize the differences between his view and the standard biological thinking of his time. While children and animals are, as he puts it, compelled to play by their instincts (*ibid*.: 7–8), adult play is a free and conscious activity. Though animals and humans share a disposition to play, the difference is that in humans this disposition is developed and elaborated in culturally complex and various ways. Huizinga is sceptical of the biologists' view of play as functional in origin, something which has arisen to serve something else:

> The numerous attempts to define the biological function of play show a striking variation. By some the origin and fundamentals of play have been described as the discharge of superabundant vital energy, by others as the satisfaction of some 'imitative instinct', or again as simply a 'need' for relaxation. According to one theory play constitutes a training of the young creature for the serious work that life will demand later on. According to another it serves as an exercise in restraint needful to the individual. Some find the principle of play in an innate urge to exercise a certain faculty, or in the desire to dominate or compete. Yet others regard it as an 'abreaction'—an outlet for harmful impulses, as the necessary restorer of energy wasted by one-sided activity, as 'wish fulfilment', as a fiction designed to keep up the feeling of personal value, etc.

> All these hypotheses have one thing in common: they all start from the assumption that play must serve something which is *not* play, that it must have some kind of biological purpose.
> (*ibid*. 1949:2)

Today Huizinga's scepticism is not as irreconcilable with all biological approaches to play as it was when formulated. There is in evolutionary theory a controversial suggestion by Gould ([1980] 1990) that species sometimes take a feature originally evolved for one purpose and develop it for another—in a process referred to as evolutionary 'exaptation', in contrast to evolutionary 'adaptation'. A classic example is the exaptation of the oral cavity—originally adapted for eating—for speech.[13] Though Huizinga did not have the benefit of this insight, his thesis may be expressed in similar terms. Human children, like the young of other animals, play. 'Civilization' has developed as an adult exaptation of this childhood characteristic. Though we may have an innate disposition to play, our cultural organization, developed as an extension of play, arises as a secondary effect.[14] Societies are created and held together by institutionalized activities which are essentially play-like: art, religion, education, warfare, philosophy, law. All that we take most seriously is an exaptation from play! From this theoretical starting-point, Huizinga proceeds to analyse the history of the most weighty institutions of culture as the development of games.

Huizinga's approach is in some senses a universalist one, in that it describes, as his title suggests, an aspect of the human species, but it is also one which posits a sharp discontinuity between humans and animals, and provides a framework for the presentation of variation between cultures and historical periods. As a historian and linguist he is able to draw upon a type of etymological and textual evidence generally ignored by evolutionary psychology to suggest that what is considered as 'play' is not at all universal, and that it was quite different, and far more extensive, in earlier periods of European history than it is today (*ibid.*: 28–45).[15] This is strongly implied by the etymology of many words which, while now denoting very serious matters, share roots with words denoting more playful ones. ('School', for example, derives from the Greek for 'leisure'.) On the other hand, as a linguist he is able to show a remarkable similarity in the relation of the concepts of play to non-play in a range of languages such as Arabic, Blackfoot,[16] Chinese, Greek, Hebrew, Japanese, Sanskrit—the use of the same or related words, for example, to denote free movement, leaping, combat, and sexual love. We can see this in English, where uses of the words 'game' and 'play' in disparate contexts are a key to considerable changes in the conceptual range of these words. We still use them, for example, to describe drama ('plays'), music ('playing'), sex ('foreplay'), hunting ('game'), and fighting ('swordplay'). 'Swordplay', for example, seems an odd way to refer to mortal combat. Textual evidence of the uses of these words suggests the same. In *Hamlet*, for example, the stage direction 'they play' precedes the duel between Hamlet and Laertes which leads to the death of both.[17] In one particularly striking example Huizinga cites (*ibid.*: 41) verses from the 1611 Authorized Version of the Bible:

And Abner said to Joab, Let the young men now arise and play before us. And there came twelve from each side, and they caught every one his

fellow by the head and thrust his sword into his fellow's side, so they fell down together.
(2 Samuel 2:14)[18]

Interestingly, as Huizinga points out, this disturbing use of the verb 'play'—so anomalous from a modern point of view—has equivalents in both the Latin *ludant* ('that they play') and the Hebrew *sahaq* ('to do something jestingly', 'to dance'), suggesting both a strong similarity in the play concept across cultures and languages, and a tendency for the gradual removal of areas of life originally associated with it. It challenges modern perceptions of clear boundaries between the playful and the serious, and suggests a certain narrowness of perspective in contemporary studies which confine 'play' to the study of children and animals.

All hangs, of course, upon definition, and Huizinga here might be accused of taking two bearings at once. For the most part he adopts an 'etic' perspective in which he forces upon modern society a view of activities as play which it does not use itself. Yet in analysing the past, and particularly the life of classical and medieval Europe, he seems to adopt an 'emic' perspective, and classifying activities as play on the grounds that that is apparently how they were widely perceived at the time. Huizinga gives the following very concise definition of play at the outset of his argument:

> Summing up the formal characteristics of play we might call it a free activity standing quite consciously outside 'ordinary' life and being 'not serious', but at the same time absorbing the player intensely and utterly. It is an activity connected with no material interest, and no profit can be gained by it. It proceeds within its own proper boundaries of time and space according to fixed rules and in an orderly manner. It promotes the formation of social groupings which tend to surround themselves with secrecy and to stress their difference from the common world by disguise or other means.
> (Huizinga [1944] 1949:13)

Abstracting from these comments (and adding to them an earlier comment that 'in [the] faculty of repetition lies one of the most essential qualities of play' (*ibid.*:10), we can summarize Huizinga's conception of play as having the following 14 characteristics.

Play is:

1 a free activity
2 conscious
3 outside 'ordinary' life
4 'not serious'
5 absorbing the player
6 bounded in time and space
7 rule governed

8 orderly
9 serving no material interest
10 profitless
11 promoting social grouping

and it has:

12 a tendency to secrecy
13 a tendency to disguise
14 a faculty of repetition

This is certainly not without its problems and paradoxes. It seems to contradict other statements by Huizinga, and to run partly counter to intuition and experience. We can no doubt think of instances of play which do not display one or more of these characteristics. In the modern world, many activities which might count as play, or at least as play-like, do not seem to be entirely free and conscious activities. People feel compelled to participate by social pressure, by the prospect of gain, or by some inner compulsion. Argyle (1996: 36), for example, reports that although watching television is the largest of all leisure activities and 'the third biggest use of time in the western world after sleeping and working' (*ibid.*: 182), surveys show that 'TV is never mentioned as a source of happiness or joy' (*ibid.*: 88). A similar problem arises with the claim that 'no profit can be made' by play. In many games there is clearly a profit to be made, whether it be the literal financial profit made by the professional player, or, more metaphorically, the profit of increased prestige or popularity for the amateur. These are quibbles over one criterion or another. More damningly, one might attack the whole notion of an 'etic' definition of play, since it could be argued that Huizinga's definition is both self-fulfilling and arbitrary, for once the components are itemized, we may then identify behaviour as play which has these characteristics, exclude behaviour as non-play which does not, and then proceed to show with utter circularity that play indeed does have these characteristics.

Yet to take issue with Huizinga in this way, either in detail or in general terms, is perhaps to miss the point. The ways in which contemporary play-like activities diverge from these criteria may reveal exactly the kind of change in attitude to play of which Huizinga is writing. Play is, moreover, as Huizinga himself points out, the slipperiest of concepts: 'the fun of playing . . . resists all analysis, all logical interpretation. As a concept, it cannot be reduced to any other mental category' (Huizinga [1944] 1949: 3). Consequently any itemized definition will fail alongside some particular instance, which manifestly is play, and yet diverges from one criterion or another. Yet the alternatives to such a faulty definition—none of them satisfactory—are either to confine play to the study of children and animals, to abandon the study altogether, or to embark on an analysis of adult play without a definition. Huizinga provides us with an image of prototypical play, and a useful idealization against which to measure the playfulness of any activity. It is the kind of flexible and adaptable definition which an activity such as play demands.

Agôn, Alea, Mimicry, and *Ilinx*: the theory of Roger Caillois

Another major theorist of play is the French writer, Caillois. Like Huizinga, he includes among the distinguishing characteristics of play its separateness and boundedness in space and time, its lack of productivity, its rule-governed nature, and its creation of a make-believe alternative reality. Yet he also adds important new features and emphases of his own. In his seminal article, 'The Structure and Classification of Games' ([1955] 1969),[19] Caillois acknowledges Huizinga as his starting-point and his inspiration, but also notes Huizinga's almost exclusive focus upon agonistic play, and observes how many instances of play do not seem to be accounted for by it. His list includes an apparently unrelated variety of non-agonistic playful activities:

> betting and games of chance—that is gambling houses, casinos, horse races, lotteries (. . .) kites, crossword puzzles, and rocking horses, and to some extent dolls, games of patience, Chinese puzzles, hoops, most toys, and several of the more widespread diversions (. . .) the giddiness induced by high speed, the kind one experiences on skis, in a motorcycle or in an open car.

To bring order to this diverse list of examples, he adds to Huizinga's agonistic play three other categories of his own, thus creating four major categories of play, as follows:

agôn	in which competition is dominant: the desire to win in regulated competition; ('football, billiards, or chess')
alea	in which chance is dominant: submission of one's own will in favour of anxious and passive anticipation of where the wheel will stop; ('roulette or the lottery')
mimicry	in which simulation is dominant: the desire to assume a strange personality; ('pirates or Nero or Hamlet')
ilinx	in which vertigo is dominant: ('dances like the waltz', rock-climbing, the merry-go-round, children's swings, 'the giddiness of high speed')

At the end of his essay Caillois summarizes the four as follows:

> In *agôn*, the player relies only on himself and he bends all his efforts to do his best; in *alea*, he relies on everything except himself and he surrenders to forces that elude him; in *mimicry* he imagines that he is other than he really is and invents a fictitious universe; *ilinx*, the fourth fundamental tendency, is an answer to one's need to feel the body's stability and equilibrium momentarily destroyed, to escape the tyranny of perception, and to overcome awareness.

The power of this taxonomy is its apparent capacity (despite the datedness of some of Caillois's examples) to account for all activity perceived as play. The categories are useful for our understanding and categorization of language play. They also highlight problems for theories of play based on evolutionary psychology, and for our understanding of the function of language play. For whereas *agôn*, however complex, is fairly easily traced to an origin in animal behaviour, and *mimicry*, which is also present in animals, can in part be explained as a means of learning new behaviour, the other two *categories— alea* and *ilinx*—are less easily explained, and consequently often neglected in functionalist evolutionary approaches.

To this fourfold taxonomy Caillois adds another useful graded distinction between *paedia* (play's 'primary power of improvisation and gaiety') and *ludus* (its 'rules . . . institutional existence . . . civilising power' and 'the taste for gratuitous difficulty'). This can be applied to play under each of the four headings, as shown in the table below.

	Agôn (Competition)	Alea (Chance)	Mimicry (Pretense)	Ilinx (Vertigo)
paedia ↑	races combats, etc. } not regulated	*comptines* heads or tails	childish imitation masks costumes	children's swings merry-go-round teeter-totter waltz
noise agitation	athletics			
laughter dance	boxing fencing	betting roulette	theater	outdoor sports skiing
hoop solitaire	football checkers	lotteries		mountain- climbing
games of patience crossword puzzles	chess	compounded or parlayed		
↓ **ludus**				

Note: In each vertical column, the games are classified very approximately in such order that the *paedia* element constantly decreases, while the *ludus* element constantly increases.

Table 4.1: The structure and classification of games (Caillois [1955] 1969)

In the terms of this diagram, Huizinga's theory is concerned primarily with the institutionalized forms of agonistic play (in other words with the bottom left-hand corner): that is with the most complex and formal types of play which are exclusive to human beings, and associated more with adults than with children. Evolutionary psychology, on the other hand, keen to demonstrate the similarities of human and animal play, is also concerned with agonistic play, though in its more spontaneous and less organized forms (the top left-hand corner). The strength of Caillois's taxonomy is that it includes both of these focuses of interest, but also broadens the scope of inquiry in a principled and organized manner which will embrace both evolutionary and cultural explanations of play, but also point in other directions too. Yet useful as Caillois taxonomy will be, it still leaves many questions unanswered—about the relationship between categories, and the forces which make them universally attractive. For our purposes, we need to see how language play can be accommodated to this model. It is to this issue, and in particular to the appeal and role of *alea* in human games and language play, that we shall turn in the next chapter.

Notes

1 See for example Geertz 1993. To a degree this view was compatible with the behaviourist paradigm of psychology with its view of the mind (deriving from the philosophy of Locke) as a blank slate on which experience could write many patterns. Yet in another way it departed from behaviourism—which sees human and animal learning as essentially similar—in the central role it attributed to human cultures, which were regarded as qualitatively different from the sum of their individual components.

2 As language is such a crucial aspect of humanity it is not surprising that both universalist and relativist theories of behaviour have been closely tied to different movements in linguistics. One major influence upon the relativist tradition has been the writing of Whorf, who claimed in the 1930s that the North American language of Hopi did not encode the notion of time as an objective phenomenon as 'Western' languages do (Whorf [1940] 1956). This finding seemed to lend strong support to the so-called 'linguistic relativity hypothesis' of Sapir (1966): that our world view may to a large degree be determined by the language we speak. Such ideas in linguistics about language echoed ideas about culture that were current in anthropology at the time. Mead, for example, under the tutelage of the anthropologist Boas, claimed that the traumas and complexes of Western adolescence were unknown among the teenage girls of Samoa, as a consequence of the sexual freedom they were allowed (Mead 1928). This seemed to show that something as 'natural' as societal restriction of adolescent sexual promiscuity was in fact culturally conditioned. From these seminal starting-points, a research paradigm was launched, dedicated to amassing evidence cataloguing similar variations, and on their basis, some extreme statements were made. 'The genetic elements which may determine personality' declared Boas (1934), 'are altogether irrelevant as compared with the powerful influence of cultural environment.' A theory of play following this injunction would clearly expect to find, and have to account for, substantial and surprising cultural differences.

Unfortunately, and embarrassingly for this tradition, the evidence of Whorf and Mead has now been shown to be spurious. Whorf's report of time categories in Hopi was simply wrong! Hopi *does* encode time as an objective phenomenon (Malotki 1983). (For an account of how Whorf's views have been distorted by subsequent commentators, however, see O'Halloran 1997.) Mead's informants were playing jokes on a gullible and overworked young anthropologist (see Freeman 1983). Understandably, the errors of Mead and Whorf have been gleefully seized upon in recent universalist literature (Pinker 1994: 57–64; Brown 1991: 9–38). However, it is important to realize that these errors are not evidence *against* cultural determinism, though they do remove some of the evidence *for* it. Every discipline has its errors and frauds. The excesses of one side or the other need not be taken as grounds to see either 'inherited characteristics' or 'the cultural environment' as—in Boas' unreasonable phrase—'altogether irrelevant'. Linguistic theory should be capable of accommodating both.

To a degree, cultural and linguistic relativism has also drawn support from interpretations of the linguistic theory of de Saussure, whose emphasis upon the arbitrariness of the linguistic sign, and upon how meaning is a function of differences between signs within the system, can be read as supporting the view that reality can be carved up in arbitrarily different ways by different languages. Linguistic structure, moreover, in de Saussure's writing is described as 'a social product' and 'a body of necessary conventions' ([1915] 1983: 9–10) with a kind of quasi-autonomous existence independent of its actual speakers, rather than rooted in—as Chomsky would have it—the biological structures of the brain. Yet it would be a mistake to assume that there is anything in Saussurean linguistics which implies that there is no objective and external reality, that language is not delimited by a universal human nature and needs, or that language is somehow not used to convey individual intentions. On the contrary, Saussurean structuralism is rather a universalist theory whose broad principles are taken to apply across languages and cultures. It is only in some post-structuralist extensions of these views that a denial of external determination of the human world, coupled with an excessive elevation of the role of cultural determination, can be found (Foucault [1969] 1977). In effect, such post-structuralist writings, though they make use of structuralism, do so by rewriting it rather than adding to it. The relation of structuralism to post-structuralism is, as Carroll (1995: 246) has aptly described it 'a kind of disciplinary kidnapping'.

Just as relativist views of human behaviour have drawn upon certain interpretations of linguistics, so the evolutionary humanities have been able to draw in general terms upon Chomskyan cognitive linguistics. In confrontation with the relativist view of language as unexpectedly variable, and the human mind as almost infinitely plastic, Chomsky has developed his programme to describe the principles and parameters of an innate Universal Grammar. These, he believes, in interaction with only a minimal environmental stimulus, determine the unfolding of the individual's linguistic competence: a 'mental organ' whose development he likens to the maturation of any other organ in the body (1980: 38–45). The originality and coherence of his position, his apparent compatibility with genetics and neuroscience, and the dramatic character of his attacks on those who disagree with him (see Botha 1989) have made his argument a favoured point of reference for the evolutionary humanities. There are, however, important differences between Chomsky's view and that of many evolutionary psychologists. He does not, for example, link his theories, as Pinker does (1994:354–64) to the notion that language emerged in gradual stages during evolution, nor to the notion that it is directly encoded in the genes.

3 The new interest and faith in the power of genetics and evolutionary theory is also witnessed by the success of popularizations of these disciplines, notably those of Dawkins (1976, 1982, 1986, 1995) and Jones (1993, 1997). As these works suggest, however, the general view in biology of cultural and genetic determinism is rather more balanced than in evolutionary psychology, which in effect often discounts the role of cultural variation in human behaviour as negligible. While suggesting that cultural and mental phenomena may obey evolutionary principles of a very general type, most biologists argue that such changes are qualitatively different from those arising in DNA (Dawkins 1986: 189–201; Wills 1994:10; de Duve 1995:229–70). Steve Jones, for example, writes that

> Our brains and our behaviour are what separate humans from any other animal. They probably involve a few genes whose importance is lost in a measure of average genetic difference. There is also, of course, a whole set of intellectual and cultural attributes which appear once a crucial level of intelligence has been reached and which *are not coded for by genes at all.*
> (Jones 1993:130, emphasis added)

Other leading geneticists express even stronger opposition to the relevance of biology to the study of cultural behaviour, in effect siding more with the relativists. Lewontin (1993:98), for example, observes that

> The incredible variety of human social circumstances would require an amount of DNA which we simply do not possess. There is enough human DNA to make about 250,000 genes. But that would be insufficient to determine the incredible complexity of human social organization if it were coded in detail by specific neuronal connections. Once we admit that only the most general outlines of social behaviour

could be genetically coded, then we must allow immense flexibility depending on particular circumstances.

4 In this sense, claims to be playing belong to the class of declarative speech acts (Austin 1962; Searle 1975b), in which saying and doing are one, and realize Hymes's (1972a) 'contextual function' of language, in which an utterance changes the social nature of the event.

5 Contrary to popular beliefs, incest is generally avoided by animals as well as by humans.

6 Aston, analysing encounters between shopkeepers and their customers, argues that a desire for comity is a major factor in public discourse between strangers.

7 A realization of the beneficial psychological effects of play was behind the 'Play Therapy' movement, popular in the 1960s, which used play in the treatment of disturbed children (Axline [1947] 1969).

8 Where such games involve competition, they may also, like play fighting, defuse aggression (Aldiss 1975; Bruner 1976).

9 Standard contemporary undergraduate introductions to psychology either do not include sections on play (e.g. Hogg and Vaughan 1998) or have very brief sections dealing only with children's play: (Eysenck 1998 (3 pages out of 825); Gross and McIlveen 1998 (1 page out of 804); Scott and Spencer 1998 (2 pages out of 778); Malim and Birch 1998 (5 pages out of 922); Myers 1998 (no pages out of 606)!

10 In the original German, Huizinga uses the genitive to suggest that play is inseparable from culture rather than something merely contained in it. He argues in his Foreword of 1938 that the English phrase 'the play-element of culture' captures this point more accurately than the phrase (used by the anonymous translator into English of the 1944 German edition) 'the play-element in culture'.

11 At least when it is constrained by some degree of convention.

12 See, for example, Ridley 1994:127–63.

13 This *ad hoc* hijacking of one feature by another fits with the image of evolution as tinkering (Jacob cited in Chomsky 1996:30) or repairs to a boat which is always at sea (Neurath cited in Aitchison 1996:148), and the idea that many features, far from displaying perfection, from the point of view of rational design often display severe shortcomings. Frequently cited as examples of such 'bad design' in humans are the apparently useless but potentially lethal appendix, and a vocal tract which allows us to choke (Williams 1996) (for further discussion see Cook and Seidlhofer 1995: 2–4). This belief in imperfection arising from evolution is, however, strongly contested by Behe (1998: 222–5).

14 Species-specific features—and this could well include language, language learning, or the disposition to play—may not be genetically encoded at all, but arise as epiphenomena from the encoding for some other ability.

Gould and Lewontin (1984) explain this by analogy with an architectural phenomenon called 'spandrels'. Spandrels are 'the tapering triangular spaces' which inevitably appear at 'the intersection of two rounded arches at right angles'. They are not constructed, as such, but they always arise. One possibility is that language itself is a kind of mental spandrel. As Piattelli-Palmarini explains:

> The innate, very specific and highly abstract structures governing language and cognition may also be seen as 'spandrels', that is biological traits that have become central to our whole existence, but which may well have arisen for some purely architectural reason (perhaps overall brain size, or the sheer duplication of existing modules), or as a by-product of evolutionary pressures driven by other functions (say, an increase in connectivity, or in sub-modularisation). (Piattelli-Palmarini 1989)

These claims are violently dismissed both by other evolutionists (Tooby and Cosmides 1992) and by other linguists (Pinker and Bloom 1992). In a disparaging analogy, Pinker (1994) dismisses the notion of language arising as a spandrel as being as likely as a hurricane blowing through a warehouse full of scrap metal accidentally constructing an airliner.

15 A similar point is made in Bakhtin's studies, already referred to in Chapter 3, of the relationship of the medieval carnival to the serious rituals of medieval life (Bakhtin [1940 and 1965] 1968; Bakhtin [1934] 1981).

16 An Algonkian language from North America.

17 Act V, ii, 295.

18 The words 'And there came twelve from each side' are Huizinga's summary paraphrase of a longer sentence.

19 Subsequently expanded into the book *Les Jeux et Les Hommes* (Caillois [1958] 1961).

5 The play of nature: randomness and creativity

For a thousand years in Thy sight are but as yesterday: seeing that is past as a watch in the night. As soon as Thou scatterest them, they are even as a sleep: and fade away suddenly like the grass. In the morning it is green and groweth up: but in the evening it is cut down, dried up, and withered.
Psalm 90 (part of The Order for the Burial of the Dead in the 1552 *Book of Common Prayer*)

When Lucy was a baby, a baby Lucy was,
She went, 'waaa, waaa, waaa, waaa, waaa'.

When Lucy was a toddler, a toddler Lucy was,
She went toddle, toddle, toddle, toddle, toddle.

When Lucy was a schoolgirl, a schoolgirl Lucy was,
She went 'Miss, Miss, I can't do this.
I've got my knickers in a right-hand twist.'

When Lucy was a teenager, a teenager Lucy was,
She went 'Ooo Aah, Cantona,
I've left my knickers in my boyfriend's car.'

When Lucy was a mother, a mother Lucy was,
She went smack, smack, smack, smack, smack.

When Lucy was a granny, a granny Lucy was,
She went knit, knit, knit, knit, knit.

When Lucy was a skeleton, a skeleton Lucy was,
She went click, click, click, click, click.
(Children's clapping rhyme)[1]

The previous chapter examined theories of human play in general. In this chapter we return to language play, and consider what other factors (in addition to those outlined in the last chapter) may be needed to account for it. We shall also address more directly the questions raised earlier: why is language play so widespread, and why does it exert such a compelling attraction for human beings, as a species, as societies, and as individuals?

Implicitly, the first section of this book has already taken a theoretical position on language play by assuming that play at the three levels of form, meaning, and use is connected, and by treating under a single heading of 'language play' a wide range of apparently disparate genres. Thus we have examined nursery rhymes, children's lore, poetry, fiction, verbal duels, riddles, play languages, jokes, puns, magical spells, and religious prayers and liturgies— all as though they were instances of a single phenomenon. We have also considered the most trivial patternings of sound and exploitations of coincidence (for example in puns and rhymes) as comparable with language carrying the most profound meanings (for example in literature and religion). In modern society at least, where the meaning of language is generally held to be more important than its form (on the assumption that the two can be separated), the different levels of play and the genres which carry them differ wildly in status and in the degree of seriousness accorded to them, as well as in the contexts in which they are used. Yet there is a good deal of similarity between them. They have an evident social significance and emotional import. They are widespread—probably universal—in human societies, and they are among the uses of language which people most enjoy, remember, and value. Despite their obvious difference, the two comments on death at the head of this chapter have a good deal more in common than their subject-matter alone.

The purpose of this chapter is to suggest that there is a causal relation between play at the three levels of linguistic form, semantics, and pragmatics. The patterning of form, though apparently random, leads to the creation of alternative realities, and this in turn performs essential functions in human life. In previous chapters we have seen how this process contributes to social interaction, and in particular to competition and collaboration. Here, we shall look at this connection again, though from a slightly different perspective. The main thrust of this chapter, however, is to consider how the exploitation of formal patterns and random coincidences is a key to creativity and adaptability. This is not only the case in language play, but also in games, and in complex and adaptive systems in nature. We shall consider this effect in each of these three areas.

In order to develop a more explicit understanding of the similarities between different genres, and of the way in which play at one level interacts with play at the others, we need to state more formally the features identified so far which typify—even define—language play. They are grouped below under the headings of linguistic form, semantics, and pragmatics, and coded for ease of reference.

The features of language play

linguistic form	(L1)	patterning of forms (rhythms, phonological, and grammatical parallels)
	(L2)	emphasis on exact wording
	(L3)	repetition (both of parts and of whole texts)
semantics	(S1)	indeterminate meaning (foreign or archaic language, unknown or obscure words, ambiguities)
	(S2)	vital or important subject-matter (birth, death, sexual relations, health, etc.)
	(S3)	reference to an alternative reality
	(S4)	inversion of language/reality relation
pragmatics	(P1)	focus upon performance and upon the speaker and/or writer
	(P2)	use in congregation and/or intimate interaction
	(P3)	creation of solidarity and/or antagonism and competition
	(P4)	no direct usefulness
	(P5)	preservation or inversion of the social order
	(P6)	enjoyment and/or value

Not all features are present in every instance, nor are they equally prominent in each genre. Yet the degree to which they unite radically disparate discourses is illustrated by the fact that they are all[2] present, for example, in the children's clapping rhyme, and the words from the Anglican funeral service at the head of this chapter.

The very variety of contexts and genres in which these features occur, and the different functions which they perform, ensure that language play is a substantial part of the lives of all members of very different societies. We find it at every stage of life; in solitary, intimate, and public uses of language; in prestigious and non-prestigious discourse; in diverse societies, and throughout history. When some forms of language play are rejected as childish, immoral, or lowbrow, other more elevated forms may substitute for them—or vice versa. Children grow *out of* their games of make-believe, only to grow *into* fiction and ritual. The individual who finds 'high literary fiction' too taxing may pay more attention to tabloid newspapers or soap operas. A puritan society which brands games and drama as immoral may compensate by taking a greater interest in sacred texts or 'improving' fictions. Thus the presence of language play (though disguised) seems to remain fairly consistent. The impression is of a general human need satisfied in various but constant ways, independent of the immediate functions (entertainment, humour, contest, magic, worship, etc.) attributed to particular forms, in particular societies and contexts. One of the main burdens of the argument so far has been that this ubiquity of language play demands more attention in applied linguistic theory. Given that language play is marked by apparent uselessness, explanation is needed as to why so much human time, effort, and emotion is invested in it.

One rather obvious result of play is enjoyment. But we should beware of letting this in itself be used as an explanation. There is a certain circularity in explaining the prevalence of an activity by saying it is enjoyable. In the absence of harmful consequences—and sometimes even despite them—we of course do things we enjoy. The activity stems from the enjoyment, and the enjoyment from the activity—but the harder and the larger question is to seek out the reasons for both. It is, however, a premise of both evolutionary and cultural theories that the enjoyment of play is an epiphenomenon rather than a cause. Our feelings of pleasure have developed to ensure the maintenance of activities which are—at least potentially or in moderation—beneficial to us, though the benefits may not be immediate, apparent, or even permitted by the reigning social ideology. As one of the universal sources of human pleasure, play belongs with sex, parenthood, friendship, gaining social acceptability, eating, and sleeping; but as with these other basic and universal activities, its benefits are often treated as rather obvious and straightforward, and then pursued no further. Play, it is assumed, is for relaxation or stimulation, or to burn off energy, and that is all. One of the purposes of this chapter is to explore the functions, and thus the pleasure, of an aspect of language play which is not easily accounted for by any of the theories examined so far—the sheer delight which seems to arise from surrender to chance and unpredictability. This notion of the functionality of all aspects of language play, however, leads to a paradox. If one is arguing for a notion of play as something free from utilitarian influence, then the notion that it is after all useful can be regarded as a reduction of play to non-play. Perhaps we should not exclude the notion that some play may simply have no usefulness at all.

Language play: evolutionary and cultural explanation

So far we have encountered, broadly speaking, two types of explanation of play in general which might also be extended to embrace language play. Both are satisfactory, and convincing to a point, but ultimately insufficient. The first is an evolutionary explanation which can encompass language play as continuous in function with play in the animal world, even though it makes use of the species-specific attribute of language. We *play* with language as a means of improving a skill essential to our species.[3] Once acquired we continue to *display* it as a way of demonstrating our proficiency and thus our claim to social status and desirability as a mate. There are, however, a number of limitations to this rather straightforward evolutionary explanation. Although the origin of language play may be its primeval usefulness in training and competition, it does not follow that this is now its only function, nor that all genres dominated by language play have come into existence solely for these purposes. Such original uses may have later given rise to epiphenomena, with functions of their own, which have outgrown and superseded their origin. From the competitive insult, the joke, and the riddle may have arisen imaginary worlds which, developed into fully-fledged fictions, then allowed their creators to explore hypothetical circumstances and events. This in turn would have increased flexibility in dealing with unforeseen eventualities. This enhanced resourcefulness might in turn have augmented a general understanding of the world, and the ability to think creatively and theoretically.

The second type of explanation is cultural and historical in nature. It sees human society as essentially different from that of animals. It may see the *origin* of play in activities common to humans and animals, but regards it as having assumed a character and nature of its own. Such a view is at the root of Huizinga's thesis that primeval agonistic play transmuted into cultural institutions such as law, art, religion, philosophy, warfare.[4] This then allows considerable cultural variation—despite the general universality of play, and its influence on cultural institutions. It is on this issue of cultural diversification that evolutionary psychology and the cultural approach decisively part company. For it remains axiomatic in evolutionary psychology that while both biological and cultural inheritance determine human behaviour, the influence of the former is always stronger, and more important to anthropology, psychology, and linguistics (Tooby and Cosmides 1992; Pinker 1994). Cultural approaches, on the other hand, tend to be equally dogmatic in their relegation of biological determinants to a minor role (Huizinga [1944] 1949: 2). The dichotomy is, as already argued, both unfortunate and impoverishing. The difference is a matter of emphasis rather than contradictory claims, and it is the argument of this book that a theory of play is stronger if it acknowledges the complementarity of the two positions, rather than seeing them in opposition.

Despite their differences, however, the evolutionary and cultural accounts of play share a common limitation, especially when applied to language play in particular. They explain the fact *that* there is play, but not *what* it is, and *why* it should take the forms that it does. Why does it involve the patterning and repetition of linguistic forms, and the creation of imaginary worlds, rather than some other use of language? Considered from the evolutionary perspective, the connection between actual language play and its training function is not as straightforward as that between, say, the chasing and catching play of kittens and the hunting of adult cats. Linguistic performance skills could just as easily be improved through the practice of logical argument, or the fluent recitation of facts. Similarly, there is no evident necessary connection between rhyme, rhythm, and fantasy, and the symbolic display of adult aggression. Other verbal skills might suffice just as well. Considered from the cultural perspective, there is no particular reason why these linguistic and semantic forms of play should persist within diverse societies.

The omission of *alea*

The major limitation of the evolutionary and cultural approaches is that they address some types of play while ignoring others. If we return to Caillois' taxonomy of four types of game (set out schematically on page 115), we see that only two of his categories—*agôn* and mimicry—can be easily accounted for. *Agôn*, being concerned with competition, which is viewed as both the driving force of evolution and the main concern of social institutions, is self-evidently central to both kinds of theory. From an evolutionary perspective, mimicry can be seen as an aid to learning, and thus continuous with imitative behaviour in animals (as when lion cubs pretend to be hunting lions) but far more various. It also serves to develop the theory of mind[5] (the ability to assess the thoughts of others, discussed more fully below) by allowing those involved in imitative games to experience what it is like to be, or to deal with, other people in unfamiliar situations.[6] From the cultural perspective, mimicry not only serves to initiate the young through role play into social structures which are—by definition in this view—learnt rather than inherited; in adult life, it is also a key element in both art and ritual, in which cultural values are expressed by individuals taking on new and artificial roles.

Both *agôn* and mimicry, then, are accounted for by theories of general play. *Ilinx* remains problematic. The examples of this type of play given by Caillois are physical rather than verbal, and for this reason can seem distant from language play. However, it may be that sensations of vertigo, in which our 'equilibrium [is] momentarily destroyed' and we 'escape the tyranny of perception', can be achieved through surrender to the flow of language, whether one's own or—in recitation—somebody else's. To some degree *ilinx* fits Csikszentmihalyi's theory of play as flow (see page 106), although the pleasure of *ilinx*, unlike that of flow, seems to be in a loss of control rather than in the mastery of challenges. *Ilinx* seems to be constituted by a deliberate denial of the normal, and, like *alea*, to manifest a desire for disruption. Caillois himself expresses some unease about it as a separate category, and for our purposes here, it may be best considered as a branch of *alea*, though in the physical rather than the mental spheres.

It is upon this category, *alea*, that I wish to focus in this chapter. *Alea* is defined by Caillois as a kind of play, typified by roulette, in which 'chance is dominant' and the player 'relies on everything but himself and surrenders to forces that elude him'. As such, it is not substantially explained by any of the theoretical approaches to play which we have examined so far. The appeal and benefits of this surrender to the forces of chance are widespread in other aspects of human life, and in nature, and the purpose of this chapter is to consider how it may operate in language play. As a prelude to examining how it works in language, however, we look at its role in games, where its function may be clearer, and more readily recognized and understood. At the end of the chapter, we shall also consider its creative role in natural processes.

The appeal of chance: games

So far in this book the words 'game' and 'play' have been used almost interchangeably. Here, we need to be more specific. The term 'game' is notoriously difficult to define (Wittgenstein [1953] 1968:31),[7] and its relationship to 'play' is problematic. Is every instance of play a game? Is every game an instance of play? In a general sense 'game' is used to describe a range of activities, including such unstructured ones as the rough and tumble of young animals and the *ad hoc* improvisations of children's make-believe ('We're playing a game'). It is also used metaphorically—in the plural—to describe the deceitful or trivial behaviour of adults ('He's playing games'). In a more specific sense, however, (the one in which I shall use it here) it refers to intricate, rule-governed, and culturally variable competitive activities. Games in this sense can provide insights into language play for a number of reasons. They are, like language itself, uniquely human; they generally involve a substantial role for chance; they are used as instruments of competition; and they express and create cultural value and identity.

The relation of games and language

On the surface, the extent to which games actually involve language varies considerably. Some, such as chess or football, may be played in complete silence, and do not seem to involve language at all. Others, such as cryptic crosswords, involve playing *with* language, using it as both the object and the instrument of play. Between these two extremes there is an intermediate category of games (such as the children's game 'I spy') which, while they are conducted in language, use it to refer to and play with something non-linguistic ('what I can see' in the case of 'I-spy'). Despite these differences in their use of language, all games have notable affinities with it. Even apparently non-verbal games may involve incidental language (as when the chess player comments on a move); they can be described and analysed in language; often they are partly learnt via the use of language. Indeed, although a game like chess can be played in silence—and one can imagine two people who have no language in common doing this quite successfully, in effect using the game as a means of communication—it is hard to imagine how chess could have been either developed or learnt without language.

Non-verbal games, too, are also often structured in ways comparable to language, whether at the level of the sentence or the whole text. Thus, while each playing of the game may be different from every other, they are all constrained by the same underlying constitutive rules, just as utterances in a given language may be novel and creative, but constrained by a finite set of abstract structures. The distinction between competence and performance drawn for language by Chomsky (1965: 3–4) can validly be applied to games; there is a fixed competence in the rules of the game underlying the variations of every performance. If we accept the view of structuralist critics that genres of literary texts also have underlying combinatorial constraints (Propp [1928] 1968; Todorov 1966) then we can 'level shift' the similarities between grammar and games upwards to the level of the text itself. Instances of genres are variations within a constrained structure, in the same way as particular sentences and instances of games. Like the unfolding of a fairy tale or a detective story, the playing of a particular game follows predictable patterns and stages, but with infinite variations. There is a 'games competence' involving knowledge of particular games, in the same sense that there is 'literary competence' (Culler 1975: 113–31) involving knowledge of particular genres. This 'grammar' of the game, however, does not preclude the occurrence within it of fixed sequences, such as standard chess openings, copied from other games. In a similar way, actual language use contains assemblages of ready-made chunks as well as unique utterances (Pawley and Syder 1983; Sinclair 1991).

As well as having similarities of structure, non-verbal games and language have similar uses. Players of non-verbal games communicate meaning; they collaborate or compete through the game, and create relationships by playing. Like conversationalists, they employ elaborate turn-taking procedures. Games, like language use, offer the same opportunity for individual display and communal enjoyment.

Games often involve deception and a subtle calculation and monitoring not only of what each player is thinking, but also an estimation of what each player *thinks* that the other thinks.[8] It is this which makes what are structurally quite simple procedures, such as betting in poker or bidding in bridge, inordinately psychologically complex, as each player reasons along the lines of: 'I think she thinks I think she thinks' or 'I know he knows I know he knows'. In evolutionary psychology, this ability is known as 'theory of mind'. It is believed to be innate, and to have developed through natural selection during the hunter-gatherer phase of evolution. There is now evidence for a 'theory of mind' module associated with quite specific areas of the brain (Leslie 1987), and it may be a lack of this neuronal apparatus in the autistic which makes their use of language, however grammatical and meaningful, fail as communication (Frith 1993).[9] One function of games may be to develop or maintain this faculty of assessing the thoughts of others, for even if it is largely an innate skill, it presumably needs environmental stimulation to develop, and be capable of improvement through practice.

These many analogies between non-verbal games and language can also be reversed. Games are like language, but language is also like a game. Many canonical statements in linguistic theory about the nature of language use this comparison, as in de Saussure's famous analogy of language with chess ([1915]1983:88–9),[10] or Wittgenstein's use of the term 'language games' ([1953] 1968:5).

Although games and language have much in common, it is not the case, necessarily, that all play with language is also a game. Much language play is characterized by that same undirected exuberant outpouring of energy which characterizes the spontaneous improvised play of children and young animals: that is, in Caillois' terms, *paedia*. To some degree, it too might seem comparable to animal play, with the difference that instead of using objects and limbs it uses words and the organs of speech. Much language play is non-competitive, and therefore has no conclusion and no victories. It is simultaneously anarchic and ordered, obsessed with breaking free of constraints, but also with creating new patterns and new realities where there were none before.

Chance and competition: Game Theory

Often, games are vehicles for competition and collaboration, and as such they have a very similar social function to the language play (verbal duels, jokes, rituals) which we examined in Chapter 3. (In fact, that chapter began by comparing language play to ball games.) Yet competition is often sharpened, and made less predictable by the addition of an element of chance. In many games, indeed, the competition is with chance, rather than with another player. In recent years, competitive games, and the role of chance within them, have been the subject of an area of inquiry known as Game Theory. This is very much in Huizinga's 'etic' tradition of analysing serious cultural activity as play. It has been used, for example, in the analysis of economics (von Neumann and Morgenstern 1944), of military strategic planning (Sigmund 1995:159), and of voting behaviour (Colman 1982: 195–234).

Defined as 'the logic of decision-making in social situations in which outcomes depend upon the decisions of two or more autonomous agents' (*ibid.*:1), Game Theory sets out to describe how in competitive games, the *strategy* of each player will be affected by his or her calculations of what the other player or players will do in pursuit of the *pay-off*, the desired benefit of the game. (The two words are used as technical terms.) Games, in other words, are conceived as ways of exercising and stretching each player's theory of mind to the limits. Game Theory can be applied to the simplest of games such as variations on 'Chicken', the potentially lethal contest of nerve said to have been popular among teenage joy-riders in the United States, in which two cars were driven towards each other at top speed. The driver of the first car to swerve was considered to be 'chicken', and thus the loser—but then, if neither car swerved, or if both swerved to the same side, both drivers would be losers—in a much more serious way. The problem for each driver was to estimate what the other driver was likely to do, in a calculation which—even in this comparatively simple instance—quickly became inordinately complex, as each player needed to make judgements based on mathematical calculations of possibilities, their experience of previous games, their knowledge of the other player, and their assessment of what the other player was calculating about what *they* were calculating—a factor which meant that almost any decision might need to be reversed, on the grounds that the other player realized it has been realized! In the game of Chicken there are only nine possible combinations.[11] In more complex games for two players, the mathematics are obviously far more intricate. In chess, for example, there are around 160,000 possible positions after the first four moves. Yet in any game with two players, the psychological factors—such as estimating whether the opponent is bluffing, or likely to take risks, and so on—remain much the same. It is only when the number of players in a game increases that these factors multiply.

Competitive games, then, tend to exploit the multiple possibilities generated by the rules, pitting the competing players not only against each other, but also—as it were—against the game itself. To further complicate matters, in many cases these 'forces of the game' are by no means logical or susceptible to skill. In addition, there are also games, such as Patience, in which there is no other player, but *only* the game—and in these, as in games with a human opponent, Chance may play a greater or lesser part. To deal with such instances, Game Theory personifies inanimate or random factors as another player, 'Nature'.

Game Theory has important implications for the question of the relation between animal and human play, and the degree to which the former can throw light upon the latter, for it suggests aspects of human play which are quite unique to our species. There is, it is true, evidence for higher animals having some 'theory of mind' (thoughts about the thoughts of others), even if there is nothing approaching the complex empathy present in even the most rudimentary human social interaction. Game Theory, therefore, could be used to calculate how individual animals make decisions in specific conflicts by balancing the risks against the potential pay-offs—how a dog, for example, might decide whether to bite, or just bark. There is also a branch of Game Theory—Evolutionary Game Theory (Maynard Smith 1988)—which draws an analogy between evolutionary competition and the conduct of human games, and seeks to assess how one species may fare in conflict with another.[12] Yet although the adaptations of species can be analysed as though they were moves in a game whose pay-off is survival, this application is, in an important sense, metaphorical. There are no conscious calculations of moves in evolution; each adaptation gives only the impression of decision-making, in much the same way as—it is claimed—evolution itself creates an illusion of design (Dawkins 1986, 1995).[13] The notion of decision-making, which is so crucial in human games, is not applicable in the same sense to animals as it is to humans. This is not simply a question of greater intelligence and a more developed theory of mind, however. In both individual and evolutionary conflicts, the pay-off for animals which determines the strategy is always the same: survival (whether of the individual itself or of its genes in its offspring). Consequently, animals act in more predictable and automatic ways. In human games, however, all calculations are complicated by the fact that different individuals seek different pay-offs in different circumstances. Three frequent alternatives are summarized in Game Theory as 'praise, prize or price' (words which interestingly share a common root in the Latin word *pretium*, Sigmund 1995:167) to which we might add the pay-off of 'practice' and, of course, 'fun'.

Game Theory has interesting insights to offer into the use of random and inanimate factors in competitive games. Yet it also has a number of limitations. By defining games as activities involving competitive decision-making, it embraces a number of very serious activities—such as warfare—which are not generally described as games by the players themselves. (In this it shares Huizinga's 'etic' approach.) This, however, does not capture the nature of games from an 'emic' point of view. There remains some indefinable element of difference distinguishing those activities known as 'games' in the societies in which they exist, such as (for it is easier to exemplify than define) patience, poker, bridge, chess, football, tennis, I-spy, and scrabble. There is a difference—perhaps an element of fun—which makes them decisively different from arms races and election campaigns.

A further criticism levelled at Game Theory is that it misrepresents and underestimates the complexity of variation in individual attitudes and motivations. Danielson (1992), analysing his own failure to calculate outcomes in computer simulations of moral decision-making, accuses it of 'motivational monism' for focusing only upon 'an ideal situation where all agents reason in the same way', and for assuming that all agents are 'symmetrically rational' and (recursively) believe each other to be so, too.

A more serious criticism is that levelled by the French philosopher Jean Duvignaud (1980), who regards 'Game Theory' as a misnomer, and its use in calculating outcomes as quite antithetical to the essentially unpredictable quality of play. 'Simulation ... as practised by technocrats and administrators ... construct(s) a future which is determined, predictable and secure even in the event of nuclear catastrophe. Such a procedure is inimical to the essential caprice and freedom of play' (Burke 1994: 29).

In seeking to understand the role of chance in language play we shall need to take these criticisms into account, and search for a model which will account for an insider's view of play, allow for individual variation, and—above all—acknowledge that once an element of chance is introduced, outcomes are unpredictable. The next section looks a little further into the issue and benefits of this unpredictability, which is central to the concept of *alea*.

Games of chance

Games may be divided into three types, according to the role of chance (Figure 5.1). First, it is arguable that there are games which involve no chance, but only skill. Chess is an example, as every move is decided and controlled by the players (although the incalculable range of possibilities makes the future course of the game very similar to one dictated by random factors). Other games, such as bridge, combine elements of both chance and skill. Indeed, it is the element of chance in them, on balance favouring all opponents equally, which ensures that greater skill will ultimately be the deciding factor. Other games depend entirely on chance, and involve no skill at all. Such is the case for example, when two people wager money on the throw of dice. In this last category, the submission to chance takes on a value of its own, rather than merely acting as a catalyst enhancing the role of skill. It is this third category—games of 'pure chance'—which will provide the greater insight for the argument at this point.

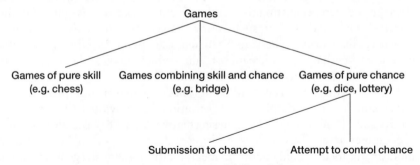

Figure 5.1: Games of skill and chance

Games of pure chance are often played competitively. Yet, by definition, victory in them does not indicate any superiority in the winner. So they cannot be explained by an evolutionary theory which sees the function of competition as the selection of the fittest. Nor are they entirely explained by a cultural theory. They may have a limited social function in shaking up the established order, or giving hope to the disadvantaged (thus also perhaps keeping them under control), but this does not seem to be an adequate reason for their appeal. Some other explanation is needed. Even when played socially and used in competition, they seem to be events in which the player competes with, or appears to submit to, arbitrary, random, and illogical forces. The other player is in effect not another competitor, but Chance—a power which, significantly, is often personified. A classic example of such a game is a lottery in which the winning sequence is generated by a method which must—if the rules are fair—guarantee that it is random. Modern lotteries use purpose-built machines in which numbered balls spin until released one at a time by the push of a button. There is no element of choice or design. In contrast, the human players, who *can* choose their numbers, may either try to match the machine by using a random sequence of their own,[14] or by following some guiding principle, such as listing the ages or birth dates of members of their family, seeking by so doing, to increase their chances of winning. Such superstitious gambling practices share with magic the notion that some secret pattern can control natural forces; and like Kabbalism, they see significance in apparently meaningless numbers.

There are thus two very different ways of approaching games of pure chance (Figure 5.1). The first is epitomized by the lottery player who seeks to impose or find order in the apparently unpredictable. Here the player acts as though no force, even the most illogical, is beyond control, thus providing, presumably, some degree of comfort in the face of the unknown. (If we regard unpredictability as an essential element of play, this is not playful at all. It seeks, in effect, to show that there is no such thing as a game of chance.) The second is epitomized by the lottery player who chooses numbers at random, abandoning all influence over the situation and submitting to factors beyond their control. This is harder to explain. It does not yield to either the standard evolutionary or cultural approaches, or to Game Theory, yet it seems to exert a fascination—to drastically different degrees—for everyone. A full theory of play, however, needs to explain this peculiarly human inclination.

Randomness

This fascination with chance in games has a particular relevance to the theory which I wish to develop in the following sections of this chapter about language play—and conversely, an understanding of chance in language play may illuminate its attractions in games. Yet before returning to language play in particular, it is necessary to say more about a concept which is central to this discussion: randomness.

The word 'random', though often used rather loosely, has at least three distinct meanings (Boden 1992: 223). A first sense (A-randomness) refers to the absence of any order or structure. An A-random sequence of events or numbers cannot be compressed, or expressed in any simpler or more concise form than itself. A second sense (E-randomness) refers to the absence of any explanation or cause of the sequence.[15] In practice the difference is often unimportant. Many sequences are both A-random and E-random at once. But there is always the possibility that a structured sequence will arise by accident. If, for example, four throws of a pair of dice were to produce the sequence of even numbers 2, 4, 6, 8, this would be E-random but not A-random.

A third sense (R-random) refers to the lack of any order or structure relevant to some specific consideration. Thus, although the position in which tumbling dice eventually come to rest may be at least partially determined by factors such as speed, friction, initial position, and so on, these influences are all random 'with respect to the knowledge and the wishes of the players' (Boden (*ibid.*)). Games of pure chance are random in this third sense: what happens could have structure or order by accident, and may have a cause, but it is random with respect to the outcome. In human affairs, it is R-randomness which magic and augury attempt to overrule. Some order of events (such as a magic rite) or configuration (for example the patterns of a bird's entrails, or the tea leaves at the bottom of a cup) are claimed not only to have an internal structure and order of their own—which they may have—but also to be relevant to and thus predictive of the structure of something else: typically the fate or fortune of a known individual. In this sense, magic is not play.

R-randomness in language

This third type of randomness—R-randomness—is particularly important in linguistic theory, for it lies at the heart of the dual structure (or 'duality') which enables language, in von Humboldt's well-known formulation, 'to make infinite use of finite means' (Chomsky 1996: 8). According to this principle of duality, all languages have two levels, each of which has an internal but independent structure (Hockett 1958: 574; Lyons 197: 71–6). The first is the level of phonology, the second the level of lexis and grammar. The units at the first level are phonemes; at the second level they are lexemes. (Except by coincidence in a word such as I = /aɪ/, phonemes are not meaningful in themselves.) Each level has rules specifying permissible combinations; but these rules say nothing about the acceptability of the sequences they specify in the other level. Thus for example, in English, at the phonological level, both 'gop' (/gɔp/) and 'gap' (/gæp/) are permissible phonologically. Nothing in the rules of phonology, however, predicts that 'gap' is an English lexeme while 'gop' is not. The same stretch of language can thus be analysed in two quite different ways, but the two descriptions have no relevance to each other. They are, in other words, in an R-random relationship.

It is this R-random relationship which underpins the extent and variety of the lexicon, and the capacity for word coinage, in all languages. For if each phoneme were itself a lexeme, this would permit the language to have a set of lexemes of the same number as the phonemes. Although in principle, in such a hypothetical language, the use of compound lexemes would allow both extension and innovation,[16] in practice the combination of meaningless components adopted by actual languages is far more elegant and effective, and can more easily generate enormous numbers of unambiguously distinct lexemes. When these are in turn combined through the combinatory rules of grammar the possibilities available become, literally, infinite. This creative combinatory power is one of the principal features distinguishing human from animal communication.[17]

Dual structure is a feature of all spoken languages. For this reason there is no 'control' comparison against which to measure its efficiency. Its generative capacity, however, and the consequences of its absence, are clear when we compare writing systems which have adopted the principle of dual structure, with those which have not. In alphabetic writing,[18] which uses a small set of meaningless graphemes (typically between 20 and 30, depending on the alphabet), the combinatorial possibilities are quite staggering. Quite how large they are has been calculated by Umberto Eco as follows:

> the 21 letters of the Italian alphabet can give rise to more than 51 billion billion 21-letter-long sequences (each different from the rest); when, however, it is admitted that some letters are repeated, but the sequences are shorter than the number of elements to be arranged, the general formula for n elements taken t at a time with repetitions is n^t and the number of strings obtainable for the letters of the Italian alphabet would amount to 5 billion billion billion.
> (Eco 1997:55)

In actuality, of course, mathematically possible combinations of graphemes are severely restricted by the rules of graphology, and of the phonology to which they loosely correspond. Yet as Eco's figures illustrate, there is hardly need to use the mathematical potential to anything like its full extent. Even restricted by graphological and phonological rules, the possibilities of combination remain astronomically large. This power is clear when we compare alphabetic writing systems to those which do not exploit the principle of duality. In contrast to the 20 to 30 letters of modern alphabets, the contemporary Chinese writing system, even after the drastic pruning imposed during the 1950s, uses some 2,238 characters (Li 1992).

The relationship of forms and functions

There are, then, two systems in language, the phonological and the lexical and grammatical, occupying as it were the same space, and existing in an R-random relationship. The usual assumption, both in the popular view and in many schools of linguistics, is that the lexical and grammatical system is in turn related to a third non-linguistic level: that of meaning. (I use the term 'meaning' here to cover both *pragmatic* and *semantic* meaning.) The status of the three systems, however, is not regarded as equal. It is the desire to mean something which is regarded as the starting-point for each utterance. This view is shared both by formalist linguistics (on those occasions when it does consider performance) and by functionalist linguistics. It is assumed that lexical and grammatical choices are made in order to realize this meaning, and that these in turn are realized through phonological and graphological strings. In other words, it is conceived of as a hierarchical relation, in which meaning is the master, and lexis and grammar, and phonology and graphology, are the servants. Meaning is also seen as autonomous, and independent, and valuable in itself; linguistic forms are regarded as dependent and of no value in themselves. (Significantly, the word 'meaningful' can be used as a synonym for 'worthwhile', and 'meaningless' for 'futile'.) The general order of events in language production is thus assumed to be as shown in Figure 5.2.

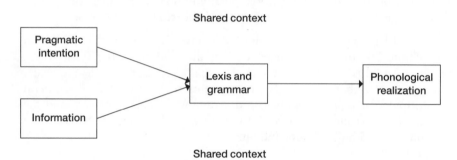

Figure 5.2: A standard functionalist view of communication

In reception, according to this view, the order is reversed. Meaning remains dominant, not in the sense that it as the prime mover, but in the sense that recovery of it is the final goal. Linguistic forms are enlisted only as a means to that end. A similar direction is also often assumed in functionalist views of language acquisition. Halliday (1975), for example, argues that the starting-point for the child is the desire to mean. This is expressed initially through an idiosyncratic use of phonology which in turn connects to the adult lexis and grammar.

There are, it is true, more or less sophisticated versions of the model and in particular some distinction is needed between what Reddy (1979) has referred to as the conduit view of language, in which communication is seen as a simple encoding/decoding process (de Saussure [1915] 1983:11–13), and a view of communication as discourse (Widdowson 1979:89–153, 1984: 5–137), in which interpretation is derived from a combination of decoding with relevant contextual factors. Some such tripartite view of communication, however, is shared by otherwise apparently opposed schools of linguistics, and the essential belief is that in performance form follows meaning. The only possible dissension might appear to be an extreme relativism, in which available meanings are seen as determined by the linguistic system and, in performance, emerging from its use.

This emphasis on the primacy and autonomy of meaning is not undermined by the fact (noted by many linguists) that even in the most humdrum or factual discourse, apparently purely aesthetic considerations of phonological or grammatical parallels occur. Tannen (1989), for example, notes repetitions and echoes in casual conversation; Werth (1976) uncovers parallelisms in a newspaper report on pest control; and Carter and McCarthy (1995) report frequent plays upon sound and words in their extensive corpus of spoken English. These facts, however, are not taken to undermine the general assumption that the overriding direction of influence in production is from meaning through grammar to phonology, and that minor embellishments are allowed and possible, but do not interfere with the meaning.

Formalism in linguistics is closely allied to evolutionary psychology; functionalist linguistics is a descendent of cultural relativism (Halliday 1985:xx). It is not surprising, then, to find that the notion that form follows function is taken for granted in the study of human behaviour in general, as it is in ideas about language. Both evolutionary and cultural explanations of language play, taking group identity and competition as the driving force behind play, seem based upon this assumption. Yet neither offers an explanation of why these motivating forces give rise to the playful patterning of linguistic forms, and to the description of fictional events.

One reason why play takes these directions may be as follows. The speaker begins with a social purpose: to exclude someone through contest, or to establish or reinforce solidarity. These aims are best accomplished by extended discourse, rather than some brief allusion to the fact that they exist. Yet there is little to be imparted by way of information. The speaker might refer to the rival's actual shortcomings if the purpose is to exclude them from the group, or to their virtues if the purpose is to include them. Yet doing this, and nothing else, will neither last long, nor demonstrate any great mental or linguistic agility in the speaker. Hence a rapid move towards invention. At the most basic level, for example, in agonistic play, the speaker might refer to some imagined shortcomings of the rivals, rather than real ones. This departure from the tyranny of facts, combined with an imperative to keep speaking, seems to be a central characteristic of language play.

At this point, however, with choices no longer constrained by reality, it may become easier to impose some sort of grammatical or phonological pattern upon successions of insults or endearments. The fictional events and linguistic patterns themselves become motivating forces, each complementing and stimulating the other. The two may be in balance or—in extreme cases—the source of choices may shift over towards the formal system, so that the direction of flow is not just balanced but reversed. Meaning is no longer an autonomous level. Now meaning and effect are dictated by patterning of forms, rather than the other way round. The speaker becomes concerned with three goals simultaneously: the patterning of linguistic form, the creation of imaginary facts and events, and the maintenance of an original purpose, to insult or to flatter. The first two of these augment the third by demonstrating inventiveness and linguistic fluency.

Let us examine how such a process might work in more concrete terms by looking at a simple example of a playful insult, taken from *The Lore and Language of Schoolchildren* (Opie and Opie 1959:179).

> You're daft, you're potty, you're barmy
> You ought to join the army.
> You got knocked out
> With a brussel sprout
> You're daft, you're potty, you're barmy.

It is very likely that on the occasion when this was recorded (in Market Rasen in Lincolnshire), the child recited it by memory, thus appropriating the wit of the originator, and also demonstrating his own repertoire rather than originality. For our purposes, however, let us imagine it being invented— as presumably it was on at least one occasion. The speaker begins with an intention to insult and simultaneously—one may imagine—to demonstrate his or her own superiority, to win admirers, and to establish or consolidate his own position in the hierarchy of the playground. He begins with a bald and unimaginative insult, a mere assertion of opinion, but expressed in an established rhythm (best scanned as stress verse with four beats) and ending fortuitously with:

> You're <u>daft</u>   you're <u>potty</u>   you're <u>barmy</u>

The rhythms and the conventions of rhyme (as much as any previously conceived idea) then lead into the next line, which both echoes the rhythm of the first, and by repeating the sequence /ɑːmɪ/, creates a relationship at the lexical level out of the apparently irrelevant (i.e. R-random) relationship of 'barmy' and 'army' at the phonological level.

> You <u>ought</u>   to <u>join</u>   the <u>army</u>.

So far there is nothing particularly inventive. But then—almost in order to continue—and prompted presumably by the notion of joining the army, which in turn was prompted by the word 'barmy', the rhyme now becomes (with a cavalier shift of timescale and tense) a small-scale fiction about the object of derision and what happened to him.

> You <u>got</u> knocked <u>out</u>
> With a <u>brussel</u> <u>sprout</u>

This development, however, though taking its cue from the barmy/army rhyme, is neither illogical nor contrary to the original intention to insult: for violent events are to be expected in the army, and only someone who is both slow-witted and physically weak could be floored by a sprout. The lines also create a joke, explicable by Raskin's script-incongruity theory of humour, in that Brussels sprouts are not among the objects capable of knocking somebody out. Two forces, then, are in balance, and exerting a mutual control upon each other: the intentions of the speaker, on the one hand; the patterns demanded at the level of rhythm and rhyme, on the other. They are—as we have seen—in an R-random relationship. From the tension between the two emerges the fictional world of the miniature incident. The speaker wants to say something insulting about his opponent and to illustrate his silliness, but the precise reason for joining the army (rather than the navy) and being knocked out with a Brussels sprout (rather than a cabbage) are R-random events from the phonology. It is as though the levels of linguistic and phonological form, originally used to realize or amplify a social intention, rebound upon it, introducing a random determinant, in varying degrees of balance with purpose.

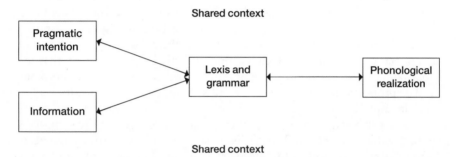

Figure 5.3: A language-play view of communication

This particular example of the children's insult is relatively easy to follow through, not only because of its brevity and structural simplicity, but because it so neatly unites purpose—the exclusion of one child, and a bid for superiority by another—with linguistic means: rhythm, rhyme, fictional incident. Other instances of language play might be similarly analysed—though with distinguishing and complicating features. Nursery rhymes, for example, motivated by the need to create and maintain a social relationship, are free to use the denotative and phonological resources more or less as they wish, provided that they do not contradict that overriding purpose by, say, frightening the child too much, or introducing markedly adult subject matter. Crucially, what seems to have happened in language play of a literary nature is that, even where the rudimentary social intention to insult or unite is no longer dominant, the dynamic interaction of the patterning of linguistic form with fictional worlds, has taken on an independent value of its own.

The random in complex systems

This notion that play introduces into language use a random element which works against more rational forces and destabilizes them, fits well with the understanding of complex adaptive systems developed in recent science. The new interdisciplinary science of 'complexity studies' considers language to share characteristics with other systems of this kind, as apparently diverse as economic orders, musical traditions, evolution, organisms, the weather, and ecosystems (Gell-Mann 1992, 1994; Kauffman 1995). In opposition to the older scientific notion that a system would move towards a state of entropy if left to itself, complexity theory suggests that a common distinguishing characteristic of such complex adaptive systems is an internal propulsion towards change, adaptation, self-organization, and increasing complexity. Typically, they alternate between periods of order and periods of chaos, in which a sudden transition from one to the other (Briggs 1992) is triggered by causes which are disproportionate to their effect, and whose precise influence is unpredictable (Gleick 1987). The most famous hypothetical illustration of this is the so-called 'butterfly effect' (now a part of popular folklore) in which it is imagined that the effect on the weather system of a butterfly flapping its wings in one place might be to bring in devastating storms in another. This dramatically captures the consequences of a fact of mathematical calculation which has only recently been discovered: that the approximation of apparently insignificant decimal points can make enormous and disproportionate differences to results. Axiomatic in complexity studies are the notions that the development of a complex system cannot be precisely predicted, that its properties cannot be reduced to the sum of its parts (Waldrop 1992), and that it is sensitive to feedback from the effects which it itself produces. It follows from all of this that it also cannot be in a state of equilibrium. In the words of Kauffman (1995:52) 'for a living system, equilibrium corresponds to death'.

Also crucial in all such systems is the presence of destabilizing R-random influences, which by ensuring that equilibrium is never reached, imbue the system with the capacity to adapt to new environments. Gell-Mann (1994: 164) suggests that it is 'the mixture of regularity and randomness that favours the evolution of complex systems [and] conditions between order and disorder which guarantee its change' (*ibid.*: 116). The interaction in language play between the opposed forces of linguistic choices made to reflect intention or to denote reality on the one hand, and the need to create formal patterns on the other, would seem to be a perfect example of such a dynamic and destabilizing interaction: one which perhaps works both as an agent of language change, and as a creator of new meanings and relationships.

This effect of random forces in underwriting change, dynamism, and adaptability can be illustrated by reference to another complex adaptive system which is often compared to language, and in which the effects of random change have been particularly closely studied: the genes. Though there are obvious limitations to the analogy, to be spelt out shortly, there does seem to be an essential similarity. In both cases, the complexity and adaptability of the system depends upon the interaction of a random and a non-random force, and for this reason, it is worth looking into further. It may be that our understanding of language play, and the reasons for its universality and attractiveness, are to be understood by regarding language, not as entirely unique, but as a system which shares properties with complex systems in general (Cook 1995). In all such systems, the presence of R-random influences is a necessary factor in imbuing the system with the capacity to adapt to new environments.

An analogy: the random in genetics

Genetics is an area of study in which the importance of the random has received a great deal of attention in recent years. Appreciation of the essential contribution of random mutation to change has in turn contributed to a new understanding of evolution. Darwin's notion of natural selection did not offer an explanation of the origin of the variation which is essential to such a process. A new view of evolution (sometimes referred to as 'neo-Darwinism') proposes that the cause of change is not environmental pressure alone, but environmental pressure in combination with the random mutation of DNA (Crow and Kimura 1970). Selection operates in an apparently rational and ordered way, but it can only select among features which have arisen—as the phrase significantly puts it—without rhyme or reason.

The key to adaptation and inheritance depends upon factors which are R-random with respect to their outcomes, but it was not until the development of modern genetics that these random factors could be described and understood. Essentially there are two ways in which randomness is present in genetic inheritance (Lewin 1994:59–80). First, in sexually reproductive organisms, when the sex cells (gametes) are formed, the chromosomes from the father and the chromosomes from the mother divide randomly, and there is some shuffling of alleles within each chromosome. Second, as the DNA sequences are copied into the cells of the new generation there are occasional random copying errors. Many of these have little effect on the organism; others create problems which may, in the worst cases, prove fatal; others still, accumulating in the population as a whole (following complex mathematical laws, see Crow and Kimura 1970; Wills 1994:200–20), provide a range of potential variations on which natural selection can then act, driven by environmental pressures.

Comparisons of genes and language

The genetic system is frequently compared to a language, and biologists make extensive use of the comparison, not incidentally or decoratively, but as the central structuring concept in their explanations. DNA is described as a 'text' assembled with a four-'letter' 'alphabet' which is then 'transcribed' (de Duve 1995:79) into RNA then 'translated' into the proteins of the organism (*ibid.*: 56–71). Since DNA can be sectioned hierarchically it can further be described as having 'sentences' and 'words' (Hodson 1992:83), and even (as there are codons whose function is to signal the end of a section), as having 'punctuation marks' (Pollack 1995:82). RNA is described as 'reading' the 'dictionary' of DNA (Dawkins 1986:120, 123). Each individual genome is 'the unique edition of a manual', and the activity of genetics is 'a bit like reading a foreign language by looking up words in a dictionary to see what they mean' (Jones 1993:79). The metaphors even keep pace with writing technology, with printing presses being replaced first by typewriters and then by computers. In 1903, Archibald Garrod described hereditary disease in individuals bearing two copies of a regressive gene as a 'misprint' (Hodson 1992:27). Dawkins (1986:123) depicts mutations as 'typos' which occur in lines of millions of typists each copying from the person on their left. For Pollack (1995:90–118), the same process happens on a 'molecular word processor'.

Indeed the parallels are striking. By some they are treated not as merely illustrative, but as literal. Dawkins (1986:111) asserts very boldly that the comparison is 'not a metaphor'. In justification of this claim he observes that genetic engineering could, by setting up systematic correspondences between sequences of the four nucleotides and the Roman alphabet (or any other writing system), transcribe a substantial linguistic text (his example is the New Testament) into the DNA of a bacterium (Dawkins 1986:116). When this organism multiplied, the same sequence of nucleotides would be copied into each offspring. A geneticist who knew the correspondences could then translate the nucleotide sequences back into the alphabet and recover the original text! In this sense, the alphabet of DNA could in principle be used to represent actual language. (A rather daunting practical disadvantage to the procedure is that, in Dawkins's estimate, it would take five centuries to transcribe the text.)

In this claim Dawkins employs a rather crude notion of language as a straightforward encoding device, without consideration of the way in which actual language understanding takes place in context. He sees stretches of language as texts carrying fixed semantic meanings, rather than as discourse yielding different pragmatic interpretations (Widdowson 1979:98). Yet even if a more sophisticated model of communciation is employed, the analogy will still hold.[19] Genes have a semantics (what the DNA sequences encode before they are translated into the proteins of the organism) and a pragmatics (what they realize as the organism develops in an actual environmental context). In biology this corresponds to the distinction between the genotype (the DNA patterns carried in an organism) and the phenotype (the observable and measurable characteristics which it develops). The former constrains, but does not entirely determine, the latter. There is—if you like— a DNA text and DNA discourse.

Limitations of the analogy

That geneticists should seize upon language as the vehicle for explaining their findings is hardly surprising. Indeed, given that language and genes are by far the most complex known systems for the encoding and transmission of information, it may even seem inevitable. What else could genetic information be compared to? Yet it is also true that the analogy has its dangers: the existence of features on one side of the comparison can be taken as proof that they exist in the other. There are certainly significant differences between genetic and linguistic encoding which should give rise to reservations about adopting the comparison too wholeheartedly.

A first limitation is that the comparison is between genetic structure and *written* language, not between genetic structure and *spoken* language. Like writing, it is fixed and recoverable. It is even 'read' by RNA in a non-linear manner (Pollack 1995:68)—i.e. the genes are not copied by RNA in the order in which they occur in the DNA strand; RNA moves backwards and forwards in the text like a reader flicking backwards and forwards in a book. A second limitation is that in language there is no parallel to the *doubleness* of the DNA text. Nor is there a parallel to the random shuffling of information when two half-texts are brought together. A third is that the transcribed DNA codes (after transcription into RNA) do not merely signify the organism by arbitrary convention in the same way as a linguistic expression (such as 'horse') might do (de Saussure [1915] 1983:67). They actually *become* it. Sections of RNA turn into the proteins which constitute the organism itself (Pollack 1995:68–9). It is as though the written sentence 'The cat sat on the mat' were to turn as we read it into an actual cat sitting on an actual mat!

The essence of the analogy: language and genes as complex systems

We are becoming lost in detail, however. Despite these limitations to the analogy, there remain points of similarity which are important to the argument here, and may provide insights into the workings of language. Both systems employ dual structure and depend upon random change. Like graphemes or phonemes, the nucleotide units are meaningless in themselves but signify certain proteins in combination, thus 'affording great flexibility in the construction of different, unambiguous statements, for different, unpredictable purposes' (Pollack 1995:65). It is mutation at this level of pure form which provides, if we extend the analogy, 'new ideas' (Cook 1995).

The mutation of DNA is purely formal: random changes accumulating and drifting according to mathematical context-independent laws; but these formal characteristics do not in themselves determine the course of evolution, for only those mutations survive which answer the contextual needs of the phenotype. Thus evolution is not all formal. On the other hand, the phenotype does not have just *any* genetic resources available that have somehow been conjured up because they would be useful. Thus evolution is not all functional. Evolutionary theory simply cannot isolate innate form and environmental function. At the heart of both evolution and language is the interaction of random mutation and environmental constraint. A biology which studied only phenotypes or only genotypes could explain the nature of neither. By analogy, a linguistics which does not admit *both* non-functional form and functional constraints cannot fully explain either.

Conclusion

In this chapter we have examined the interaction of random forces in language use, and compared them with similar interactions in other aspects of human behaviour (games) and other complex adaptive systems (e.g. genes). Strangely, although the relevance of this to applied linguistics is an obvious one, in practice it is often ignored. It is the case that in complex systems form and function cannot be separated, and that if they are to maintain their adaptability and capacity for change, the two must remain in dynamic interaction. For practical purposes, form must follow function; yet function must also follow form, if the resources for adaptation are to be maintained. This need for the random and the irrational is perhaps greatest at times when environmental demands for change are greatest. In adult language use, such a situation is encountered in the learning of a new language and adaptation to a new culture. It is to this that we turn in the next two chapters.

Notes

1 There are many versions of this rhyme in circulation. This one was recorded in north London in 1998.

2 Arguably, there is no obscure vocabulary in the skipping rhyme (unless one counts the name of the footballer Cantona) although the reference to some items (e.g. skeleton, boyfriend's car) may well seem more mysterious, or at least taboo, to a child than to an adult.

3 That is to say we practise and develop linguistic performance. This view is not therefore at odds with the Chomskyan notion that the basis of linguistic competence is innate and only minimally influenced by exposure and practice.

4 As already remarked in the previous chapter, Huizinga views these cultural developments as exaptations rather than adaptations (Gould [1980] 1990) (see page 111) which are transmitted culturally rather than genetically, following Lamarckian rather than Darwinian laws (de Duve 1995 : 257; Gould [1980] 1990 : 71). They could be conceived as an instance of what Dawkins calls 'memes', i.e. ideas which pass from mind

to mind rather than from body to body, as genes do (Dawkins 1976: 189–202).

5 Although—in the evolutionary view—the basis of theory of mind is, like language, innate, the ability to use both can still be developed.

6 If we regard fiction as a kind of vicarious mimicry then it can also be seen as fulfilling this function of developing the theory of mind. This is essentially the explanation of the appeal of fiction advanced by those evolutionary psychologists (Dunbar 1996; Pinker 1998:538–45) and evolutionary literary theorists (Carroll 1995) who consider that the appeal of fiction resides in its capacity to develop our ability to predict the behaviour of others.

7 It was used in a famous passage of the *Philosophical Investigations*, to radically rethink the definition of the word 'definition' itself, and to suggest that in the category 'games' there are no features shared by all instances, but only family resemblances between them.

8 In a more general sphere of the study of communication, the disciplines of pragmatics and discourse analysis are essentially concerned with principles and procedures which, in combination with knowledge of the forms and semantics of a language, allow such successful interpretation of what other people are thinking (Leech 1983; Widdowson 1979, 1984).

9 Meaningful is used here in the narrow semantic sense of having reference, not in the broader pragmatic sense of having reference for some clear purpose.

10 Also developed by Wittgenstein ([1953] 1968).

11 Possible outcomes are as follows: 1 The cars collide head on (crash). 2 Car 1 swerves left and car 2 swerves right (crash). 3 Car 1 swerves right and car 2 swerves left (crash). 4 Car 1 swerves left and car 2 swerves left (no crash). 5 Car 1 swerves right and car 2 swerves left (no crash). 6 Car 1 continues straight on and car 2 swerves left (no crash). 7 Car 1 continues straight on and car 2 swerves right (no crash). 8 Car 2 continues straight on and car 1 swerves left (no crash). 9 Car 2 continues straight on and car 1 swerves right (no crash).

12 The two levels are related, as evolutionary success is the outcome of success in individual conflicts.

13 For an alternative scientific view of evolution as the product of intelligent design, see Behe 1998.

14 Although humans are not capable of simply thinking up a random sequence of numbers (Dehaene 1997:76–7).

15 E-random sequences are sometimes described as 'stochastic' rather than 'random' (Gell-Mann 1994:44–6).

16 As it does in actual languages (employing dual structure) where the meaning of the sum of many words is different from the meaning of the parts. The fact that the syllabic components of 'carpet' (/kɑː/ + /pɪt/)

correspond to other semantically and etymologically different words ('car' + 'pit' in speech; 'car' + 'pet' in writing) neither affects nor interferes with its meaning.

17 Aitchison (1996) remarks that birdsong also uses duality in that although 'each individual note is meaningless—it is the combinations of notes which convey meaningful messages'. The two systems are hardly comparable, however. In language, different combinations convey different meanings. In birdsong, whatever the combinations of phrases, meanings remain the same: 'This is my territory', 'I am an available mate', etc.

18 Syllabaries, such as Japanese *kana*, also use units which (coincidences not withstanding) use phonological units.

19 There are other ways in which the analogy can be extended to encompass more sophisticated views of language than that employed by Dawkins. Genes have a synchronic aspect (their configuration in the cells of an individual) and a diachronic aspect (their history as they pass and change between generations). They have standard canonical realizations, and marked or deviant forms, as well as dialects and idiolects.

PART THREE

Language learning

6 Current orthodoxies in language teaching

O! reason not the need; our basest beggars
Are in the poorest thing superfluous:
Allow not nature more than nature needs,
Man's life is cheap as beast's.
(Shakespeare, *King Lear*, II, iv, 267–70)

The preceding chapters have examined the extent and importance of language play in social and individual life, and the key role it plays in human adaptability. There are many implications for theories and descriptions of language, both in theoretical and applied linguistics. As we have seen, understanding of language play is important in many areas of inquiry: language evolution, first language acquisition and literacy, literary theory, discourse analysis, psycholinguistics, and sociolinguistics. These final two chapters, however, deal in detail with the relevance of language play to one area of applied linguistics: language teaching and learning. Earlier chapters have made only passing reference to this field, although to language teaching professionals the extent of the implications may already be apparent.

Many currently influential approaches to language teaching take for granted a number of related assumptions, both about language use and the way in which it should be presented to students. Their aspiration is often to create classroom language use which is needs-based, meaning-focused, 'real', and culturally conventional. The language system is presented inductively (i.e. to be derived from examples) rather than deductively (i.e. with the teaching of explicit rules preceding practice), and analytically (i.e. holistically) rather than synthetically (i.e. as separate and sequenced components) (Wilkins 1976). Taken together, these approaches to language use and presentation are commonly described as 'communicative' rather than 'traditional' (Nunan and Lamb 1996:14–15) or 'task-based' rather than 'form-focused' (Skehan 1998a:4). In the light of our analysis of language play in previous chapters, this chapter examines these current assumptions. My argument will be that the understanding of language play considerably complicates our perception of many of the conclusions, terms, and distinctions currently in vogue.

A disclaimer, however, before we begin! It is not the purpose of this or the next chapter to propose that language teaching and learning should be conducted through play. On the contrary, I shall argue that learning and play should be distinguished from each other, but also from work. The most fruitful approach is not to set up a dichotomy of play and work, and then force learning to belong to one side or the other (or perhaps to alternate between the two), but rather to view play, work, and learning as a triad, each having parts which overlap with one or both of the others. Learning has elements in common with both work and play (as they have elements in common with each other) but is nevertheless distinct from them.

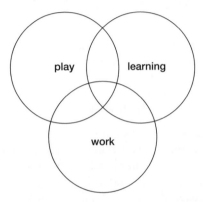

Figure 6.1: Play, learning, and work

Language learning does not need, then, to become play, any more than the classroom has to become the playground; but neither does it need to be exactly like work or 'the real world', in the core senses of these terms. What I am seeking to develop is the notion of a play element in language learning, in which understanding of language play may influence ideas about every aspect of teaching and learning: from the initial motivation, through the interim means, to the final goals.

Language play is, as we have seen, universally important, both cognitively and socially. Yet it may appear to the hard-pressed worker as a waste of time. It thus throws into doubt the dichotomy between 'useful' and 'useless' activity. For children acquiring a first language, for example, 'useless' pattern manipulation and the creation of alternate realities seems to promote both mastery of the language system and acculturation. This key role of language play in first language acquisition suggests the possibility of a similar role in adult second language learning. Yet for both the first and the second language learner, language play is much more than merely a potential *means*. As a widespread, highly valued use of language, of social and cognitive importance, it is also an *end*. Knowing a language, and being able to function in communities which use that language, entails being able to understand and produce play with it, making this ability a necessary part of advanced proficiency.

This chapter first looks at three key and connected criteria often invoked in contemporary discussion as characteristic of the 'best' language use for learners: that it should be 'needed', 'meaningful', and 'real'. Then in the concluding chapter we shall turn our attention to the implications for how languages are taught.

Needs and wants

How do we distinguish play, work, and learning? On the surface it might seem that play is driven primarily by wants; work primarily by needs; and learning by both in varying proportions. Yet as we have seen in Chapter 1, the issue is by no means straightforward. The three activities are simultaneously interconnected but distinct. Learning, for example, can be a preparation for either work or play, but can also be conducted for its own sake. We need to consider much more closely the degree to which language learning is—or should be—determined by needs as opposed to wants, and, more fundamentally, whether the two can be readily distinguished.

In the traditional humanist curriculum, the issue of why a language was learnt was often not of immediate interest (Clark 1987:5–13). Applications— if any—seemed distant, deferred to the time when school or university would be completed. The reasons for learning a language were largely a subject of consensus. It provided general mind training, access to great literature, and an understanding of civilization. It also perpetuated the study of that language as an academic discipline. Although such views originated in the teaching of the Classics (which self-evidently can have little practical application) this kind of rationale for learning passed into, and continues to be present, in the teaching of many modern languages (Howatt 1984:129). Applied to English, it has been described by Abbott (1980:123) as TENOR (The Teaching of English for No Obvious Reason). From the late 19th century onwards, however, the demise of Classics, the new confidence and ascendancy of the more widely spoken European languages, especially English, and increased trade and immigration, all led to the steady growth of adult language courses with immediate and practical use, and to a general consensus that such courses should be driven by student needs (Howatt 1984:198–207).

Defining 'needs'

At first sight, this contemporary wisdom that language courses should be determined by learner needs seems both self-evident and unobjectionable. It can also seem politically desirable, empowering students by responding to their demands rather than those of the academic institution, and rejecting the implication, inherent in the traditional humanist curriculum, that knowledge of some languages and civilizations is intrinsically more valuable than others. Yet, as amply recognized in the extensive literature on needs analysis developed since the 1970s, this apparently straightforward criterion for course design raises and begs many questions (West 1994). What sort of needs—or perhaps more pertinently *whose* needs—are we talking about? Those of students, institutions, employers, or governments? And if the first of these, do we mean simply their economic job-related needs, or some deeper spiritual need for knowledge, self-development, and enjoyment? And do we mean final goals, or interim pedagogic targets leading towards those goals, and if so what is the relationship between the two? And are language needs simply the vocabulary and conventional grammatical choices associated with some particular subject-matter, or are they specialized aspects of more general communicative abilities—such as the sociocultural, discourse, and strategic competences suggested by Canale and Swain (1980)?

The final goal of using language for work is often a reflection of the demands of governments and companies, and as such likely to be at odds with the more general educational needs of both individuals and society. The recognition that students have their own needs in addition to those imposed by their work complicates the issue of the relation between 'needs' and 'wants', and the problem of differentiating the two in any clear or meaningful way. One apparent possible solution is to distinguish two categories of need: those generated by external demands (such as the need to earn a living, or to deal with bureaucracy in a new community) and those generated by internal demands (such as the need for friendship), and then regard the latter as synonymous with 'want'. To their credit, many 'learner-centred needs analyses' (Tarone and Yule 1989:46–7) include 'what the learners want or feel they need' (Hutchinson and Waters 1987:57) as a subcategory of 'needs'. This apparently straightforward distinction, however, soon runs into difficulties. Even with the good intention to include wants as a kind of need, there is always the danger that overweening economic pressures will make externally-motivated needs appear in the student's own perception as internally-generated wants. Indeed, the two are often inextricably linked. Someone learning a language in order to get initial employment or to claim a social security benefit is clearly driven by need; it is harder to say whether someone seeking promotion in a job which already provides a good living is responding to a need or a want.

A further complication—also frequently addressed in the literature on needs analysis—is that recognizing a desired outcome, such as the ability to use language in a particular occupation, does not automatically tell us the best route to that outcome. The end is not necessarily the means. There are interim pedagogic needs as well as terminal objectives. Contrary to the work ethic, fulfilment of needs may be furthered by doing what we want. It is true, of course, that the need to master the language used for some particular job or course of study (or more generally, to survive and form part of the workforce in a given society) is often of paramount importance to students. Very often it is also a precondition for the prosperity and success necessary for further self-development, especially for the disadvantaged. As a consequence, it may be pragmatically justifiable in many circumstances for teachers and course designers to give it priority. However, it does not follow that the best way to give this need priority is to simulate the final goal immediately, or even that intermediate goals should be determined by working backwards from that final goal. In specific-purpose language teaching a realization of this fact was marked in the 1980s by a general shift of attention from an earlier naive obsession with the *what* to a more sophisticated concern with the *how* (Widdowson 1983). Success in playing games is an example of such an intermediate goal. Their outcomes are of no immediate practical benefit, but taking part in them may increase performance in some practical activity later on. The play hunting and fighting of carnivorous mammals is the archetypal example. Just as these skills are not first learnt by *actual* fighting or hunting—indeed to do so might be fatal—so in humans (as we have seen in Chapter 1), although the acquisition of a first language enables us to use that language for practical transactional purposes, it is not developed by using it exclusively for such purposes straight away, but largely indirectly, through the most useless uses of language imaginable: nursery tales and rhymes. Similarly (as we have seen in Chapter 2) the ability to engage successfully in actual, everyday social interaction is largely developed through interaction with fictional characters in games and stories.

Educational and interim needs: traditional, process, and procedural syllabuses

As in play, the goals of learning can appear to those involved to have intrinsic value, not only for their practical spin-off, but also for the feeling of well-being they create, regardless of whether or not they are later used for work. Surprisingly, perhaps, belief in the promotion of such educational aims over outside pressures can cut across the usual opposition made between traditional and communicative syllabuses, and be found in some realizations of both. In the traditional syllabus the refusal to consider practical applications of knowledge, combined with an insistence on competitive examinations, means that its goals were inevitably a mixture of the intrinsic and the pedagogic. At its best, a relative independence from the utilitarian demands of employers and governments allows the traditional syllabus to recognize or create a space in which students can perceive themselves as more than the tools of industry and the state. This positive aspect is reflected in its high regard for literature, which, being enjoyable, uplifting, but apparently useless, is closely related to play. On the other hand, at its worst, the traditional language syllabus can also promote the interests of the institution or the academic community over those of the students, making even the teaching of literature a means of inculcating establishment values. Some task-based communicative syllabuses seek to overcome such shortcomings by elevating learners' and teachers' wishes above those of both employer and institution. The Process Syllabus, for example, promotes the notion of a learner-centred curriculum, in which goals are determined by negotiation between learners and teachers rather than by external institutional or economic pressures (Breen 1987; Candlin 1987). This is done on the grounds that:

> targets for language learning are all too frequently set up externally to learners with little reference to the value of such targets in the general educational development of the learner.
> (Candlin 1987: 16–17)

This radical championing of internal motivation over external demand, however, can bring with it its own dangers and contradictions. Students may not want to exercise so much control. Or they may simply present their externally-motivated needs as wants. If they are used to a more teacher-centred educational tradition, then being made to conform to the apparent freedom of the Process Syllabus may, paradoxically, become a form of cultural imposition. In such circumstances, some institutional authority, independent of both learners and their financial sponsors, may be the best guarantor of their freedom to conform to tradition. The experience of a sense of freedom within constraint is paralleled in the experience of games. Obeying the rules of a game into which one has—by definition—entered freely, is less oppressive than having to obey the rules of a job which one is obliged to do by some external pressure. For this reason, perhaps, players seldom seek to renegotiate the rules and structures of a game, and they willingly accept the authority of trainers, referees, and judges. They may feel that a greater sense of freedom is to be found within these structures, by submitting to the game's tradition and authority. 'Freedom', in other words, has a different sense at play and at work. By extension, it seems reasonable to suppose that it may also have a different sense in learning. Whether or not compulsion in learning is actually felt as oppression may depend upon the degree to which that learning is voluntarily entered into. While the 'work sense' of 'freedom' might be relevant to compulsory secondary education, it is not necessarily so relevant to adult language learning, which is the main focus of second language teaching theory.

Like a belief in educational aims other than those stipulated by employers, attention to interim rather than final goals can be found in both traditional and communicative syllabuses. The Procedural Syllabus advocated by Prabhu (1984, 1987), for example, though adamant in its rejection of the traditional attention to language structure, is made up of tasks whose completion is an end in itself. In Prabhu's view it also acts as a trigger to language acquisition. Success in such 'pedagogic tasks' (as they are called), rather like the winning of a game, may not appear at the time to have any value beyond itself. Yet it can also develop skills which may prove to be useful in the 'real' world (by 'real' here, I mean activity which is neither learning nor play). The use of pedagogic tasks is thus highly compatible with the exploitation of play for learning.

Despite their differences over the grading and separate presentation of language items, therefore, there are important ideals and principles in common between traditional and some types of communicative syllabuses using tasks. Both acknowledge broader educational aims than mere utilitarianism, and both distinguish interim from final goals.

'Target' and work goals: needs in Task-Based Language Teaching

Other approaches, however, are unrelenting in their conviction that only final aims should dictate the syllabus, and that interim goals should reflect these directly and immediately. The Task-Based Language Teaching advocated by Long and Crookes (1992), for example, like early approaches to specific-purpose language teaching, suggests that all 'pedagogic tasks' should be derived from 'target' tasks determined by an analysis of a particular group of learners' future needs. In an earlier publication, Long (1985) had defined a target task as:[1]

> a piece of work undertaken for oneself or for others, freely or for some reward. Thus, examples of tasks include painting a fence, dressing a child, filling out a form, buying a pair of shoes, making an airline reservation, borrowing a library book, taking a driving test, typing a letter, weighing a patient, sorting letters, taking a hotel reservation, writing a check, finding a street destination and helping someone across a road. In other words, by 'task' is meant the hundred and one things people *do* in everyday life, at work, at play, and in between.
> (Long 1985:89)

As this 'definition' explicitly mentions work and play, and has exerted considerable influence on language teaching, it is worth subjecting it to some scrutiny. At the outset each item is described as 'a piece of *work*' (emphasis added). At the end, however, we are told that the list has included 'things people do at work, *at play*, and in between' (emphasis added). These 'things' are done either 'freely' or 'for some reward'—but it is not clear whether they are considered to be opposites, nor what is meant by 'reward'. Does it mean payment of some kind, or does it include such inner 'rewards' as a sense of achievement, social acceptance, or the sense of flow described by Csikszentmihalyi (see Chapter 4, page 106)? Any of the listed activities *could* be part of paid employment, or not; but none of them seems remotely connected to play. They are all rather drab instrumental subsidiary activities, without intrinsic interest or value, necessary in order to fulfil some other larger purpose. They are thus in a general sense part of the world of 'work', paid or unpaid, though not of work conceived in terms of final goals—such as making money, providing a service, producing goods, educating people, and so on—but only in terms of subsidiary activity. In some circumstances they might be creative or enjoyable, or even form part of a game; but people do not normally do such things as dressing a child, buying an airline ticket, or painting a fence for their own sake. They are described as things people actually do 'in terms of the real world' (Long and Crookes 1992), but it is hard to see why this criterion justifies them *per se*. In the real world, people do a whole host of things, both trivial and significant, which one would not want to reproduce in a language class simply for that reason. It would seem more sensible, if one is to deal only in 'real world' target activities, to select those which are intrinsically educational, valuable, or enjoyable—including telling stories and playing games.

In Task-Based Language Teaching, however, being 'real' is only one reason for taking target tasks as a starting-point. The other reasons are that they are 'compatible with SLA theory', and 'provide a vehicle for the presentation of appropriate target language samples to learners' (*ibid.*), as well as the conversational interaction believed to be beneficial to acquisition (Long 1996). We shall return to these *psycholinguistic* justifications at the end of this chapter. In this first part, however, we shall keep to the essentially *sociolinguistic* argument that 'target tasks' reflect the kind of language use which students will encounter in social contexts outside the classroom. For the moment, however, it is worth remarking that most of the activities listed in Long's 1985 definition only involve language minimally or incidentally. On both counts—as a list of motivating or needed activities, or as a stimulus for language acquisition—it is a limited and limiting list. Its relevance to language learning is questionable, and it seems to equate the aims of learning entirely with the aims of subsidiary work.

Tasks and work

Perhaps this equation is inherent in the whole notion of using tasks, of whatever kind, for language learning. An association with work remains inherent in the word's etymology and connotation, even though, as we shall see below, the meaning has since been extended to include a much wider range of activities. When Long and Crookes talk of using the term 'task' with its 'everyday, nontechnical meaning', this may, ironically, be rather truer than the authors intended. Originally meaning a tax to a feudal superior, the word is still used to denote something obligatory, and is defined as such in contemporary dictionaries:

> a piece of work that must be done as a duty or as a part of a regular routine, and which may be difficult or unpleasant
> (COLLINS COBUILD ENGLISH LANGUAGE DICTIONARY)

> a specific piece of work required to be done; an unpleasant or difficult job or duty
> (COLLINS CONCISE DICTIONARY PLUS)

a piece of work imposed, exacted or undertaken as a duty
(SHORTER OXFORD ENGLISH DICTIONARY)

As an example of its use, *COBUILD* gives the phrase 'the endless task of classifying the samples'. A task, in short, is a chore, and the 'everyday use' of the word—as opposed to its use in applied linguistics—connotes something tedious and burdensome. Its collocations are similar. We 'take someone to task' when we confront them in anger; a 'taskmaster' is someone who makes us work too hard; a 'tasking activity' is one which is exhausting and difficult. In many languages, the word used in language teaching to translate 'task' can carry the same sense of obligation and drudgery: 'tarea' in Spanish; 'Aufgabe' in German; 'zadaniye' in Russian. Of course, words change their meaning, and take on technical senses within specialized fields. There is also a valid case for introducing new terminology to signify, if only symbolically, a break with the past. It could be argued that this is all that has happened to 'task' in applied linguistics and language teaching. But why was 'task' chosen to describe 'classroom activities' in the first place, and what if anything substantially differentiates a 'task' from a 'game' or 'exercise'? There seems to be in the choice of the word 'task' an implied alignment of language education with work. It is not to be treated as play ('games'), nor to be allowed the self-contained identity ('exercises') which was felt to characterize the traditional syllabus.

We shall return to later developments and definitions of task-based instruction shortly. For the moment, let us pursue a little further the implications of the merger of learning with work, and the dissociation from play, which is implied by a syllabus based on 'target tasks' or 'occupational purposes'. There are several different kinds of reason, which often become entangled, behind the advocacy of this merger. One concerns which language use is most interesting; a second the language use which best reflects the students' work needs; a third is a psycholinguistic argument about the kind of uses which, consciously or subconsciously, promote acquisition of language structures.

The discourses of work and play

A good deal of current language pedagogy directs attention towards the sort of interaction found in the contemporary working environment. In terms of Wolfson's bulge theory (see Chapter 3:62) the focus is upon the use of language in the 'bulge' rather than on the two narrower 'tapers'. In other words, it is civil and practical, but neither particularly intimate nor overtly competitive. In contrast to the features of play (see Chapter 5:123) we might say that discourse in the bulge is concerned with the following:

information	rather than	linguistic parallels and repetitions (L1–3),
exact	rather than	indeterminate meanings (S1)
mundane	rather than	vital subject-matter (S2)
actual	rather than	alternative reality (S3)
medium-sized groups	rather than	solitude, intimate pairs, or large congregations (P2)
collaboration	rather than	competition or affection (P3)
usefulness	rather than	pleasure (P6)

In summary, 'up-to-date' language teaching tends not to concentrate upon linguistic patterning, controversial and imaginary content, or emotionally charged interaction. As there is a tendency for these linguistic, semantic, and pragmatic characteristics to occur together in language play, the avoidance of any one is likely to entail decrease in the occurrence of the other two. Consider, for example, the effects of limiting subject-matter. Many international publishers, marketing textbooks in a variety of cultural contexts, explicitly prohibit the use of potentially contentious topics in language teaching materials. For example, one set of guidelines to authors (cited in Gray, in preparation) forbids mention of the following topics:

Alcohol	Nudes and flesh	Religion	Sexism
Anarchy	Names (without	Racism	Stereotypes
Abuse	permission)	Rape	Terrorism
AIDS	Politics	Science (altering nature,	Violence
Israel	Pork	e.g. genetic engineering)	
Narcotics	Pornography	Sex	

There is a strong association between these twenty topics and language play. Almost all are to do with sexual relations, religion, or aggression between social groups. Of the possible exceptions to this generalization, alcohol and narcotics are associated with release from inhibition (and banned in various legal and religious contexts for that reason); anarchy is by definition the absence of authority, and thus associated, like much language play, with its overthrow; the use of names although presumably banned by publishers for fear of libel action is also frequent in language play (whether as affection or abuse) and in magic (see Chapter 3:86). The avoidance of such topics as these—the substance of language play—will lead almost automatically to a reduction of a focus on language patterning, and upon relationships of solidarity or aggression.

A good deal of contemporary language teaching, then, deliberately turns its attention away from language play, and focuses more or less exclusively upon simulation of the discourse of the 'bulge'—in which students go about their daily business, motivated by external pressures, doing the things they will have to do in the language, and interacting with the people they have to negotiate their needs with along the way. This is of course what many of them are learning language for. Yet as an analysis of play demonstrates, it is not necessarily the case that the best way to equip them for these needs is to tackle them directly, any more than it is the best way for children to prepare for adult life by working rather than playing (whether with language or in general) or for adults to gain understanding of the complexities of social interaction by reading fact rather than fiction.

Although the civil and transactional discourse of the 'bulge' may be, as Wolfson points out, quantitatively greater in modern urban life, it does not follow that it is also the most important and interesting to its users. The most popular leisure genres deal with precisely the kind of vital subject-matter and interaction which is avoided in the bulge and outlawed in language teaching. It is not the language emanating from work which attracts people when they are free to choose, but that of songs, games, fictions, gossip, humour, aggression, intimate relations, and religion. Indeed, publishers' lists of what should *not* go into a language teaching textbook could be read as recommendations for what *should* go into a bestselling novel, lead news story, or blockbuster TV series. One has only to wonder how successful a soap opera or novel based on target tasks, or avoiding controversial topics, might be!

From the standpoint of evolutionary psychology (discussed in Chapter 4), this avid human interest in conflict and intimacy is hardly surprising. In this view, the innate attributes of the human mind were not environmentally selected to deal with the demands of modern urban society, but with those of much smaller bands of hunter gatherers. What mattered there was to establish a small number of close relationships, to gauge who could be relied upon, to compete with others in the band for status and mates, and occasionally to engage in conflicts with other bands. This focus on personal relations and inter-group rivalry, it is argued, remain characteristic of our species even in contemporary urban society. As a consequence, many people view their work not as an end or source of interest in itself, but as a means of supporting their families and gaining status in society; in contrast, outside work, they become passionately involved in actual or symbolic clashes between nations, ethnic groups, religious sects, and localities. At the same time, work itself takes on something of this tribal nature, with internal squabbles and factions, rivalry for promotion, and contests between departments and companies assuming greater importance to those involved than the actual work activity. Good personal relationships make or break successful working collaboration. From the perspective of evolutionary psychology, it is feasible that an aptitude for language play was selected for its crucial role in social inter-actions (as described in Chapter 3), as well as for its role in first language acquisition (Chapter 1) and in creative thinking in general (Chapters 2 and 4).

It is true that descriptions of hunter-gatherer society and its lasting effect on the human mind are partly speculative and not amenable to empirical investigation. Yet they are based upon those facts which are available, and do seem to be borne out by corroborative evidence of modern human behaviour and interests. There is, at the very least, a case to be made for their relevance to language teaching. There is also a need for much more investigation into what students like and want. In this context it is strange that many current approaches to language learning assume, without either reflection or evidence, that it is the mundane transactional discourse of modern work, rather than the ancient playful discourse concerning intimacy and power, which should stimulate interest in language learning. There is confusion between what is relevant and what is motivating.

The matter, of course, is not so simple, and there are many commercial and pedagogic reasons to avoid controversy in the classroom. Publishers want to keep their markets; private institutions do not want to offend their customers; teachers and learners want to avoid embarrassment and argument. Language learners, moreover, by definition, lack the proficiency necessary to do justice to sensitive topics in discussion, and this may cause embarrassment and resentment if these are too personal. In addition, an evolutionary perspective may seem to emphasize aggressive and competitive behaviour over altruism and egalitarianism, emotion over rationality, and in general to be at odds with the values promoted in modern urban democratic society and necessary for large-scale collaborative work. To exploit universal human preoccupations, however, need not entail promoting them. One can make use of the fact that people are interested in intimacy and conflict without encouraging actual intimacy and conflict in the classroom! Subject-matter of inherent concern need not involve students directly. On the contrary, an educational setting is well suited to detached critical discussion of human behaviour. Our inherent fascination with the controversial, combined with the need to avoid actual antagonism, is a further argument for the reinstatement of literature in language teaching. This is partly because literature, like language play, has an affinity with the topics avoided in many ELT materials, but also because it has the advantage (recognized in the traditional syllabus) of being able to introduce controversial issues at a distance. There are, of course, students and sponsors whose ideologies are such that they will not even discuss views with which they disagree, and their custom may also be a needed source of income. In such cases, institutions and publishers may face a difficult choice between commercial and educational criteria.

Broader interpretations of 'task'

It would be unfair, however, to suggest that all developments in task design have kept to the narrow vision of work-oriented tasks advanced by Long for task-based language teaching. Others have used the term more creatively to focus upon more interesting subject-matter. In the task taxonomy proposed by Skehan and Foster (1997), for example, 'personal tasks' contain explicit focus upon cultural differences ('talk about the ways life in Britain is different from your country'), while decision-making tasks use precisely the type of moral and political topics censored by publishers. In one set of tasks

(Skehan 1998b), students are asked to act as judges deciding on appropriate sentences for criminals in cases such as the following:

1 The accused found her husband in bed with another woman. She took the breadknife and killed him.
2 The accused is a prisoner of war. Your country has just defeated his. He was a pilot. He dropped an atom bomb on your tenth largest city, killing 200,000 people and injuring many more.

In another set they must respond to problem page letters in a magazine:

Dear Sue,
I'm 14 and I am madly in love with a boy of 21. My friends have told him how I feel and he says that he likes me, but he won't take me out because he says I am too young. I'm very upset. Age doesn't matter does it?

Dear Sue,
My wife and I separated two years ago. Our three-year-old son lives with his mother, who now has a new boyfriend. They live in a house with other people and I am sure that many of them use drugs (. . . *more details given* . . .) What should I do?

Students are also asked to create their own tasks—a procedure which abdicates direct control of subject-matter—and to reflect upon how 'culture-bound' their ideas are.

Such interesting 'tasks' as these are symptomatic of an ever broadening interpretation of the term. Tasks are no longer confined to routine topics involving work or other uncontroversial subject-matter, nor to mere information exchange or problem-solving, and are more likely to be of personal interest and relevance to students. They can be active as well as passive, written as well as spoken. There are now 'open-ended tasks' with no final answer, as well as 'closed tasks' with a single solution, and 'divergent tasks' (such as those above) encouraging differences of opinion, as well as 'convergent tasks' in which the aim is to reach agreement. There are even tasks which, abandoning the older precept that a task must not specify language items but only activities, attempt to elicit, practise, or make students notice particular structures. Such an expansion, however, raises the issue of whether the concept of task now embraces traditional classroom activities such as games, the study of literature, and grammar exercises. If so, it seems that there is nothing which is *not* a task—and the term has become too general to be useful.

Amidst all this diversification and reinterpretation, however, there are those who seek to rescue the term 'task' from overgenerality by stating more precisely what it is, and what it is not. Skehan (1998a: 95), for example, helpfully lists the following characteristics:

– meaning is primary
– there is some communication problem to solve
– there is some sort of relationship to comparable real-world activities
– task completion has some priority
– the assessment of tasks is in terms of outcome.

He also lists the following things they do *not* do. Tasks

– do not give learners other people's meanings to regurgitate
– are not concerned with language display
– are not conformity-oriented
– are not practice-oriented
– do not embed language into materials so that specific structures can be focused on.

This list has the virtue of stating clearly and explicitly many of the value judgements implicit in contemporary task-based language teaching. It also reveals—especially in the list of what tasks are not—a fundamental opposition to many of the characteristics of play in general and language play in particular. For play is often form-focused, separate from the real world, and inconclusive.[2] Language play is often characterized by repetition of other people's meanings ('regurgitation' if one wants to be pejorative), by display, by conformity (though also by creativity), by practice, and by choices based on specific linguistic structures. In the next sections we shall examine two key assumptions which feature prominently in this list: that the best language use for learning is meaning-focused, and that it is related to the real world.

Problems with 'the primacy of meaning'

The belief that meaning is primary in language use is one of the most cherished in current applied linguistics. Its pedagogic counterpart—that it is better for language learners to focus upon meaning than upon form—draws upon a long-established tradition dating back to content-based approaches, the communicative approach, immersion programmes, the natural approach,[3] and procedural syllabuses. As we have seen, it is still central to contemporary task-based instruction. Another frequently quoted, and approving, definition of 'task' based on the centrality of meaning, for example, is the following by Nunan:

a piece of classroom work which involves learners in comprehending, manipulating, producing or interacting in the target language while their attention is principally focused on meaning rather than form.
(Nunan 1989:10)

Such approving formulations of desirable language teaching activity seem to receive almost universal acceptance, and are very seldom subjected to scrutiny.

We need, however, to distinguish two versions of the argument for the primacy of meaning. One, which I shall call the *meaning-only* view, proposes that students should pay exclusive attention to meaning. Krashen, a major proponent of this view of language teaching, for example, used to declare in lectures, rather crudely, that where acquisition is concerned, 'the only thing that counts is giving people comprehensible messages'.[4] The other, more sophisticated view, which I shall call the *meaning-mainly* view, allows some limited attention to form, but only on condition that this arises out of activities, or as part of a syllabus, in which focus on meaning is ascendant. Nunan, for example, in the quotation above, talks of students 'interacting in the target language while their attention is *principally* [rather than *exclusively*] focused on meaning rather than form', and includes '*manipulating* . . . in the target language' (by which he presumably means some sort of formal pattern practice) as a valid activity. This kind of *focus on form* within the framework of a general attention to meaning, however, is distinguished from *focus on forms*, where form is perceived as being taught in isolation from meaning, for its own sake, and without reference to use (Long and Crookes 1992; Nunan 1998). To this there is still strong opposition.

The separability of meaning and form

Behind the claims of the meaning-only standpoint is a *pre*supposition that form can be separated from meaning in language learning. (If this were not the view, there would be no point in objecting to traditional approaches for focusing upon form without meaning.) Let us consider this presupposition first, before turning to the rather more complex view of the meaning-mainly standpoint.

What is meant by the notion that form has, in traditional syllabuses, been presented without meaning? At first glance, it might seem that there are two areas in which we can (if we wish) present form without also of necessity invoking meaning. One is phonology, the other is grammar. In both cases, after all, we can state abstract rules without using actual words. In phonology, for example, we can say that the English syllable is structured:

(C)(C) (C) V (C)(C) (C)
(Where C = consonant, V = vowel, and round brackets represent optional constituents.)

We can also say that there are phonotactic rules governing which consonants can occur together and in which order: /str/, for example, is possible at the beginning of a word, while /rts/ is not.

Similarly, in grammar, we can say that

S   V   C
Subject Verb Complement

is a possible (and indeed common) syntactic structure for an English clause. We can also state morphological rules. In this clause structure, for example, the verb should agree with the subject. Thus if the subject is a singular noun phrase and the verb is in the present tense, an 'S' morpheme (pronounced /s/ or /z/ or /ɪz/) will need to be added to the base form. And so on.

Attention can also be diverted away from the syntagmatic flow of language, and which linear combinations are possible, and towards the paradigmatic choices possible at each point within that flow. For the SVC clause structure, for example, learners could be taught paradigmatic options for the verb 'to be', to fill the verb slot:

am   was
are   were
is   was
are   were
are   were
are   were

In English, such verb conjugations are of less use than in languages where verb form changes more significantly with person. For many learners of English, however, one familiar though brief mnemonic of this sort is the three-form paradigm for an irregular verb: present, past, and past participle:

go   went   gone
give gave   given
ring rang   rung

and so on.

Such abstractions and tables are important in linguistics, and they can also be useful to language learners; paradigms, for example, can be learnt and recited rhythmically, like multiplication tables or verse. In addition, they may or may not have some kind of psychological reality for first language users. Yet it is presumably not abstract statements of rule and paradigmatic tables which are being referred to in the summary dismissals of a focus on forms. If so, the critics are tilting at windmills, for there are no language courses which present abstract rules or paradigms without also instantiating them in example sentences. What needs to be considered, if we are to assess whether form can be divorced from meaning, is not such abstract rules and paradigms in themselves, but what happens when they are realized with actual sounds or words, and whether there is any difference in the relation between form and meaning in examples invented for language teaching or linguistics, and those found in attested use elsewhere.

In the case of phonology, it might seem, as phonemes are in themselves meaningless (see Chapter 5:134) that we can indeed create realizations which conform to, or exemplify, the rule but have no meaning. Early audiolingual textbooks made use of this fact by asking students to practise sequences of sounds which, while phonologically possible, are not instances of actual words—a technique which is still recommended to a more limited extent in some contemporary works on pronunciation teaching (Celce-Murcia, Brinton, and Goodwin 1996). Such sound coinages also occur in use outside the classroom: in affectionate language play, both between children and adults, in popular music, in avant-garde poetry, and in nonsense. Thus, when my daughter was four, she answered the greeting 'hello' by saying:

1 Hello sloonie woonie.

When I talk to my one-year-old son (whose name is Toby) I call him:

2 Toby the boby (or alternatively) Turbot the burbot.

In the Valentine's Day messages in the press we find people calling their partners by such names as:

3 Weedee wiggy woo woo
   Wiglet will always love you.
   (*The Guardian*, 13 February 1999)

The Little Richard rock song 'Tootie Fruitie' begins with the well-known line:

4 Wo bop a loo bam a lop bam bam.

The Dada poet Hugo Ball produced poems[5] with lines like:

5 gadjama bimbalo glandridi glassala zingtata impoalo ögrogöööö
   viola laxato viola zimbrabim viola uli paluji maloo.

and Edward Lear wrote the following letter to a friend:[6]

6 Thrippsy pillivinx,
   Inky tinky pobblebockle abblesquabs?—Flosky! beebul trimble flosky!—Okul scratchabibblebongibo, biggle squibble tog-a-tog, ferrymoyassity amsky flamsky ramsky damsky crocklefether squiggs.
       Flinkywisty pomm
       Slushypipp

All these were spoken or sung as though they conformed to the rules of English phonology. Yet this does not make them instances of form without meaning. Although the 'words' have no meaning in the sense of a precise denotation known widely in the speech community, they certainly achieve social meaning in their own context. Indeed we cannot stop them taking on such meaning as soon as they are uttered. Pragmatically, they mean things like, respectively,

1 'I'm a cheeky child'
2 'I'm your Dad and it's nice to be with you'

3 'we are lovers with secrets from everyone else'
4 'listen to me I am full of energy and happiness'
5 'I'm an avant-garde poet breaking the conventions'
6 'I'm in an exuberant lighthearted mood'.

They can quickly take on denotational meanings too (Sloonie and Burbot, Wiggy and Wiglet, Pillivinx and Slushypipp, become names) and as such can even 'enter the language'. The verbs 'burble', 'chortle', and 'galumph', were originally 'nonsense' words in Lewis Carroll's *Jabberwocky*; the name 'Wendy' was coined from 'I'm your friendy-wendy' (rather like 'sloonie woonie') in J. M. Barrie's *Peter Pan*. Yet even when they do not enter the general language, they still enter some limited private language between parent and child or lover and lover, where they serve both as an index of that intimacy, and may also take on precise private denotations. Social relations produce speech sounds; speech sounds create social relations. As in the infant's perception of the piggy rhyme (Chapter 1:13ff.) it seems that any speech sounds are immediately and simultaneously phonological and pragmatic, and that they also exert a kind of pressure to become semantic.

Words like 'Wendy' and 'burble' are exceptions, however, since very few such coinages do actually enter the semantic realm. Though they all have potential to take on denotations, the majority are simply wasted. In this they resemble the 'unused' genetic mutations discussed in Chapter 5, and like them only represent an unrealized resource for change. In the strictly semantic sense, they do remain as forms without meaning. Who can say what 'Shooba dooba doo' means?

In the case of the abstract grammatical rules at which most of the criticism is directed, however, it is quite impossible, once we 'lexify' by putting actual words in the place of grammatical categories, to prevent them from taking on semantic meaning. If, then, we cannot interpret the resulting sentences as referring to actual reality (whether literally or metaphorically), we interpret them as referring to an alternative reality—as being, in other words, fiction. This is true in the case not only of utterances intended to be fictional ('The Owl and the Pussy-Cat went to sea'), but also of example sentences invented by linguists or teachers, even when—as we have seen in the case of 'Colorless green ideas sleep furiously' (Chapter 2: 50)—the inventor vainly attempts to make them meaningless. Any isolated invented sentence, however peculiar or contrived, can be interpreted as meaningful, and thus has the potential to become the first line of a story.[7] It is not the case, then, as is often suggested, that the contrived examples of traditional grammar teaching and translation exercises have 'no meanings at all' (Skehan 1998a: 93), although it may be that their potential for use is not pursued, or is not very interesting.

The presupposition that there can be presentation of form without meaning seems, then, to be wrong. To some extent we may talk of there being form without meaning in abstract statements of rules, and in paradigmatic tables, but as soon as these are instantiated in sentences, they assume meaning. The relevant question, then, is not *whether* language examples used in teaching should have meaning, but rather *what kind of* meaning it should be. Here it may be useful to introduce a further distinction, not between meaning and form as such, but between two types of language use: *meaning-driven* and *form-driven*, corresponding roughly to that between the transactional and the playful. We may say that language use is meaning-driven when words and structures are chosen primarily to represent some extra-linguistic state of affairs, and to fulfil some practical need. In form-driven language use, on the other hand, they are chosen primarily to fulfil some formal consideration, for example to create a rhythm or some other pattern. In practice, this is not an absolute distinction; the two are in constant dynamic interaction, and there are a whole host of interim cases. Meaning-driven utterances make use of formal patterning without distorting their purpose (Tannen 1989), while form-driven utterances may (as we have seen in Chapter 5) create or provide useful insights into the extra-linguistic world, and help us to pursue practical purposes.

The general wisdom in recent years has been to favour meaning-driven over form-driven language use in language teaching. This has been achieved either by creating or simulating practical purposes in the classroom ('tasks') or by borrowing bits of language which have already been used for some practical purpose in another context ('authentic' texts and dialogues). In meaning-mainly teaching, where some focus on form is allowed, and understanding of some particular language item is felt to be needed, it is hoped that the tasks will elicit it, or that the authentic example will illustrate it, in a way which makes it clear to the learner. However, the invention of texts and sentences to exemplify some particular word or grammatical structure is ruled out as meaningless, unauthentic, and contrived. Before turning to the rival claims for reality and artificiality in general, let us look a little further at this issue of the meaningfulness of invented and 'real' examples.

'Real' and invented examples

Opposition to invented examples in language teaching has a long history. At the end of the 19th century, Sweet, one of the leaders of the Reform Movement, parodied them by inventing examples of his own, such as:

> The merchant is swimming with the gardener's son, but the Dutchman has the fine gun.

and quotes one which he remembers his Greek teacher actually using 'with a faint smile on his ascetic countenance':

> The philosopher pulled the lower jaw of the hen.
> (Sweet 1964:73)

In the 1930s, Firth expressed similar antagonism.[8] Like that of Sweet, his argument relies heavily upon parody:

> I have not seen your father's pen, but I have read the book of your uncle's gardener.
> (Firth 1957:24)

Firth argued that even though such a sentence may be an apt illustration of grammar,[9] 'from the semantic point of view it is just nonsense' (*ibid.*). It cannot be related to any 'observable and justifiable set of events in the run of experience' (Firth 1968:175). In the 1980s, Sinclair, commenting on the invented examples used in dictionaries, remarked that:

> teachers and learners have become used to a diet of manufactured, doctored, lop-sided, unnatural, peculiar, and even bizarre examples through which, in the absence of anything better, traditional dictionaries present the language. It is perhaps the main barrier to real fluency.
> (Sinclair 1988:6)

What are the reasons for this long-standing objection to invented examples? There seem to be several, entangled together. One is that they have 'no meaning'. This, as already discussed, seems to deny the ability of form-driven language to create its own context, and to refer to alternative realities. As has been argued throughout this book, this capacity of language underpins human creativity, and is central to both social and individual existence. If we can make such constructive use of language in this way in games, fiction, humour, ritual, hypothetical thinking, and in our most important social and personal relationships, it seems odd to abandon it summarily when we come to language teaching.

A second objection is that they are not accurate reflections of the way the language is 'really' used. This implies that there is a clear distinction between the language of 'real' and 'invented' examples. The logic of this, however, is not clear. The distinction seems to apply to the motivation for producing a stretch of language rather than to the stretch of language itself. This is why, given a sentence out of context, it is impossible to tell whether it is 'real' or 'invented'. 'The Owl and the Pussy-Cat went to sea' was not real until it was written down, but became so instantly when it was. Are we to assume that if the same sentence had been composed as part of a grammar exercise it would be 'invented', but that because it was written in a poem it is 'real'? If 'reality' is not a quality of a stretch of language itself but only of its use, then the terms 'invented' and 'real' cannot be used as exclusive opposites in assessing a stretch of language, as it may be both. The relevant distinction seems rather to be between meaning-driven stretches of language extracted from another context, and form-driven examples composed for language teaching or linguistics. A valid objection to such form-driven examples could be that they do not exploit sufficiently their capacity to refer to an alternative reality—

but this is different from objecting to them *because* they are invented or form-driven, as many critics do. There is nothing 'unauthentic' about form-driven language use *per se*. In language play the choice of words is often guided by formal considerations such as rhyme, rhythm, and parallelism, but this does not prevent meanings from emerging from them. If these are often vague and illusory, fictional or bizarre, they are also often interesting and exciting.

The charge of a lack of authenticity might be applied to the over-use of meaning-driven examples in many language teaching materials. As we have already seen, the use of attested data as a source of 'real' examples for language teaching textbooks is subject to censorship, and a distorted image of language use is created through doctoring and manufacture by selection. The tendency is to favour the meaning-driven language of the bulge, and particularly that associated with work. There is little use of form-driven genres dealing with vital subject-matter and personally significant relationships, although these are just as real as business letters or meetings. It is true that language teaching examples chosen to illustrate a structure are often uninteresting, but this is not *because* they are form-driven. On the contrary, being form-driven, in the hands of a capable inventor, has the potential to improve them as examples, allowing them to be more interesting, high-lighting the language item in the way required, and if adjusted to the level and needs of a particular group of students, avoiding those inaccurate but authentic uses of language which occur in non-pedagogic interaction.

A third objection to invented examples seems to be that they are peculiar and bizarre. Sinclair treats this quality as part of being 'manufactured' and 'doctored', and also assumes that it is bad (only to be allowed 'in the absence of anything *better*'). Again, neither of these claims seems to be logical. There are plenty of 'peculiar' and 'bizarre' instances in attested language use. Pedagogic examples, on the other hand, can strive to be as bland or as bizarre as they wish. (In practice, most are lamentably bland.) There is no necessary connection either between bizarreness and being invented for language teaching, or between bizarreness and being attested in language use for some other purpose. Behind the objection to invention there seems to lie an objection to 'bizarreness' in itself. This is strange, for as we have seen throughout our discussion of language play, it is the bizarre and unusual uses of language which, outside the classroom, seem to capture attention, take on importance, and remain in the mind. Indeed, there is a conundrum for language teaching here when it attempts to use data on frequency as an insight into psychological salience: that frequency and familiarity may in themselves contribute to making some particular usage uninteresting and unnoticed. Humans (like all intelligent hunters) seem innately disposed to notice things that move rather than things that stand still. This seems to apply to communication too, where we notice contextual change (Sperber and Wilson 1986), and new uses rather than old ones. It is the unusual, creative, and playful use of language which catches our attention most surely: a fact well known to advertisers, whose copy almost invariably seeks out original and unusual combinations of words. A similar imbalance may well exist between quantity and importance in language learning too. We may pay far more attention to words of personal significance, such as a joke or an insult, a sarcastic or loving comment, or to public discourse which is valued for its personal significance (such as the line of a song, a prayer, an utterance in a soap opera) than we do to quantitatively greater stretches of discourse. People remember the wording of short utterances of personal emotional significance more accurately than other more factual discourses (Keenan *et al.* 1977; Bates *et al.* 1980).

An example like 'The Owl and the Pussy-Cat went to sea' is entertaining because it is unusual, and as good an illustration of a particular grammatical structure as, for instance, 'My brother and my father went to sea'. It could be argued that the meanings of language teaching examples should be weird in order to make them both memorable and effective. Sweet cites the sentence 'The philosopher pulled the lower jaw of the hen' as a 'bad' example, but he also admits that it is a sentence 'which I remembered long after I had forgotten all the rest of my Greek', and even quotes the Greek translation from memory. So in achieving memorability it seems to be a rather successful example. I certainly did not need to look it up before quoting it.

One obvious problem with this argument is that there is a strong connection between form-driven and interesting language use, and idiosyncratic or genre-specific grammar and vocabulary, which may not be at all appropriate for students to use themselves. What may be seen as inventive or original when produced by native speakers, may seem simply wrong when produced by language learners. The discussion so far has focused entirely upon student reception rather than production, upon the examples which are given to students rather than those which they themselves produce. The aspiration to playful language may create a problem when it comes to student production. How is the student to gauge the degree to which something departs from convention to a permissible extent? But this problem only exists—both in reception and production—if one leaves the teacher out of account, and tries to assess language by some impersonal and absolute criterion (such as being 'real'). Both in the choice of language presented to the student, and in the assessment of the language they produce, intervention and guidance by the teacher can exert the control necessary to avoid such pitfalls. However, it may be better to leave this to professional judgement in particular contexts than to any absolute rules.

'Real language' versus authentic artifice

There is a close relationship between the notion of 'real' language and the 'real world' activities advocated in task-based teaching—apart from the obvious one, which is that each should give rise to the other. Both are based upon two implicit assumptions, which, when made explicit, are anything but self-evident. The first assumption is descriptive: that a clear and ready distinction can be made between what counts as real behaviour or language and what does not. The second is evaluative: that, once the two are distinguished, the real is better. Knowledge of play makes both assumptions open to doubt.

In play, those features rejected by advocates of 'real' language and activity feature prominently: they include mimicry and repetition, the explicit discussion of rules, the structuring and atomization of processes, the creation of alternative realities, and a liking for form-driven rather than meaning-driven behaviour. Play, as we have seen, is widespread. It is also 'real', in the sense that it actually happens. It takes up time and space, uses up energy, and so on. But is what happens *within* play real? The answer to this must be equivocal, and relative. On the one hand, if the term 'real' applied to human behaviour is to maintain any meaning at all, and not come to include everything, then we must say that it is not. People commonly recognize the events and relationships of play and games as in some sense distinct from 'real' ones. On the other hand, we can see play as a different rather than a non-reality: what is real outside the game is not real inside it, and vice versa. Suppose, for example, that the managing director of a company plays squash with a junior employee. They are not equal in the working context, but they meet on equal terms at the beginning of the game. If the employee beats the boss then the game produces a relationship opposite to that at work. Or consider two children pretending to be pirates and boarding an enemy ship in the playground, when a teacher comes and tells them not to climb onto the roof of the bicycle shed. Then, like the squash players, they are involved in two relationships simultaneously. In one they are fearless villains, in the other they are obedient children. One relationship is considered to be 'real', and the other 'not real'. In another sense, however, both are 'real'—though from different perspectives.

But it is not only in play that we find a systematic and substantial use of activities which from a working or practical perspective might be categorized as 'unreal'. The use of a temporary dissociation from 'reality'—or the sense of stepping into another reality—is common in work too. This is well documented by the sociologist Goffman in his book *Frame Analysis* (1974: 40–82). His taxonomy of behaviour considered as not 'real, actual, or literal' includes both play activities (such as make-believe, contests, and ceremonials), and also a class of activities which he terms 'technical redoings' which are frequently a part of work. These include: running through a course of action mentally or physically before actually doing it; formal rehearsals (which may concentrate selectively upon some aspect of the act to be performed); demonstrations (showing someone how to use something is not 'actually' using it); and replications, such as the use of recordings or enactments (when we refer to notes, or study a record of something, we are not experiencing the 'real' event).

In one sense of the term, many activities at work and at play are not 'real'. Yet this does not make them useless. On the contrary, it would seem that the complexity of human social and economic affairs depends upon such 'unreal' behaviour. Reality and artifice are complementary, and each strengthens our understanding of the other. Why language teaching alone should be singled out as an area where everything should be real, and where the 'real' is somehow better than artifice, is unclear.

Although the term 'authentic' is often used superficially as a synonym for 'real', there has also been a great deal of careful discussion distinguishing the two terms in language teaching theory. Widdowson (1978:80) introduced an important distinction between language use which is *genuine* and language use which is *authentic*:

> Genuineness is a characteristic of the passage itself and is an absolute quality. Authenticity is a characteristic of the relationship between the passage and the reader and it has to do with appropriate response.

It is what we do with a stretch of language, in other words, rather than the mere fact of its having once occurred in some conventionally 'real' environment, which is, in pedagogic terms, authentic. This raises, however, the issue of what authentic 'relationship' and 'response' to language actually are. In Widdowson's view, they should be 'to learn something relevant and interesting about the world' rather than 'to learn something about the language itself'. Our examination of play suggests that activities often associated with a focus on form (such as repetition, rote learning, and structural analysis and manipulation) *can* take on personal and social significance, and both draw attention to the language, and be 'interesting and relevant'. We shall return to the issue of *how* they may do so in the next chapter.

van Lier (1996:127–8) takes a slightly different stance on authenticity, but one which also distances it from the simple concept that something is good because it is 'real' or 'genuine'. In his definition of the term, authenticity

> has nothing to do with the origination of the linguistic material brought into the classroom (Widdowson's 'genuine' text), nor even with the kinds of uses to which material is put, i.e. the tasks and exercise devised for and executed in language lessons. (. . .) Authenticity results from self-determination (knowing-what-you-are-doing), a commitment to understanding and to purpose, and transparency in interaction (. . .) authentication is basically a personal process of engagement, and it is unclear if a social setting could ever be clearly shown to be authentic for every member involved in it.

and he goes on to suggest, significantly, that:

> In a curious way it seems to me that the traditional language lessons of the grammar translation type which I remember from my school days might

lay greater claim to that sort of authenticity than some of the so-called communicative classrooms that I have had occasion to observe in recent years. I must emphasize that the old lessons seem to have been authentic *for me*, although they may well have been unauthentic for some of my classmates.

It is artifice, in other words, which may on occasion be more authentic than reality.

Given the problems with the identification of what is real, and the fact that 'unreal' activities are far from useless, it may be that the term 'authentic' is a better alternative for language teaching. Behaviour or language in the classroom, as argued by Widdowson and van Lier, may be unreal, but, nevertheless, authentic, in the same sense that games, rehearsal, imitations, and invented examples are. Conversely, language and behaviour which is real (with reference to some context outside the classroom) may easily become unauthentic within it. It is again a question of the impact of individual teachers and learners upon material, rather than a question of some abstract rule. As Skehan (1998a: 96) puts it:

> skilled teachers (and 'aware' learners) can bring meaning to the most unpromising material, just as the reverse can happen when a task with great potential is rendered mechanical through unimaginative implementation.

Dubious premises: SLA arguments for a focus on meaning

In this chapter we have looked at three dichotomies: needs/wants, meaning/form, and reality/artifice. In language teaching, the three run in close parallel. Current orthodoxy makes a clear judgement in favour of the first term in each pair. Needs, meaning, and reality are lined up as the criteria to be revealed by good teaching and good materials. The arguments we have encountered so far in favour of this trio of values might broadly be described as sociolinguistic. They derive from beliefs about the kind of language use which students will need in the social contexts they encounter outside the classroom, and the assumption is that this will be meaning-driven and work-oriented. This is tempered by an implicit pedagogic assumption that goals and means should be the same. Focusing upon *meaning* is what students will *need* to do when they use the language in *real* situations, the argument goes, so why not get on with it straight away? There are also, however, psycholinguistic arguments (briefly alluded to earlier) for this policy of attention to meaning. They have a very different intellectual pedigree, but are used nevertheless to point towards the same pedagogic practices.

The psycholinguistic argument for the focus upon meaning is based upon theories developed in the study of Second Language Acquisition (SLA), one of the dominant academic influences on language teaching. Some researchers in this area have extended Chomsky's ideas about first language acquisition, and claimed that an innate knowledge of the principles and parameters of Universal Grammar (UG) is still—fully, partially, or indirectly—available to the second language learner, and is necessary and sufficient for SLA to take place (White 1989; V. Cook 1993). This theory of SLA is clearly universalist rather than relativist—more compatible with the evolutionary psychological than the sociological approach to language play (discussed in Chapter 4). It assumes implicitly that second language acquisition is driven by an innate and general human capacity which has developed during the course of evolution, and is only minimally subject to cultural or environmental variation. Even from an evolutionary standpoint, however, this is a tenuous claim. For although it seems reasonable to assume that first language acquisition has been required for an evolutionarily significant period of time, little is known about our species' prehistoric need to acquire *second* (as opposed to first) languages.

During the 1970s and 1980s a large (though largely self-contained) literature developed cataloguing factors judged to affect the 'natural' acquisition of second language competence. Although a great deal is written by those inside this area about its scientific rigour and relevance to language teaching practice, my intention here is to query both of these qualities. I shall also take an outsider's view, and group together shades of opinion which insiders might regard as significantly different.

As in Chomskyan linguistics, 'language' was narrowly conceived as phonology, syntax, and morphology, and the acquisition of semantics, pragmatics, and discourse were often ignored. Little or no attention was paid to knowledge of cultural and contextual appropriateness (Hymes 1972b) or of memorized lexical collocations (Pawley and Syder 1983), or to the ability actually to put knowledge from any of these areas—formal or contextual—to use (Widdowson 1989). In extensions of this UG-based approach, theories were advanced that second language acquisition would be triggered by comprehensible input (Krashen 1985) or by interaction in which there was negotiation of meaning (Long 1983)[10]. Conversely, acquisition would be only minimally affected—if at all—by instruction, graded syllabuses, or conscious attention to form. These hypotheses about second language acquisition (that it resulted from UG, comprehensible input, interaction, or a combination of the three) were then tested against observation of learners' language behaviour, and through controlled experiments.

It would be wrong, however, to assume that this UG-derived tradition is the only one in SLA. There are many alternatives (see Mitchell and Myles 1998) some of which are highly compatible with the views expressed in this book about language play. Among them are theories which stress the social and pragmatic aspects of language acquisition, viewing the acquisition of formal systems as inseparable from the social context of their use. These include ethnographic studies, which seek to understand the process from the learner's point of view (Bremer *et al.* 1996); acculturation theory, which examines language acquisition as a form of entry into a new community (Schumann 1978b); sociocultural approaches based upon Vygotskian learning theory (Lantolf and Appel 1994); and variable competence models which seek to account for the fact that learners produce different versions of particular constructions (Ellis 1985; Tarone 1988).

Of these alternative theories, the last two—Vygotskian learning theory and variable competence models—are particularly compatible with the notion of play as a use of language in which form, meaning, and function are in dynamic and mutually-determining interaction. Vygotskian learning theory provides the notion of socially-constituted 'scaffolding' activities, in which the learner, guided by others, first participates before internalizing what has been practised. The constraining rules of games may be viewed as such a scaffolding, while the self-directed egocentric patterning of linguistic form to no obvious communicative purpose may be viewed as part of the internalization. Play takes place within what Vygotsky described as 'the zone of proximal development', an 'area' in which the learner is able to try out new behaviour with appropriate scaffolding and support. Variation theory, meanwhile, suggests that variation in interlanguage form is sensitive to changes in psychological state, social context, function (Tarone 1988), or even to random factors (Ellis 1994:134). In her most recent work, Tarone (1999) has specifically taken up the notion of language play as an activity which contributes to language acquisition in specific ways: by lowering affective barriers; by destabilizing interlanguage; by providing practice in the use of interlanguage for creative and hypothetical purposes; and by enabling the learner to internalize many different voices appropriate to many different roles.

Such approaches are inherently more open-minded than the UG-derived tradition and, unlike them, do not seek to separate off the formal language system from its social and psychological uses. Under their influence, a different climate of opinion is perhaps beginning to emerge in SLA studies. Although some within the UG-derived tradition have advocated the need for 'a unified theory' of SLA (Long 1993), such ideas have also been subjected to increasing criticism and doubt (van Lier 1994; Block 1996). The criticism emanates not only from those who doubt the validity of using empiricist scientific methodology in the humanities; it is also voiced from within the SLA community.

It is not my intention here to comment on the details of those SLA findings which subscribe to the view that UG is still available to the second language learner, or that it can be triggered by meaningful input or interaction. My purpose is rather—with reference to some of the criticism from within SLA studies—to raise doubts about whether the research supporting such a view is reliable science. It is not simply that, even within its own terms, this branch of SLA has not produced evidence that a focus upon 'real interaction' and 'meaning' in language teaching have triggered language acquisition in a way comparable with first language acquisition (Sheen 1994; Ellis 1997:55). Nor is it only that much research in this mould has treated 'the learner' as an information-processing device producing decontextualized 'output' in laboratory settings, rather than as someone engaging in interaction with others (Tarone 1997). The main weakness of broadly UG-based SLA is not to be found in the details of experiments and observation. The problem runs much deeper, to the underlying assumptions about appropriate methodology for the scientific study of language teaching and learning. In particular the issue arises as to whether the methods of prediction based on observation and experimentation are suitable to so complex an area, involving so many variables. Rod Ellis, the most authoritative historian of SLA (1986, 1994), comments on the tension between reliability and validity in much SLA research. He observes how, as reliability increases through the control of contextual variables, its validity decreases for actual contexts in which variables are not controlled (Ellis 1997:93). The more apparently 'scientific' the findings, in other words, the less relevant they are to teaching.

There are added complications when scientific findings (even reliable ones) are applied directly to social action—such as teaching—without taking people's beliefs and motivations into account. Ironically, opposition to the application of psycholinguistic theory to pedagogy is expressed with particular force by Chomsky:

> Psychology and linguistics have caused a good deal of harm by pretending to have answers to those questions and telling teachers and people who deal with children how they should behave. Often the ideas presented by the scientists are totally crazy and they may cause trouble. (. . .) The truth of the matter is that about 99 percent of teaching is making the students feel interested in the material. Then the other 1 percent has to do with your methods.
> (Chomsky 1988:180–2)

A different line of criticism of SLA research—though one leading to similar conclusions—is followed by Larsen-Freeman (1997). Although in earlier work, she too accepted the view that language learning is amenable to scientific testing by means such as controlled experimentation (Larsen-Freeman 1991), she now suggests that this SLA tradition, by treating second language learning as a simple linear process in which outcomes can be predicted by increased sophistication in the control of variables, lags behind current scientific methodology for studying complex adaptive systems (described in Chapter 5). It uses, for example, replication studies of the kind appropriate to the study of simple systems. The essence of complex adaptation, as we have seen, is that outcomes are far more sensitive to minor variation, including random variation (which by definition cannot be predicted), than had earlier been imagined. While in first language acquisition the relevant external environment may be far less variable, and relatively invariable innate cognitive structures may play the key part, with the result that outcomes are far more predictable and consistent, in second language acquisition the variables (age, time, and frequency of exposure, first language, context of use, motivation, personality, etc.) are simply too many and too various to be controlled.[11] If second language learning is a complex adaptive system whose outcomes are at least largely the results of variable external factors, it may be that it simply cannot be studied following the kind of methods usually advocated.

Her conclusions throw doubt not only upon the validity of the SLA research tradition (as Ellis does) but also upon its reliability. Her criticism touches not only the assumptions behind approaches based on UG, comprehensible input, and negotiation of meaning, but all investigation of SLA based on controlled experiment and observation.

> Progress in understanding SLA will not be made simply by identifying more and more variables that are thought to influence language learners. We have certainly witnessed the lengthening of taxonomies of language-learner characteristics over the years, and we doubtless will continue to add to the lists. Schumann (1976) mentions 4+ factors; by 1989, Spolsky notes 74. However, it is not clear that we have come any closer to unravelling the mysteries of SLA now than before. If SLA is indeed a complex non-linear process, we will never be able to identify, let alone measure, all of the factors accurately. And even if we could, we would still be unable to predict the outcome of their combination.
> (Larsen-Freeman 1997)

> We know from chaos theory that complex systems are comprised of many interacting parts, the behaviour of which (even the tiniest), when combined, is unpredictable. As such, it is futile to expect that by aggregating findings from simple univariate cause-effect links made in laboratory settings that we can build a theory of SLA which will hold when all factors are combined.
> (*ibid.*)

Yet it is the belief that causes can be isolated, controlled, and replicated, and that there is a simple relation between cause and effect, which has so extensively influenced second language acquisition theory, and through it teaching and learning practice, in the last few decades. While variable competence models go some way towards taking account of these factors, UG-based approaches, seeking unified and predictive theories, seem hopelessly adrift.

Discipline and practitioner-led influences upon language teaching: the road away from play

The influence of UG-based SLA upon language teaching might be described as 'discipline-driven'. That is to say, it begins with ideas developed in academic research and works outwards to what happens in classrooms. Its theoretical basis is an extension to adult language learning of ideas which were originally developed in linguistics to account for first language acquisition by children. Its supposedly scientific evidence is, however, as discussed above, seriously flawed, based on a methodology whose suitability for describing complex systems, or for reaching educationally valid conclusions, is now seriously questioned.

Approaches to language teaching influenced by theories of communicative competence (to be discussed in the next chapter), or by corpus linguistics (discussed earlier in this chapter), might also be described as discipline-driven, though their starting-point is sociolinguistic rather than psycholinguistic. They do not share the SLA faith in Universal Grammar, and are more in the tradition of cultural relativism, which views language as a social semiotic, and includes within it memorized knowledge of contextually-appropriate routines. They too, in certain interpretations, have pointed the language learner towards narrowly defined 'meaningful interaction', not as the means of language acquisition as in SLA, but as its only end.

These 'discipline-driven' influences might be contrasted with those which are 'practitioner-driven', beginning with a concept of what learners need or want, and working backwards towards an appropriate theory.[12] Under this heading might come needs analysis, and syllabuses based on 'target tasks' discussed at the beginning of this chapter. What is striking about all these influences from the perspective of language play, however, is that despite their different starting points—psycholinguistic/sociolinguistic, innatist/relativist, discipline/practitioner—they all converge to promote a view of language teaching and learning which is quite antithetical to play. Emphases upon predictability, reality, narrowly-defined need, and meaning divorced from form, are all features quite at odds with the playful use and development of language as I have described it in the first part of this book. In the next chapter we shall consider how this current view of language teaching might change if it incorporated a play element.

Notes

1 He refers to this as a definition, though it is perhaps better described as a string of examples. In a later publication (Long and Crookes 1992) where this list is again cited, various academic tasks are added, such as 'reading a technical manual, solving a math problem, reporting a chemistry experiment, taking lecture notes, and so on'.

2 Although a game comes to an end, it can always be played again.

3 Both the late 19th-century version (see Howatt 1984:198–202) and the 1970s version (Krashen and Terrell 1983).

4 BBC 2 *Horizon*. 1983. *A Child's Garden of Languages*.

5 Ball was a native German speaker, and the poem was performed in Zurich (Richter 1965:41–4). Presumably the poem was originally spoken with German pronunciation.

6 Quoted in Lecercle 1990:1.

7 It becomes, in other words, an utterance *as well as* a sentence.

8 From an address to the Philological Society in 1935.

9 Arguably, this particular parody, with its odd possessive construction, is not.

10 I regard them as broadly UG-based approaches because they conceive of language as grammar and its acquisition as a universal cognitive process.

11 For ethical reasons the control of variables is in any case too limited to be of use.

12 A similar distinction is drawn by Bartholomew and Adler (1996).

7 Future prospects for language teaching

Drawing upon the insights into language play developed in earlier chapters, Chapter 6ʹ has critically examined some current widespread beliefs and practices in language teaching. As such, it has been largely retrospective (and to some may seem unduly negative). In contrast, this final chapter is more prospective, and more positive. Its purpose is to consider how an understanding of language play may contribute to language teaching practice in the future, and to the applied linguistic theory which underpins it. At a time of radical change in social organization, in modes of communication, and in the nature of work, it is also appropriate that assumptions about the nature of learning in general should be reconsidered.

To its detriment, 20th-century language teaching has been pulled from one extreme position to another. Stated in simplified terms, an earlier emphasis upon the manipulation of linguistic forms without sufficient reference to their use was replaced by an emphasis upon successful communication (both as a means and an end). At times this meant that insufficient attention was given to the language system in itself. There was also a reluctance to simplify or separate the components of communication as an aid to learning. (In actual practice, the division has perhaps never been so stark, and whatever the fashion of the moment, discerning teachers may have always followed a more moderate middle way.) This chapter considers the relationship between the formalist and functionalist positions, and their roots in linguistic and applied linguistic theory. It argues that an awareness of language play can help to unite and exploit the best elements of both, making this damaging dichotomy—and the bitterness which has accompanied the rival claims of each side—no longer relevant.

Before embarking upon this argument in more detail, however, it is necessary to counter in advance two possible misunderstandings. The first concerns the relationship of play to traditional language teaching activities, the second the relationship between play, work, and learning.

The play element in learning: neither traditional nor trivial

Many observations in earlier chapters (about the pleasures of patterning linguistic forms, the ubiquity of fiction, or rote repetition, in important social activities) seem to provide a degree of support for the revival of activities which have fallen out of favour as dull, irrelevant, or artificial, and to suggest that they may be more enjoyable, useful, and authentic than commonly believed. There is certainly a case to be made, based upon an understanding of language play, for an informed reconsideration of explicit attention to rules, deductive teaching, manipulation of forms, repetition and rote learning, translation, literature teaching, and the encouragement of competition between students. In what follows, all of these are reconsidered, together with the relationship between teacher and student, and between the classroom and the real world. What this chapter does not argue for, however, is the reinstatement without adaptation of traditional language teaching activities or relationships. It seeks rather to consider how their focus upon form and upon artifice can be recast in ways which combine playfulness and usefulness. An understanding of language play does not alter the fact that the capacity to communicate should remain the ultimate aim of language teaching. What it may do, however, is substantially alter our notions of what that capacity involves. It shows us that the ability to manipulate form without reference to meaning, to allow alternative realities to emerge from that activity, and to use both formal patterning and fictional worlds for competition, collaboration, and creative thinking, is as essential to the development and deployment of communicative competence as the ability to conduct practical transactions and communicate facts.

The second misunderstanding which may arise is that an argument for the relevance of play implies that teaching is to be conducted only through games and 'fun' activities: that learning, in other words, should be replaced by play, and never involve anything resembling work. The concept of language play advanced in this book, however, embraces a far wider range of activities than the trivial games often associated with its use in language teaching. In addition, it would be a contradiction in terms to equate play, which is essentially a free activity, with learning, which is often necessary or compulsory. The argument here is that play, broadly defined, should exert an *influence* upon learning. This is not the same as saying that it should *replace* it. For this reason I talk about a *play element in learning*, and not about play as learning.

In order to develop these points we need first to consider the relation of play, learning, and work in education more fully, and to understand this relationship in a historical and theoretical context. From here, in the second part of the chapter, we shall move on to the role of language play in reconciling emphases in teaching which have often been treated as mutually exclusive: structures versus communication, artifice versus reality, solitary and whole-class study versus group and pair work, authority versus freedom. Finally, we shall consider the particular relevance of play in learning to the kind of societies in which we find ourselves at the end of the 20th century.

Play, learning, work

There is certainly nothing new in suggesting a role for play in language learning. In the 16th century Montaigne and Erasmus both recommended games as mnemonic devices, while in the 17th century Comenius advanced the view that seven elements found in games were particularly helpful: movement, spontaneity, social mixing, combined effort, order, ease, and relaxation (Kelly 1969:126). Yet although the use of play in learning has a long history, the manner and reasons for its inclusion in the language syllabus have varied considerably. In some approaches, there seems to be a genuine attempt to enlist play in the service of learning; neither to allow it to take over, nor to exclude it entirely. In others, however, the tendency has been to *equate* learning with play, as in, for example, the 'Learning Through Play Movement', which was first advocated in the early years of the 20th century and again in the 1960s (Kelly 1969:100). Partly in reaction against this, and partly under pressure from the utilitarian educational policies of governments and business, language teaching has in recent years often taken its cue from the work needs of the student, and tried to replicate them within the classroom. In this climate, although play persists, it is often severely marginalized, and tends to be used for some ephemeral pedagogic purpose—such as 'getting the class in the right mood', 'filling a gap', and so on—but not as an end or a means of language learning. Its function is seen as affective, and specifically relaxing. (This is a rather different view of play from the one in this book, in which play is also considered to express aggression, and to have a cognitive function in promoting creative thinking.) The general belief that anxiety is unhelpful to learning (Lozanov [1971] 1978; Schumann 1980), and more specifically, that the lowering of an affective filter promotes language acquisition (Dulay, Burt, and Krashen 1982), has led to a general acceptance that play of a non-competitive kind is a way of inducing a friendly and relaxed atmosphere. Yet whether motivated by pedagogic concerns or by debatable theories about receptive states of mind, play is seen as quite separate from work, while learning is condemned to be now one and now the other.

It is the work elements of learning which have tended to be over-stressed recently. Therefore it is perhaps worth re-emphasizing, and re-integrating those elements which learning *does* have in common with play. In examining the extent of the similarities between the two, Caillois' distinction between *ludus* and *paedia* and Huizinga's notion of play as the origin of serious social institutions (both discussed in Chapter 4) are useful. If play varies, as Caillois suggests, along a continuum whose extremes are, on the one hand, its most ordered and conventionalized ones (*ludus*), and on the other hand, its most spontaneous and exuberant instances (*paedia*), then learning (at least in conventional practice) is closer to *ludus*. In Huizinga's terms, learning begins at a 'borderline' where play transmutes into another activity with a different purpose and cultural significance. To state the matter more simply, what happens in the classroom is perhaps most fruitfully thought of as resembling an ordered game, of the kind played by adults or older children, rather than the spontaneous improvisations of infants.

Common elements in learning and games

There are many resemblances between such games, and learning in conventional educational settings. Both typically take place within a separate bounded area (the classroom/board/pitch) and time (the lesson/game) especially set aside for the purpose. Both are conceived as being apart from ordinary life, somehow outside of the real world, and for this reason behaviour can be practised in games and lessons without fear of serious consequences of error. Both set up temporary relationships between participants (students/players) which are different from those which pertain outside the classroom or off the pitch. These can be intense, and may involve both collaboration and competition. In both situations novices submit to direction by an expert (teacher/coach), and this expert—or another—acts as a judge of performance and an arbiter in disputes (examiner/ umpire).

There are also significant differences between learning and games. Sometimes these are difficult to pin down because of their subtlety, or the scope for exceptions. Paradoxically, there may also be instances of a 'game', or a 'lesson', which displays all the features commonly associated with the other activity. There are also activities which are both at once. Clearly it is necessary to talk in terms of typical qualities rather than essential components. In general terms, the following differences seem to be important.

Both games and learning can establish their own goals and needs. Yet while these may remain internal to a game, it seems necessary for learning finally to connect to something outside itself, to cross the bridge, in other words, to the 'real' world. For this reason, perhaps, while many games are 'not serious', a period of learning, taken as a whole, is generally perceived as being a serious activity. In a game, the authority of the coach or umpire is voluntarily accepted by the players (indeed, the players very often assume these roles themselves), and the relationship is freely entered into; this is not always the case in education, especially in compulsory schooling.

Connected to this issue of compulsion is that of rules, and the balance between freedom and authority. Games and learning are both rule-governed activities, but the rules which dominate them are not necessarily of the same type. A useful distinction is that between constitutive rules and regulative rules (Searle 1975b; Widdowson 1979:141–53). Constitutive rules are those whose observance is essential to the identity of the activity, and they tend to be voluntarily accepted by participants. In chess, for example, a constitutive rule is that each player must begin the game with 16 pieces; they are free to depart from this rule, but if they do so, they are no longer playing chess.

Regulative rules, on the other hand, are imposed and enforced, sometimes against the will of those involved, but they are not essential to the identity of the activity. Many institutional rules and laws are of this type. In schools, for example, children may be banned from carrying cigarettes; but they are still pupils at school even if they disobey. Generally speaking, we might say that games are characterized by an emphasis on constitutive rules, and certain types of educational practice by regulative rules. However, although the distinction is a useful one, it may not always be easy to make in practice. Classification may be more a question of attitude to the rule than any absolute definition. In language learning, for example, if students were forbidden to translate into their first language we might wonder whether that rule was regulative or constitutive.

In addition to the similarities and differences between games and learning listed above, there are also a number of typical features in games whose relevance to learning is debatable. Games are marked by explicit attention to constitutive rules; they are consciously artificial; they can involve individuals acting independently or whole groups acting in concert; they appear to be undertaken for their own sake rather than to serve directly a material interest; they are ritualized vehicles for competition and collaboration; they are simultaneously expressions of conformity and opportunities for radical experimentation. Learning, on the other hand, does not *have to* have any of these qualities. What is in dispute is whether it benefits when it *does* have them. However, it is precisely these elements of games which are now widely considered to be inappropriate for learning, both in current educational thinking in general, and in language pedagogy in particular. Against this general current of opinion, the argument in this chapter is that language learning might benefit from an incorporation of these features of games, even in a climate where usefulness for work is regarded as an essential criterion of syllabus design. In the second half of this chapter we shall look in more detail at the advantages of increasing these particular play elements in language teaching. To set the scene we must first step back into the past to understand how those elements which are constitutive of games, but not necessarily constitutive in education, came to be cold-shouldered in both traditional and contemporary language teaching.

Negative attitudes to play

Historically the pedagogic potential of game elements in learning has often been stifled by negative attitudes to play. This subordination of play to 'the serious' is often reinforced by religious, political, and philosophical traditions emphasizing the virtues of work, and the triviality or even immorality of play. There have been many times and places where play has been expressly outlawed in places of learning. The following two quotations, for example—

one from each side of the Atlantic—illustrate this attitude in 19th-century Western schooling.

> Play of whatever sort should be forbidden in all evangelical schools, and its vanity and folly should be explained to the children with warnings of how it (. . .) works destruction to their immortal souls.
> (Schmidt, quoted in Groos 1901:399)

> We were sent into this world, not for sport and amusement, but for *labor*; not to enjoy and please ourselves, but to serve and glorify God and be useful to our fellow men.
> (*The New Englander* 1851, quoted in Oriard 1991:14)

Yet we would be wrong, perhaps, to associate this puritanical disapproval only with periods earlier than our own. Although contemporary Western society is not among the most repressive in its attitude to play, it does tend often to see it as childlike—even childish. Play is conceived as something immature, trivial, and superfluous, an appendage to be tagged on to the serious business of life.

On the one hand, the suppression and marginalization of play may simply arise from the fact that certain modes of social organization have an interest in stifling the psychological benefits which arise from its encouragement. Authoritarian societies and institutions are threatened by lateral and creative thinking. On the other hand, variation in attitudes may hang upon how play is defined. In societies which marginalize play, valued activities tend to be categorized as far away from it as possible. As adults take their activities seriously, even their most blatantly play-like activities are seen as something else. Scribbling and daydreaming are discouraged as wastes of time—but not when the scribbler is a Matisse, or the daydreamer an Einstein. Modern society is very keen to portray play as separate from worthwhile activities such as learning, and 'play' is popularly defined not only as the opposite of 'work', but also of 'study'. Study is even referred to as 'work' by students and schoolchildren alike. Teachers let the children out to play *between* lessons and teach them to make a distinction *between* playing and learning. Thus, while work and learning are merged (see previous chapter), play and learning are kept separate. Paradoxically, this view is only reinforced by the occasional use of games in the classroom, for they are admitted under sufferance as a separate kind of activity different from the regular activities of the lesson. If a play element were present in learning as a whole, as work element is, this contrast would be harder to make.

If we consider in very broad terms the relationship between work, learning, and play in language teaching over the last century, it seems fair to say that one kind of work orientation has been replaced by another, and the play element consistently ignored. The traditional syllabus, by divorcing knowledge of the language system from its use, whether for work or play, often created an atmosphere of drudgery, and it could only justify this by appeal to a work ethic in which labour was seen as an end in itself, a means of self-improvement, or a token of success within the educational system. Functional approaches, while they ended this austere regime, and in many ways improved language teaching and made it more interesting and enjoyable, nevertheless tended to view it in utilitarian terms, as a preparation only for practical and social applications. However, this is a very broad, and consequently simplified picture. In the next section we shall look at these issues in more detail.

The structural/communicative divide

The traditional grammar-translation syllabus was built around the staged presentation and practice of points of grammar, graded according to a notion of increasing difficulty. Presentation took place through the explanation of grammar rules in the students' own language; practice was through the translation of sentences containing the structures currently in focus, and those already covered in earlier lessons. New items of vocabulary were provided, together with translation equivalents to be learnt by rote. In many direct method syllabuses—which began at the end of the 19th century and grew, especially in English language teaching, throughout the 20th—this procedure remained essentially intact, except that, by definition, recourse to translation was now outlawed. Teachers were thus faced, in the presentation stage, with the almost impossible tasks of explaining the rules of grammar or the meaning of new words in the target language, even though the level of proficiency needed to understand the explanation was likely to be higher than that assumed by the rule or word being taught! At the practice stage, translation of sentences was replaced by manipulation exercises such as substitution tables, blank filling, or the rewriting of one structure as another—of active as passive sentences, for example, or of direct as indirect speech. Under the influence of behaviourist learning theory, the audiolingual method added to these procedures rote learning, association of linguistic items with non-linguistic stimuli, and individual and choral repetition.

The advent of the direct method thus made little impact upon the central belief that explicit focus upon rules, and the isolation and grading of points of grammar, was the best way to prepare students for a meaningful use of the language at a later stage. Indeed, as many commentators have suggested, the change from translation to direct method was motivated more by changing demographic and economic factors than by any new theory of language teaching. Mass immigration into the English-speaking countries, the rise of language schools offering short courses to mixed nationality classes, and the export of monolingual native speakers of English as teachers, meant that in many contexts it was simply impossible to use translation, either because the students' languages were too diverse, or because the teachers could not speak the language of the community in which they were working (Howatt 1984:192–208). Although many reasons were advanced both for the superiority of direct method teaching and of native-speaker teachers (see Phillipson 1992:193–9; Pennycook 1994: 175–6), in many ways, if a structural syllabus is to be used, then an exploitation of translation in a monolingual class by a bilingual teacher makes more sense (Medgyes 1994: 71–81).

In the communicative reaction to structural syllabuses in the 1970s and 1980s, however, no such distinction between translation and direct method courses was made. (If anything it was the grammar-translation syllabus which was regarded as the greater villain.) Both were castigated for relying upon explicit explanation, for focusing only upon the grammatically possible rather than the situationally or culturally appropriate, for rewarding accuracy but not fluency, and for being almost wholly devoted to the written rather than the spoken language. They were also reproached for being boring.

In addition to these pedagogic objections, it was argued in second language acquisition research of the same period that the ordering of items, the insistence upon accuracy, and the penalization of error, ran counter to a natural acquisition order (Krashen 1982: 12–14) and to the development of an interlanguage (Selinker 1972, 1991) analogous to that of children acquiring a first language (Brown 1973: 254–82). An obvious requirement for such a position is to explain how at least some learners manage to emerge from the structural classroom with a high level of proficiency and the ability to communicate. This, however, was simply dismissed on the grounds that such success had emerged despite exposure to traditional syllabuses as a result of incidental acquisition through meaningful interaction (Krashen 1982: 86–7)! Apparent demonstrations that language learning could take place without explicit explanation, error correction, or grading of structures, were taken—quite illogically—to prove that such activities were not helpful (Krashen 1981:40–50). For a long time the valid hypotheses that both traditional and natural methods might be successful, or that the two might be complementary, or that one or other might suit different students, were not even entertained. As already discussed (see Chapter 6: 175), the veneer of scientific method and terminology in the SLA studies of this period in favour of the 'natural approach' masked a deeply unscientific stance. Despite the number of uncontrollable variables, and the impossibility of separating exposure to 'meaningful input' from conscious attention to form, many experiments were carried out which purported to prove claims for the former which were in fact simply untestable. For these reasons I shall leave aside for the moment the assertions of early SLA theory about the effects of the structural and communicative syllabuses on language acquisition, and return to the far more coherent debate about the pedagogic advantages of them both.

Many of the criticisms of structural syllabuses from a pedagogic standpoint were well founded, and seem to have caught a mood of popular dissatisfaction among both teachers and students. In many traditional courses much of the explanation was unnecessarily convoluted and unhelpful, the examples were uninspiring, and the grammatical accuracy which was taken as the criterion of success did not ensure appropriate language use in actual communication—even if it did form the basis for the later successful development of such abilities. The structural syllabus disdained influence by the outside world, and its aloof refusal to engage directly with the demands of work was matched by an equally austere disengagement from play. There were superficial echoes of play in its manipulations of linguistic forms; yet while play with language forms always reverberates with pragmatic meanings, and frequently creates alternative realities, much of the language of the traditional structural syllabus seemed to do neither. A compensation for this, however, was its emphasis on literature, to which we shall return again shortly.

From the 1970s onwards, the solution offered to these shortcomings of the structural syllabus was the elevation of communication as both the end and the means of successful language teaching. It was supposed that the acquisition of language structure would be promoted by using the language immediately for communication, either outside the classroom (Allwright 1979), or more usually through simulations of various kinds, such as information transfer, role play, and so on (Littlewood 1981). On these grounds the deductive teaching of rules was abandoned. Sometimes it was replaced by inductive teaching. At other times, under the influence of the SLA theories mentioned above, no attention was given to rules at all. Invented examples were replaced by so-called 'authentic' examples (bits of language lifted from their original context) or by student language generated by the communicative activity itself. The use of literature both as a means and an end of language teaching declined. An interactive structure in which individual students related directly to the teacher but not to each other, or from time to time acted in congregation, as in choral recitation, fell from favour, and tended to be replaced by increased work in pairs or small groups.

Arguably it may have been this change from the structural to the communicative syllabus, rather than the shift from the translation to the direct method, which marked the real sea change in 20th-century language teaching. The principles were sensible and coherent, taking as their theoretical foundation a combination of functionalist linguistic theory and Hymes's (1972b) notion of a communicative competence.[1] The leading theorists of the movement were careful to stress that the new importance attached to function should not be bought at the expense of form (Wilkins 1976; Widdowson 1978). It was, however, in the interpretation and implementation of these principles by many less thoughtful syllabus designers, that major problems emerged. As we have seen, two very different influences were largely responsible, one theoretical, the other commercial. On the theoretical side, the excessive claims of some SLA researchers about classroom language acquisition through exposure to meaningful input and interaction led many teachers to believe that accuracy can be neglected, that authentic interaction does not involve conscious attention to rules, and that language use and communication do not focus upon linguistic form. On the commercial side, publishers were concerned to avoid controversy in multicultural classrooms and markets, while at the same time, governments and businesses demanded language for specific purposes. Under these pressures, 'authentic communication' tended to be reduced to rather bland civil interactions about work or uncontroversial topics. A belief developed that both language and activity could be tailored to needed skills, and that the way to acquire these was to engage in them immediately.

Form and function

To a degree this damaging dichotomy—between structure and communication—mirrors the division in theoretical linguistics between formalism and functionalism. In the formalist view, linguistics is only concerned with the representation of the phonology and grammar, and can be studied without reference to its use; the deployment of that phonology and grammar is the concern of other, separate, branches of study, such as pragmatics. Weight is added to this position by the view in Chomskyan linguistics that the mind's language faculty is modular, making the separation apparently a matter of psycholinguistic reality rather than mere academic convenience. In the functionalist view, forms are determined by their use, and cannot be studied in isolation. On the other hand, in both ontogenetic and phylogenetic development, language and languages are regarded as shaped by the needs of their speakers. In use, linguistic choices are to be understood in terms of what social action their user is trying to effect.

We have, then, two radically different explanations of the *forms of language*. In one they are homogenized and independent, shaped by forces internal to the system; in the other, they are the servants of pre-established intentions and needs. We also have two quite different approaches to *language functions*. The formalist approach ignores them on the grounds that they are not necessary to an understanding of the system; the functionalist approach will not admit any formal relation which does not reflect some ready-made purpose. Such extremism leaves both views with unexplained problems. For formalism, there is a need to specify why an autonomous system happens to be so well suited to the functions it performs, or why it was selected in the course of evolution if not for its functionality. For functionalism, which assumes functions existing prior to forms, there is the issue of how complex functions could have come into existence without language form to realize them. The debate points rather obviously to a middle position, in which both form and function exert a dynamic reciprocal influence upon each other, leading to the ever greater complexity of both.

Classic functionalist theories of language (Bühler 1934; Jakobson 1960; Searle 1969, 1975a; Popper 1972; Hymes 1972a) are taxonomies of macro functions, each reflecting aspects of the human species' overarching need to collaborate in manipulating the environment: sharing information, and creating and maintaining elaborate social structures for this purpose. With this in mind, in Hallidayan theory the macro functions are reduced to two: the ideational, the interpersonal, together with a third, the textual, answering the need to give coherence to stretches of discourse (Halliday 1973: 22–46; Halliday 1976:19–27). Set out below (from Cook 1994a:39) is a table showing correspondences between five taxonomies, including Halliday's, and emphasizing how Halliday's textual function, and—more importantly for our purposes—Jakobson's poetic function, have no equivalent in the other four.

The taxonomy most relevant to my argument is Jakobson (1960), Jakobson proceeded by first identifying six elements in communication:
– the addresser: not necessarily the same as the sender
– the addressee: usually but not necessarily the same as the receiver
– the context: in his terms the referent or information
– the message: the particular linguistic form
– the contact: the medium or channel
– the code: the language or dialect.

Corresponding to each element is a particular function of language, respectively:
– the emotive: communicating the inner states and emotions of the addresser
– the conative: seeking to affect the behaviour of the addressee
– the referential: carrying information
– the poetic: in which the message (i.e. form) is dominant
– the phatic: opening the channel or checking that it is working, either for
  (1) practical reasons or for (2) social ones
– the metalingual (*sic*): focusing attention upon the code itself, to clarify it
  or renegotiate it.

Jakobson	Bühler	Searle	Popper	Halliday
referential	representational	representatives	descriptive	
metalingual			metalinguistic	} IDEATIONAL
phatic		commissives		
(1) practical				
(2) social				
expressive	expressive	expressives	expressive	
conative	conative	declarations	signalling	} INTERPERSONAL
		directives		
poetic	(no equivalent)	(no equivalent)	(no equivalent)	(no equivalent)
(no equivalent)	(no equivalent)	(no equivalent)	(no equivalent)	TEXTUAL

Figure 7.1: Functional taxonomies (Cook 1994a)

Neither formalist nor functionalist theory, however, has an adequate account of the human predilection, which we have studied at length in this book, for the patterning of linguistic forms. Formalist theory goes no further than the notion of grammaticality, and treats creativity as something existing within the boundaries of this concept. It is the grammar itself (the finite means) which allows the production of new ideas (the infinite outcomes). No explanation is offered either for the formal relations established *in addition* to those demanded by the grammar (such as parallelism in playful discourse), or creative departure from it. In functionalist theory, explanations are usually practical and, where playful discourse is dealt with, it is explained in practical terms. Often, play is treated only as an aid to learning (Hasan 1989: 105), and it is significant that in Hallidayan theory a play function is prominent in his description of child language acquisition (Halliday 1975), but less apparent in his description of adult language. Such an approach is essentially compatible with the kind of biological and evolutionary explanations of play which we examined in Chapter 4. We have seen, for example, how rhythm can be explained as a mnemonic, or as a means of co-ordinating social action in a large group (p. 22), and how ingenious linguistic manipulation can be used in competition between rivals (p. 64ff.). While such explanations may be valid, however, as I have commented earlier, they do not seem to do full justice to the persistence of delight in patterned language and the exploitation of systemic coincidences which is so conspicuously a feature of adult discourse.

The notable exception to this (as indicated in the table on page 191) is the functional theory of Jakobson (1960), whose taxonomy includes a 'poetic function' (defined as 'the set towards the message as such, focus on the message for its own sake'). Yet while he convincingly argued *that* there is a category of language use with this 'set towards the message', he did not attempt to explain *why* this should be the case. To say that something has a function suggests (despite the ambiguities of the word) that it has a purpose and/or an effect, that it is done *for* something. (Functional theories are often rather vague about whether this outcome is in the long or short term, for the sender or the receiver.) The usefulness of the other functions in his taxonomy is clear enough. Phatic language establishes and maintains social relationships; referential language enables the communication of facts; conative language affects the behaviour of others, and so on. Quite what the poetic function does, however, is not something which Jakobson considers, other than to imply—circularly—that a 'set towards' form has the potential to create poetry.[2] The weakness of Jakobson's theory, however, is that while he identifies and describes this kind of language use very effectively, it is not clear what it actually does. (See also Cook 1994a:38.) This gap, perhaps, can be filled by a theory of the function of language play.

What is missing in functionalist theory is a notion that meanings and social relations not only determine forms, but they can also emerge from them. The evidence we have examined in this book supports such a view, and points to the need in functional taxonomies for a ludic function (of which the poetic function is perhaps a part). This function differs from all others in the degree of backflow it involves, from forms to meanings and relationships. Like the genetic mutations described in Chapter 5, it is wasteful, although it can at times yield new ideas, alternative realities, and social relationships. Just such a function is needed to redress the weaknesses in the extreme formalist and the extreme functionalist positions, for when it is dominant, neither form nor function exists in a privileged position. They are in dynamic and creative interaction.

This ludic function has major implications for language teaching, which needs to find a means of focusing upon language form, upon rules, and structural manipulation, while also avoiding the sterile way in which such a focus has been achieved in traditional syllabuses. Recognition of a ludic function of language has the potential to guide language teaching out of its apparent dilemma. In language teaching, structural and communicative syllabuses shared the error that a focus upon form is non-functional. In the structural syllabus, which used manipulation of form as a starting-point, its potential to mean was ignored. In the functionalist syllabus it was assumed that interest in formal patterns and relations could only emerge as a result of needs to communicate. The lesson of play is that this dichotomy is unnecessary. If formal patterning is approached as an end in itself, meanings and interactions will emerge from it, if they are allowed to do so.

A play element and materials

In practice, Communicative Language Teaching often turned out to be as selective with the uses and functions of language as traditional syllabuses had been with language items. In particular, it neglected those pleasurable, emotive and controversial aspects of social interaction which are expressed through the genres of play. This is not to deny that transactional discourse can also be both authentic and important, or that its effective use is the main purpose of many students—those for example who are learning language for business. Yet as this book has demonstrated, it constitutes only a subsection of authentic language use. If language teaching were really to engage with a wide and representative sample of language use, it would include a far greater proportion of nonsense, fiction, and ritual, and many more instances of language use for aggression, intimacy, and creative thought. If personal importance, psychological saliency, and interest were taken into account in the selection of materials, then genres such as songs, soap operas, advertisements, rhymes, jokes, and prayers would figure equally with the ubiquitous discourse of business and polite conversation as the major source of teaching material.

This view leads, however, to a major problem, which is at present unresolved: how to find materials exemplifying language play (as in the broad definition used in this book) which are socially and linguistically suitable for students of various backgrounds and levels of proficiency, and which also ensure active production of playful language as well as its passive reception. Neither structural nor communicative approaches provide help. While the structural syllabus tended to pay little attention to the functions of language, including its ludic function, the communicative syllabus tended to limit uses to transactions and polite socializing. The use of language play for teaching has thus been largely neglected by both. To remedy this, a major research programme would be needed on how to select, adapt, and use materials, and on student reactions to them.

Bearing this need in mind, and the present dearth of materials, the following sections discuss in broad terms some principles behind the incorporation of a play element into language teaching. In these circumstances, the discussion is necessarily general and speculative. While the assertions here are based to some degree upon the argument in earlier chapters, it is also important to recognize that they are in need of testing out in practice.

Advantages of the play element in language teaching

One frequent result of the influence of theories of language and language learning upon teaching has been to reduce the range of activities and strategies open to language teachers and students, and thus the possibility of learners emerging from language courses equipped to engage fully and productively with the language they are learning. Thus, while translation and other structural approaches have neglected colloquial spoken interaction, subsequent communicative and task-based approaches have in their turn responded by disparaging a number of activities, such as deductive teaching and decontextualized focus upon linguistic forms. In the next sections I set out, in somewhat programmatic (but cross-referenced) form the advantages of incorporating a play element into language teaching, and the ways in which it might bring to an end what has become, in effect, a censorship of valid strategies for language teaching and learning. The main conclusions are italicized and numbered, for ease of reference.

1 Explanation

Advantage 1 *A play element would validate the explicit deductive teaching of rules (where possible in the students' first language) and frequent subsequent discussion of them by teachers and students in the light of practice.*

This can be justified by the general nature of human activity after infancy rather than by specific knowledge about language processing or acquisition. There are other factors in successful pedagogy, and the argument for explicit attention to rules, being sociological rather than psycholinguistic, would remain valid, even if it could be demonstrated that explicit attention to rules were not helpful to natural language acquisition.

Games are typically marked by discussion of rules at every stage: before they are played for the first time, prior to each game, and in extended discussion afterwards. The same is true of many other activities, such as meetings, legal and legislative procedures, rituals, political competition, and so on. For this reason it seems safe to assume that language learners (other than perhaps very young children) would find such a procedure quite normal, easy to relate to, and helpful. Conversely, the absence of a strategy so usual in other social activities might seem disturbingly *un*usual in language learning. Moreover, just as the rules of complex games are not best explained by immediately embarking upon an actual game, but rather by some prior explanation in non-technical language, or by a period of practice punctuated by explanation, so it seems sensible to allow explanation of features of the target language before actually using it—that is to say, explanation and discussion of the language in the student's mother tongue.

2 Authentic focus upon form: play genres and literature

Advantage 2a *A play element would help to remedy the apparent dilemma of needing to choose between an emphasis on structure or an emphasis on use.*

Advantage 2b *The need for authentic, varied, and motivating examples in which particular forms are foregrounded could be partly remedied by giving more prominence to literature, even in language courses for specific purposes.*

Language play focuses attention upon specific linguistic choices, either because meaning or effect is dependent upon them, or because these choices are patterned and repeated. Although, as argued in Chapter 6, it makes little sense to talk of form or meaning existing independently of the other, this interdependence is much clearer in some genres than in others. The rhyme, the pun, the joke, the advertisement, the tabloid headline, the insult, cannot be paraphrased. In them, as in literature, there can be no claimed division between form and function, no sense of alternative ways of 'getting the same meaning across', as there appears to be in more transactional discourse.

Among the genres of play, literary texts have the advantage of being attested instances of communication; they are also instances which—being fairly independent of situation—do not lose authenticity when used in the classroom. They are also linguistically and pragmatically varied, and as an inherently parasitic genre incorporating examples of other genres into themselves (Cook 1992: 31–5), they provide examples of almost every kind of language use from casual conversation to ritualistic incantation.

It is sometimes argued that much literary language is too idiosyncratic, deviant, archaic, or obscure for the language learner. This problem, however, can be bypassed if material is selected according to the level and interests of the class. Another commonly perceived difficulty is that the study of literature promotes passive reception rather than active use. Yet texts which focus—as literature frequently does—upon issues of power and intimacy, are likely both to evoke emotion and promote discussion. Particular activities built around literary texts can also avoid the dangers of student passivity. The rehearsal and performance of an appropriate play combines the best of both structural and communicative syllabuses: rote learning and repetition of a model, attention to exact wording, practice in all four skills, motivating and authentic language and activity, instances of culturally and contextually appropriate pragmatic use, and integration of linguistic with paralinguistic communication. Prose too, and even lyric poetry (as demonstrated by Widdowson (1992a) and Bisong (1995) can be used effectively to stimulate student production.

In addition to actual works of literature, there is an unexploited literary potential in materials which are specifically written for language teaching. Many of the invented sentences and texts of structural language teaching have an immanent literary quality (Widdowson 1990:78–100) in two senses. First, they refer to fictional rather than actual facts. Second, they are focused upon form, constrained by the need to illustrate a particular structure in much the same way that a line of poetry might be constrained to produce a rhyme, rhythm, or parallel grammatical structure. This literary potential, however, is seldom if ever pursued. This is not simply because, as often argued (Sweet [1899] 1964: 99–108; Lewis 1993: 40), the invented examples of traditional language teaching are isolated sentences rather than parts of connected texts. Although it is true that connected text might be an easier medium in which to produce coherent and interesting fictions, it is not the case that isolated sentences are necessarily meaningless, or do not occur. Indeed, many literary and quasi-literary genres (such as the haiku, proverb, epigram, and nursery rhyme) exploit the tantalizing potential of a brief, unexpanded statement to arouse interest and stimulate thought, simply by saying very little.

3 The authenticity of artifice

Advantage 3a *A play element would license the treatment of the classroom as an 'artificial' rather than a 'real' environment.*

Advantage 3b *A play element would legitimate the use of invented examples focusing upon particular forms.*

Advantage 3c *A play element would encourage the use of illustrative examples of a quasi-literary nature as mnemonics—the more bizarre in meaning, the better.*

Advantage 3d *A play element would reinstate rote learning, repetition, and recitation as enjoyable learning strategies.*

Like the argument for a conscious attention to rules, 3a is justified by an appeal to what is acceptable and usual in human behaviour in general rather than by anything specific to language or language learning. It is clear from a consideration of play, and of culturally significant activities with a play element (as described by Huizinga, see Chapter 4: 110ff.), that the designation of an area, time, or set of mind as separate from 'reality' is so usual in human behaviour that it calls into question the very distinction between real and artificial social activity which it assumes. The creation of such a space is typical of games (pitches, boards, and playtime), learning (classrooms, schools, and universities), rituals (churches, courtrooms, and parade grounds), and the reception of fiction (story time, theatres, cinemas, etc.). There is nothing particularly unusual, then, in seeing the classroom as a separate and different space set aside from everyday reality, for artificial and simulatory activity. Such artificiality—as Goffman (1974: 40–82) observes (see page 171)—is also characteristic of all but the crudest and simplest work. Most human jobs are so complex that they need to be preceded by demonstration, rehearsal, planning, simulation, and atomistic learning, and followed up by replication, recording, and discussion, so that only a small fraction of the activity is taken up by 'the job itself'. Many jobs have elements of performance and role play built into them.

For language teaching, these observations have important implications. The first is that, even if we take a vocational view of education, a good deal of classroom activity is not preparation for 'real' activity but for further artifice. An artificial atmosphere in the classroom—ritualistic and self-consciously separate—is not at odds with the world outside, but in harmony with it. At present language teaching takes place in a climate of opinion where real activity and language are constantly promoted as both easily identifiable and superior (see 167–73). For this reason, although classroom activity is necessarily artificial, teachers tend to feel guilty about the deliberate use or emphasis of artifice. Awareness of the authenticity of artifice might help them escape from this 'cult of the real', leaving them free to develop and use classroom artificiality in creative and educational ways. It might also legitimate the discriminating reincorporation of a number of traditional activities such as grammar exercises, rote learning, dictation, and role play, and encourage the use of authentic artificial activities which exist outside the classroom: games themselves, fictions, and ritual.

As already observed (page 170), artifice in the language classroom has two aspects: activity and language. The issue of artificial language is more complicated. Currently, a distinction is commonly drawn between 'real' examples on the one hand and 'invented' or 'artificial' examples on the other. By 'real' is meant a stretch of language which is known to have already occurred. As observed in corpus linguistics, such stretches (though by no means all) are wholly or partly unoriginal, in the sense that the same combination of words commonly occurs elsewhere, and it is assumed that a good deal of language is produced or understood via the deployment of ready-made chunks from memory without grammatical analysis. Understanding of language play, however, shows that neither a focus upon particular structures, nor originality, is unreal in the sense that it is untypical of language use in non-pedagogic contexts. As we have seen throughout this book, the language in many socially and personally significant genres is constrained as much by the need to use a particular form—in order to achieve rhyme, rhythm, parallelism, or pun—as by particular meaning. Many attested utterances, particularly in the genres of play (literature, fiction, jokes, riddles), are original and attract attention for that reason. They cannot be said to be 'unreal'.

A further complaint against the invented example in language teaching is that it makes no reference to its immediate context (Firth 1968:175). Thus, an invented example such as 'At dinner we shall eat the fish we caught this morning' (cited in Chapter 3) might be rejected on the grounds that the students using it have not been fishing, and are not going to be having dinner together. This is a strange complaint, however, for it is really quite usual for an utterance to make no reference to its immediate context. The use of contextual referents such as deictics, definite articles, and unknown names, far from being interpreted as somehow crazily meaningless, immediately creates its own context. There is no more reason for a student to point out that we did not in fact catch a fish this morning than for a reader of the first page of *Dombey and Son* to complain that they are not in a darkened room.[3]

> Dombey sat in the corner of the darkened room in the great armchair by the bedside . . .
> (Dickens 1848)

Utterances which suddenly transport us to another context are far from unusual, nor are they limited to fiction, as opposed to fact, or to high-flown fantasy rather than mundane business. The opening of a radio or TV news item has the same effect. The property of many sentences is not to reflect the immediate situation but to create without warning an alternative one (whether actual or fictional) in the minds of their audience.

Many examples in structural syllabuses have a dull, uninspiring feeling to them. This is not because they are not attested examples of use (many of which are equally uninspiring), or because they are isolated or decontextualized, but rather because they do not fully exploit the power and potential of these qualities to produce interesting, memorable, and unusual meanings.

They hover, as it were, at the edge of the sea of meaning and use, unwilling to get their feet wet. Some ('The philosopher pulled the lower jaw of the hen') are striking in the way that nursery rhymes are, but they are not typical. On the contrary, they have tended—perhaps influenced by vague notions that the best model is an ordinary one—to move away from the startling and the unusual towards the banal. The result is that they end up as neither one thing nor the other: neither strikingly original nor attested instances.

The move towards attestation, coupled with censorship of the controversial, has pulled language teaching examples in the direction of unremarkable, and therefore unmemorable examples. It may, however, be the startlingly extraordinary which is pedagogically more useful. There is a great deal in both personal experience and psycholinguistic research which suggests that it is the *unusual* instance which is more likely to be recalled verbatim. Commenting critically on the accepted belief in linguistics that it is content rather than form which is remembered, Ellis and Beattie (1986:244–51) document how this finding is based almost entirely upon laboratory research in the 1960s in the behaviourist tradition, in which subjects were given bland sentences of no interest, with slight and confusing variations. Other research shows that people do successfully recall the exact wording of certain original or emotive utterances (Keenan *et al.* 1977; Bates *et al.* 1980). The instances of language use which people most readily memorize verbatim are not from the mundane discourses of everyday life, where exact wording is unimportant, but those marked by unusual, elevated, or archaic language, those reinforced by parallel structures such as rhythm and rhyme, and those with important or emotional content.

If we accept the role of conscious and deliberate learning rather than only passive acquisition, then the use of the form-focused, strikingly unusual example (no matter whether attested elsewhere or invented for the purpose) can have a strong mnemonic motivation, and be recalled as a model for a structure or contextualized use of an item of vocabulary when needed. The genres of language play also frequently involve or provoke authentic spontaneous repetition, rote learning, and recitation. These activities should not, then, be regarded as unauthentic.

4 Types of interaction

Advantage 4 *A play element would broaden the range of permitted inter-actional patterns within the classroom.*

A variety of combinations of students is possible within all but the smallest classes: individuals may act alone, in pairs, in groups of various sizes or in concert as the whole group. Each of these units, from individual to whole class, may also enter into interaction with the teacher. Each combination has its own pedagogic advantages, and simulates the range of combinations outside the classroom, where proficient speakers need to handle the language on their own, in one-to-one interaction, and in groups of various sizes. Yet, in the swings of fashion, first some kinds of interaction suffered and then others. In traditional syllabuses, presentation was to the whole class. During the practice stage, individuals often worked alone or responded as a single body—a congregation. In the feedback stage, students were recipients of private individual evaluation and advice from the teacher. All of these modes of traditional interaction are valuable, but they are also limited and limiting. While the traditional syllabus encouraged these interactions, it also actively discouraged, and even punished, exchanges between individuals and in small groups. The new communicative order did not remedy this limitation, however, but provided an equally impoverished mirror image: elevating pair work and group work, and disparaging or neglecting solitary study, whole-class activity (including choral recitation or repetition), and intensive interaction with the teacher as mentor.

Clearly neither attitude does justice to the range of interactions for which language is used. Pedagogically, dogmatic opposition to some kinds of interaction may lead to tedium, and—worse—to repression, even, when students engage in them spontaneously. In addition, linguistic and pragmatic variety is reduced, with likely negative effects upon the development of communicative competence. In traditional whole-class teaching, for example, where students were likely to answer questions but not ask them, and to receive orders but not give them, there was a tendency for declaratives to be practised more than interrogatives or imperatives. In addition, students only practised interaction with someone in authority (the teacher) and not with equals or subordinates. This argument, however, has a flip side, and in the classroom which uses only egalitarian interaction in pairs and small groups, and teachers attempt to abdicate their privileged interactive status, students may miss out on precisely those forms and uses which are emphasized in the traditional classroom.

What is needed is a full range of interactions. In play in general, all combinations of players, from solitude to mass gatherings, are possible and authentic, and we find all types of relationship from the most intimate (as described in Chapters 1 and 2) to the most public (as described in Chapter 3), from those with clear differentials of power, to those in which participants meet on equal terms (see page 62). Games, though often ritualistic, con-gregational, and controlled by tradition and authority, are also intensely egalitarian—so much so that inequalities of nature or fortune are systematically removed, or equalized through handicaps, before the game can take place.

5 Freedom and tradition

Advantage 5 *A play element allows the forces of change and tradition to coexist, and the teacher to move freely and as necessary between the exercise and the abdication of authority.*

Ludic play (as defined by Caillois) is simultaneously one of the most constraining and one of the most liberating of activities. Players must obey the rules, both constitutive and regulative. Often they must remain within fixed boundaries. Their actions, speech, relationships, purposes, and even their dress, may not be of their own choosing, but dictated by the game. Yet at the same time, games promote individual expression, and create a sense of creativity and infinite possibility. Each playing of a game is at the same time a repetition, and unique. In these senses, games are like the human individuals and societies from which they emerge: all similar, but all different.

Play is simultaneously one of the most conservative and most radical human activities. Lore, stories, games, and rituals carry the traditions of societies, and inculcate their values into individuals. Like more ephemeral play phenomena, such as jokes, they can express both group identity and antagonism to other groups, often in chauvinistic ways. Yet at the same time, play is a characteristic of dissidence and invention. The random permutations of form (as detailed in Chapter 5) produce alternative realities which can challenge accepted wisdom and conventional morality, and—in creative art and science—yield new iconoclastic ideas. Related to this strange union of opposites is the role of the expert in many forms of play—storyteller, referee, magician—all figures whose power rests upon special skills and knowledge rather than coercion, and whose authority is accepted voluntarily by the players. Perhaps it is to such models as these, rather than those of the manager or facilitator, that the modern teacher should aspire.

Learning a language demands adaptation, but also creates insecurity (Schumann 1978b). Thus, just as students are attempting to push themselves forward into an understanding and acceptance of new ways and conventions, they are also likely to feel themselves impelled backwards towards the values and habits of mind in their own culture and language. It is an endeavour in which those involved are sometimes likely to seek the comfort of guidance and authority, and of artificiality and ritual, while at other times wishing to fend for themselves. For these reasons, the union of freedom and tradition found in games is very suitable to language learning, as is an ethos in which the authority of the teacher is sometimes asserted, sometimes put aside.

Play and learning: past, present, and future

We have glimpsed in earlier chapters how attitudes to play vary in different societies and in different ages. A fuzzier boundary between play and non-play in hunter-gatherer and agricultural societies gave way to a much clearer distinction in the ideologies of the industrial era and their belief in scientific determinism. If, under the influence of new technology and globalization, contemporary society is now undergoing a change equivalent to these major changes of the past, it may be that there will also be a change in our attitudes to the relations between play, work, and learning. In contemporary science's recognition of unpredictability and the creative power of random permutation, the theoretical basis for such a change of orientation is already established. Whether this follows, or is determined by economic factors, is a moot point.

In both agricultural and industrial societies, the economic rationale for the inculcation of a work ethic in education is clear enough. Long hours of labour are needed for survival, and they leave little time for the leisure when play might take place. This situation is exacerbated in societies where leisure and work are unevenly distributed. Yet in a 'post-industrial' society, in which many people's work is dominated by communication and the manipulation of information, the reasons for maintaining strict boundaries between play and its opposites (work, study, seriousness) are by no means always clear. There may well be benefits in abandoning such clear binary distinctions, and recognizing a play element *within* all our activities. The clearest distinction between work and play may only be felt by people who are forced, whether by necessity or external compulsion, to do unpleasant and wordless labour. While it is clear that someone silently operating a factory machine for wages is working, and therefore not playing, the distinction is harder to make in jobs where the activity described as work might, in other circumstances, be undertaken voluntarily, and described as play. This is true, for example, of aspects of work in child care, catering, the media, design, the arts, the leisure industry, marketing, entertainment, negotiation, and professional sport. Work and play are not always at odds, and a good deal of modern work, with its constant demand for flexibility and social skills, has reason to embrace a play element. This perception of an area where play and work often merge can certainly include education. In one sense, a reintegration of work, play, and learning is reaching back to the past, beyond the stern morality of the industrial revolution, to the carnivalesque mind of the pre-industrial era, even to the magic of the hunter-gatherer (see page 86); in another sense it is reaching forward to the future, to an era when work is more and more likely to demand some of the features of play. This notion of a simultaneous activation of past and future is inherent in the nature of play itself, which is the means both of radical innovation and of the preservation of tradition.

When our work is with words, as it is for an increasing number of people, including self-evidently those learning a foreign language to further their careers, the distinctions between work, learning, and play become particularly unclear. For although we are often compelled to use language as part of our work or study, or to satisfy a need, we can also play *while* we are working, and imbue our utilitarian use of language with playful elements without in any way minimizing its usefulness. In fact, those playful elements may paradoxically contribute to or even effect the utilitarian function. This is true even when people do manual work together. Their chattering does not necessarily interfere with their work. It may even help it along, by co-ordinating actions, and by making it seem lighter and more co-operative. Thus, although language may negotiate the work itself ('Pass me that', 'Put this here', 'Let's do it this way') a good deal of talk is often devoted to less immediately functional uses, such as joking and gossip and banter. This does not mean, however, that speakers are necessarily alternating between transactional and playful uses of language; the playfulness may be woven into the transactions themselves, so that even when the language *is* the work (as is often the case for teachers, writers, publishers, lawyers, marketers, politicians and a whole host of others) we can still play with language without detriment to what we are doing. For these reasons, those students learning a language for occupational purposes, and those designing courses for them, cannot neatly separate the needs of work from the needs of play. In many contemporary work contexts, where flexibility, innovation, and increased aptitude for communication are encouraged, the interests of employers and students, and the needs for economic survival and personal fulfilment, need not necessarily be at odds. In these circumstances, there seems to be an opportunity to exploit the potential of the play element in learning to the full.

These, however, are ideals. Modern life, even in the most affluent countries, is not as conducive to play as sometimes supposed. While new technology has the potential to offer increased leisure and equitably-distributed leisure without detriment to prosperity, this is far from what has happened. Leisure time seems to be diminished, and working hours (for those in work) to be steadily increasing (White 1997: 65). It is estimated that after factory workers in the Industrial Revolution, employed people in the richest modern societies have less leisure time than almost any other group in history. At the same time, studies show that modern hunter-gatherer societies—who supposedly have the most primitive and brutal way of life—may have more leisure, and give more emphasis to play, than agricultural, industrial, or post-industrial societies (Argyle 1996: 12; Blanchard 1995: 97). There is, therefore, no simple correlation between increasing prosperity and play. In societies where play is defined in contrast with work, the unemployed and the retired can often find themselves deprived of both.

There seems to be no logical reason for maintaining the rigid separation between work and play in education. Surely we have outgrown the crude notion that play is a sin, or some perceived necessity to train a workforce for a life of obedience and unimaginative drudgery? In the more distant past, as Huizinga reminds us, the conflation of the two was more readily accepted: 'school' derives from the Greek for 'leisure'. Provided we are not talking about the replacement of learning by play, or the admission of all and any kind of play, but rather about the recruitment of aspects of play in the service of learning, there is no reason to fear the kind of infantilization or trivialization which might seem to be entailed when play is narrowly defined (Blakeston 1996). Play—at least at the *ludus* end of Caillois' spectrum—does not entail a rejection of order or authority, though it does at least imply more voluntary and creative reasons for embracing them. Even in situations of hardship and economic pressure, where a play element in learning and work may be viewed with suspicion, there is an inherent benefit in encouraging it for its role in stimulating innovation and social harmony.

This effect may be especially true in language learning, not only because it involves adaptation to a new linguistic and cultural environment, but because play and language are so closely intertwined. Our explorations in earlier chapters suggest that there is good reason to regard language play both as a means and an end of language learning. It is an end for the simple reason that it constitutes a large proportion of personally and socially significant language use. In addition, like the work needs by which it may be motivated, it involves simulation, competition, the creation of social networks, and creative thinking. It is true that work also includes the duller tasks, but the ability to produce the language necessary to execute these is subsumed within the capacity to use language for play. A person who can play with a language in creative and socially-effective ways—to tell a joke or a story— could certainly also buy an airline ticket. The reverse however is not necessarily true. The ability to play with the language effectively is indicative of a broader command, and can thus be used as a test of proficiency.

Against this view, it can be argued that language play is an aspect of native-like performance, beyond the reach and irrelevant to the needs of learners. However, this does not seem to be borne out by the evidence. The notion that play is something which appears only at the later stages of language acquisition is belied by children's first language acquisition, and by a growing literature on the popularity and spontaneous appearance of language play at early stages of second language learning (Kramsch and Sullivan 1996; Lantolf 1997; Lo *et al.* 1998; Ohta 1998; McNally 1999; Tarone and Broner forthcoming). To hold the use of play in reserve only for those of native like proficiency seems patronizing and exclusive: reinforcing rather than helping to break down the sense of difference between expert and novice language user. Play—albeit with varying degrees of complexity— can take place at all levels of proficiency. Indeed, it could be argued that it is particularly evident in the discourse of children and the elementary stages of language learning, where repetition, pattern manipulation, and a degree of separation from the demands of work are most in evidence.

Language play, in other words, should not be seen as at odds with language work, nor as subordinate to it, a peripheral and somehow less important aspect of the study of language. One intention of this book has been to consider what might happen if, in the study of language and of language learning, we try to turn the usual order of importance inside out: to make the periphery the centre and the centre the periphery, so that language play is no longer seen as a trivial and optional extra but as the source of language knowledge, use, and activity. In order to do this, we need to engage in a willing suspension of deeply-rooted attitudes towards language play, and to its role in language teaching in particular: to discipline ourselves to see it as profound as well as trivial, as adult as well as childlike, as something which precedes rather than follows on from other more 'useful' activities. Above all we should not see it as something to fill a free moment, only to be guiltily abandoned when a more important duty appears. Such a change of stance may yield many benefits to our understanding of both language and language learning, and my argument will ultimately stand or fall on whether I have convinced you that these benefits are 'real'. You will be annoyed if you feel, at the end of an academic book, that I have just been 'playing games'.

Notes

1 Brumfit and Johnson (1979), for example, begin their collection of seminal readings on the communicative approach with Hymes's paper and an extract from Halliday.

2 I have discussed Jakobson's theory and arguments against it more fully elsewhere: see Cook 1989:24–8 (for its relation to functional language teaching); Cook 1992:120–46 (for its relation to 'poetic' language in advertising); Cook 1994a:38 (and *passim*) for its relation to literature.

3 In studies of narrative literature, this dramatic device of beginning a story with a definite reference as though we were already in, and familiar with, the situation, has often been noted. For further discussion, see Cook 1994a:12–14.

Bibliography

Dates in square brackets are those of a first or earlier edition than that cited, or, in the case of translations, of the original foreign language edition.

Abbott, G. 1980. 'ESP and TENOR'. *ELT Documents* 107:122–4.

Abrahams, R.D. 1962. 'Playing the dozens'. *Journal of American Folklore* 75: 209–20.

Ahl, F. 1988. 'Ars Est Caelare Artem (Art in Puns and Anagrams Engraved)' in J. Culler (ed.): *On Puns: The Foundation of Letters*. Oxford: Blackwell.

Aitchison, J. 1996. *The Seeds of Speech: Language Origin and Evolution*. Cambridge: Cambridge University Press.

Aldiss, O. 1975. *Play Fighting*. New York: Academic Press.

Allwright, R. 1979. 'Language learning through communication practice' in C.J. Brumfit and K. Johnson (eds.): *The Communicative Approach to Language Teaching*. Oxford: Oxford University Press.

Argyle, M. 1996. *The Social Psychology of Leisure*. Harmondsworth: Penguin.

Aston, G. 1988. *Learning Comity: An Approach to the Description and Pedagogy of Interactional Speech*. Bologna: Cooperativa Libraria Universitaria Editrice.

Aston, G. 1993. 'Notes on the interlanguage of comity' in G. Kasper and S. Blum-Kulka (eds.): *Interlanguage Pragmatics*. New York and Oxford: Oxford University Press.

Austin, J.L. 1962. *How to Do Things with Words*. Oxford: Clarendon Press.

Axline, V.M. [1947] 1969. *Play Therapy*. New York: Ballantine.

Bakhtin, M.M. [1934] 1981. 'From the prehistory of novelistic discourse' in *The Dialogic Imagination* (ed. M. Holquist, translated by M. Holquist and C. Emerson). Austin: University of Texas Press (reprinted in D. Lodge (ed.): 1988. *Modern Criticism and Theory: A Reader*. London: Longman).

Bakhtin, M.M. [1940 and 1965] 1968. *Rabelais and His World*. (Translated H. Iswolsky.) Cambridge, Massachusetts: MIT Press.

Barkow, J., J. Tooby, and L. Cosmides (eds.): 1992. *The Adapted Mind: Evolutionary Psychology and the Generation of Culture*. New York: Oxford University Press.

Barnacle, H. 1993. 'Lipogram Man: a review of David Bellos, *Georges Perec: A Life in Words*'. *The Independent* 11, 12, 1993.

Bartholomew, S., and N.J. Adler. 1996. 'Building networks and crossing borders: the dynamics of knowledge generation in a transnational world' in P. Joynt and M. Warner (eds.): *Managing Across Cultures: Issues and Perspectives*. London: International Thomson Business Press.

Bates, E., W. Kintsch, C.R. Fletcher, and V. Giulani. 1980. 'The role of pronominalisation and ellipsis in texts: some memorisation experiments'. *Journal of Experimental Psychology: Human Learning and Memory* 6:676–91.

Beard, R. (ed.): 1995. *Rhymes, Reading and Writing*. London: Hodder and Stoughton.

Behe, M.J. 1998. *Darwin's Black Box: The Biochemical Challenge to Evolution*. London: Simon and Schuster.

Bellos, D. 1993. *Georges Perec: A Life in Words*. London and Boston: Harvill.

Bergson, H. [1899] 1956. 'Laughter' in W. Sypher (ed.): *Comedy*. Garden City, New York: Doubleday.

Berne, E. 1968. *Games People Play: The Psychology of Human Relationships*. Harmondsworth: Penguin.

Bernstein, B. 1960. 'Review of *The Lore and Language of School Children* by Iona and Peter Opie'. *British Journal of Sociology* 11:178–81. (Reprinted in B. Bernstein 1971. *Class Codes and Control*. (Vol. 1). London: Routledge and Kegan Paul.)

Bernstein, L. 1976. *The Unanswered Question: Six Talks at Harvard*. Cambridge, Massachusetts and London: Harvard University Press.

Bisong, J. 1995. 'An approach to the teaching and learning of poetry in Nigeria' in G. Cook and B. Seidlhofer (eds.): *Principle and Practice in Applied Linguistics*. Oxford: Oxford University Press.

Blakeston, R. 1996. 'The infantilisation of adult education'. *Arena* 12:8.

Blanchard, K. 1995. *The Anthropology of Sport: An Introduction*. Westport, Connecticut: Bergin and Garvey.

Block, D. 1996. 'Not so fast! Some thoughts on theory culling, relativism, accepted findings, and the heart and soul of SLA'. *Applied Linguistics* 17/1:63–83.

Bloomfield, L. [1933] 1935. *Language*. London: George, Allen and Unwin.

Blume, R. 1985. 'Graffiti' in T. van Dijk (ed.): *Discourse and Literature*. Amsterdam: Benjamins.

Boas, F. 1934. 'Anthropology' in Edwin R.A. Seligman (ed.): *Encyclopaedia of the Social Sciences*. New York: Macmillan.

Boden, M. 1992. *The Creative Mind: Myths and Mechanisms*. London: Cardinal, Sphere.

Bono, E. de. 1970. *Lateral Thinking: A Textbook of Creativity*. London: Ward Lock Educational.

Botha, R.P. 1989. *Challenging Chomsky: The Generative Garden Game*. Oxford: Blackwell.

Boulton, M.J. and **P.K. Smith.** 1992. 'The social nature of play fighting and play chasing: mechanisms and strategies underlying cooperation and compromise' in J. Barkow, J. Tooby, and L. Cosmides (eds.): *The Adapted Mind: Evolutionary Psychology and the Generation of Culture*. New York: Oxford University Press.

Bouquet, A.C. 1962. *Comparative Religion*. (6th edition). Harmondsworth: Penguin.

Bowerman, M. 1978. 'The acquisition of word meaning: an investigation into some current conflicts' in N. Waterson and C. Snow (eds.): *The Development of Communication*. Chichester: John Wiley.

Bradley, L. and **P. E. Bryant.** 1983. 'Categorising sounds and learning to read: a causal connection'. *Nature* 310:419–21.

Brams, S. J. 1975. *Game Theory and Politics*. New York: Free Press.

Breen, M. 1987. 'Learner contributions to task design' in C. Candlin and D. Murphy (eds.): *Language Learning Tasks*. Englewood Cliffs, NJ: Prentice Hall.

Bremer, K., C. Roberts, M-T. Vasseur, M. Simonot, and **P. Broeder.** 1996. *Achieving Understanding: Discourse in Intercultural Encounters*. Harlow: Longman.

Bricker, V. R. 1976. 'Some Zincanteco Joking Strategies' in B. Kirschenblatt-Gimblett (ed.): *Speech Play*. Philadelphia: University of Pennsylvania Press.

Briggs, J. 1992. *Fractals: The Patterns of Chaos*. New York: Simon and Schuster.

Britton, J. 1977. 'The third area where we are more ourselves' in M. Meek, A. Warlow, and G. Barton (eds.): *The Cool Web: The Pattern of Children's Reading*. London: Bodley Head.

Brown, D. E. 1991. *Human Universals*. New York: McGraw Hill.

Brown, R. 1973. *A First Language: The Early Stages*. London: Allen and Unwin.

Brown, R. and A. Gilman 1960. 'The pronouns of power and solidarity' in T.A. Sebeok (ed.): *Style in Language*. Cambridge, Massachusetts: MIT Press.

Brumfit, C. J. (ed.): 1991. *Literature on Language: An Anthology*. London and Basingstoke: Macmillan.

Brumfit, C. J. and K. Johnson (eds.): 1979. *The Communicative Approach to Language Teaching*. Oxford: Oxford University Press.

Bruner, J. S. 1976. 'Nature and uses of immaturity' in J.S. Bruner, A. Jolly, and K. Sylva (eds.): *Play—Its Role in Development and Evolution*. Harmondsworth: Penguin.

Bruner, J. S. 1986. *Actual Minds, Possible Worlds*. Cambridge Massachusetts: Harvard University Press.

Bruner, J. S., A. Jolly, and K. Sylva (eds.): 1976. *Play—Its Role in Development and Evolution*. Harmondsworth: Penguin.

Bühler, K. 1934. *Sprachtheorie*. Jena: Fischer.

Burghardt, G. M. 1984. 'On the origins of play' in P. K. Smith (ed.): *Play in Humans and Animals*. Oxford: Blackwell.

Burke, R. E. 1994. *The Games of Poetics: Ludic Criticism and Postmodern Fiction*. New York: Peter Lang.

Burling, R. 1966. 'The metrics of children's verse: a cross-linguistic study'. *American Anthropologist* 68:1419–41.

Byers, J. 1984. 'Play in ungulates' in P. K. Smith (ed.): *Play in Animals and Humans*. Oxford: Blackwell.

Caillois, R. [1958] 1961. *Man, Play and Games*. (Translated Meyer Barash.). New York: Free Press of Glencoe.

Caillois, R. [1955] 1969. 'The structure and classification of games' in J.W. Loy and S. Kenyon (eds.): *Sport, Culture and Society: A Reader on the Sociology of Sport*. London: Macmillan.

Calvin, W. H. 1993. 'The unitary hypotheses: a common neural circuitry for novel manipulations, language, plan-ahead, and throwing?' in K. Gibson and T. Ingold (eds.): *Tools, Language and Cognition in Human Evolution*. Cambridge: Cambridge University Press.

Canale, M. and M. Swain. 1980. 'Theoretical bases of communicative approaches to second language teaching and testing.' in *Applied Linguistics* 1/1:1–47.

Candlin, C. 1987. 'Towards task-based learning' in C. Candlin and D. Murphy (eds.): *Language Learning Tasks*. Englewood Cliffs, NJ: Prentice Hall.

Caro, T. M. 1981. 'Predatory behaviour and social play in kittens.' *Behaviour* 76: 1–24.

Carroll, J. 1995. *Evolution and Literary Theory*. Columbia: University of Missouri Press.

Carter, R.A. and M.J. McCarthy. 1995. 'Grammar and the spoken language'. *Applied Linguistics* 16/2:141–58.

Cazden, C. 1976. 'Play and meta-linguistic awareness' in J. Bruner, A. Jolly, and K. Sylva (eds.): *Play: Its Role in Development and Evolution*. New York: Basic Books.

Celce-Murcia, M., D. Brinton, and J. Goodwin. 1996. *Teaching Pronunciation*. Cambridge: Cambridge University Press.

Chiaro, D. 1992. *The Language of Jokes: Analysing Verbal Play*. London: Routledge.

Chomsky, N. 1957. *Syntactic Structures*. The Hague: Mouton.

Chomsky, N. 1965. *Aspects of the Theory of Syntax*. Cambridge, Massachusetts: MIT Press.

Chomsky, N. 1980. *Rules and Representations*. Oxford: Blackwell.

Chomsky, N. 1988. *Language and the Problems of Knowledge: The Managua Lectures*. Cambridge, Massachusetts: MIT Press.

Chomsky, N. 1996. *Powers and Prospects: Reflections on Human Nature and the Social Order*. London: Pluto.

Chukovsky, K. [1928] 1963. *From Two to Five*. (Translated and edited by Miriam Morton.) Berkeley: University of California Press.

Clark, J. 1987. *Curriculum Renewal in School Foreign Language Learning*. Oxford: Oxford University Press.

Colman, A. 1982. *Game Theory and Experimental Games: The Study of Strategic Interaction*. Oxford: Pergamon.

Cook, G. 1989. *Discourse*. (In the series 'Language teaching: a scheme for teacher education.') Oxford: Oxford University Press.

Cook, G. 1992. *The Discourse of Advertising*. London: Routledge.

Cook, G. 1994a. *Discourse and Literature: The Interplay of Form and Mind*. Oxford: Oxford University Press.

Cook, G. 1994b. 'Language play in advertisements: some implications for applied linguistics' in D. Graddol and J. Swann (eds.): *Evaluating Language*. Clevedon, Avon: BAAL/Multilingual Matters.

Cook, G. 1995. 'Genes, memes, rhymes: conscious poetic deviation in linguistic, psychological and evolutionary theory.' *Language and Communication*. 15/4: 375–91.

Cook, G. 1996. 'Language play in English' in J. Maybin and N. Mercer (eds.): *Using English: from Conversation to Canon*. London: Routledge with the Open University.

Cook, G. 1997. 'Key concepts in ELT: schemas.' *English Language Teaching Journal* 51/1:86.

Cook, G. 1998. 'The uses of reality: a reply to Ronald Carter.' *English Language Teaching Journal* 52/1:57–63.

Cook, G. and B. Seidlhofer. 1995. 'An applied linguist in principle and practice' in G. Cook and B. Seidlhofer (eds.): *Principle and Practice in Applied Linguistics*. Oxford: Oxford University Press.

Cook, V. 1993. *Linguistics and Second Language Acquisition*. Basingstoke: Macmillan.

Cosmides, L. and J. Tooby. 1989. 'Evolutionary psychology and the generation of culture, part II: case study: a computational theory of social exchange'. *Ethology and Sociobiology* 10:50–8.

Crow, J.F. and M. Kimura. 1970. *An Introduction to Population Genetics Theory*. London: Harper and Row.

Crystal, D. 1987. *The Cambridge Encyclopaedia of Language.* Cambridge: Cambridge University Press.

Crystal, D. 1998. *Language Play.* Harmondsworth: Penguin.

Csikszentmihalyi, M. 1975. *Beyond Boredom and Anxiety.* San Francisco: Jossey-Bass.

Csikszentmihalyi, M. 1997. *Living Well: The Psychology of Everyday Life.* Weidenfeld and Nicolson.

Culler, J. 1975. *Structuralist Poetics.* London: Routledge and Kegan Paul.

Culler, J. 1988. *On Puns: The Foundation of Letters.* Oxford: Blackwell.

Dan, J. 1993. 'Language for mysticism' in L. Glinert (ed.): *Hebrew in Ashkenaz: A Language in Exile.* New York: Oxford University Press.

Danielson, P. 1992. *Artificial Morality: Virtuous Robots for Virtual Games.* London: Routledge.

Darwin, C. 1871. *The Descent of Man and Selection in Relation to Sex.* London: Murray.

Darwin, C. 1872. *The Expression of the Emotions in Man and Animals.* London: Murray.

Dawkins, R. 1976. *The Selfish Gene.* Oxford: Oxford University Press.

Dawkins, R. 1982. *The Extended Phenotype.* San Francisco: W. H. Freeman.

Dawkins, R. 1986. *The Blind Watchmaker.* Harmondsworth: Penguin.

Dawkins, R. 1995. *River out of Eden: A Darwinian View of Life.* London: Weidenfeld and Nicolson.

Dawkins, R. and J.R. Krebs. 1978. 'Animal signals: information or manipulation?' in J.R. Krebs and N.B. Davies (eds.): *Behavioural Ecology: An Evolutionary Approach.* Oxford: Blackwell.

Dehaene, S. 1997. *The Number Sense: How the Mind Creates Mathematics.* (Translated by the author.) London: Allen Lane, The Penguin Press.

Dennett, D.C. 1991. *Consciousness Explained.* Harmondsworth: Penguin.

Diamond, J. 1997. *Why is Sex Fun? The Evolution of Human Sexuality.* London: Weidenfeld and Nicolson.

Dissanayake, E. 1988. *What is Art For?* Seattle: University of Washington Press.

Doctorow, E.L. 1972. *The Book of Daniel.* London: Picador.

Dowker, A. (ed.): 1997. *Current Psychology of Cognition: Special Issue on Language Play.*

Downing, T.A. 1995. *Music and the Origins of Language: Theories from the French Enlightenment.* Cambridge: Cambridge University Press.

Douglas, M. 1968. 'The social control of cognition: some factors in joke perception'. *Man* 3:361–75.

Dulay, H., M. Burt, and S. Krashen. 1982. *Language Two.* New York: Oxford University Press.

Dunbar, R. 1996. *Grooming, Gossip and the Evolution of Language.* London and Boston: Faber and Faber.

Dundes A.L., J.W. Leach, and B. Ozkök. 1970. 'Strategy of Turkish boys' verbal dueling rhymes'. *Journal of American Folklore* 83:325–49. (Reprinted in J.J. Gumperz and D. Hymes (eds.): *Directions in Sociolinguistics.* New York and London: Holt, Rinehart and Winston.)

Duve, C. de. 1995. *Vital Dust. Life as a Cosmic Imperative.* New York: Harper Collins Basic Books.

Duvignaud, J. 1980. *Le Jeu du Jeu.* Paris: Editions Balland.

Eco, U. 1979. *The Role of the Reader*. Bloomington and London: Indiana University Press.

Eco, U. [1995] 1997. *The Search for the Perfect Language*. (Translated by James Fentress.) London: Harper Collins, Fontana.

Egoff, S., G. T. Stubbs, and L. F. Ashley. 1969. *Only Connect: Readings on Children's Literature*. Toronto: Oxford University Press.

Ellis, R. 1985. 'Sources of variability in interlanguage'. *Applied Linguistics* 6/2:118–31.

Ellis, R. 1986. *Understanding Second Language Acquisition*. Oxford: Oxford University Press.

Ellis, R. 1994. *The Study of Second Language Acquisition*. Oxford: Oxford University Press.

Ellis, R. 1997. *SLA Research and Language Teaching*. Oxford: Oxford University Press.

Ellis, A. and G. Beattie. 1986. *The Psychology of Language and Communication*. London: Weidenfeld and Nicolson.

Eysenck, M. 1998. *Psychology: An Integrated Approach*. London: Longman.

Fagen, R. 1984. 'On play and behavioural flexibility' in P. K. Smith (ed.): *Play in Animals and Humans*. Oxford: Blackwell.

Farb, P. 1973. *Word Play: What Happens When People Talk*. New York: Knopf.

Fink, E. 1966. *Le Jeu comme Symbole du Monde*. Paris: Editions de Minuit.

Firth, J. R. 1957. *Papers in Linguistics 1934–51*. London: Oxford University Press.

Firth, J. R. 1968. *Selected Papers of J. R. Firth*. (Edited by F. R. Palmer.) London and Harlow: Longman.

Fish, S. [1976] 1980. 'Interpreting the Variorum' in *Is There a Text in This Class?* Cambridge, Massachusetts: Harvard University Press. (Reprinted in D. Lodge (ed.): 1988. *Modern Criticism and Theory*. London: Longman.

Foucault, M. [1969] 1977. *The Archeology of Knowledge*. (Translated by A.M. Sheridan Smith.) London: Tavistock.

Foucault, M. [1969] 1979. 'What is an author?' (Translated by J.V. Harari.) In J.V. Harari (ed.): *Textual Strategies: Perspectives in Post-Structuralism*. (Reprinted in D. Lodge (ed.): 1988. *Modern Criticism and Theory*. London: Longman.)

Francis, W. N. 1979. 'Problems of assembling and computerising large corpora' in H. Bergenholtz and B. Shader (eds.): *Empirische Textwisenschaft*. Berlin: Scriptor.

Freeman, D. 1983. *Margaret Mead and Samoa: The Making and Unmaking of an Anthropological Myth*. Cambridge, Massachusetts: Harvard University Press.

Freud, S. 1905. *Jokes and their Relation to the Unconscious*. (Vol. 8 of *The Standard Edition of the Complete Psychological Works of Sigmund Freud*. (Translated by James Strachey.) London: Hogarth Press and the Institute of Psychoanalysis.

Freund, E. 1987. *The Return of the Reader*. London: Methuen.

Frith, U. 1993. 'Autism'. *Scientific American*. June 1993:108–14.

Fry, W. F. Jr. 1963. *Sweet Madness*. Palo Alto, California: Pacific Books.

Geertz, C. 1993. *The Interpretation of Cultures: Selected Essays*. London: Fontana.

Gell-Mann, M. 1992. 'Complexity and complex adaptive systems' in J.A. Hawkins and M. Gell-Mann (eds.): *The Evolution of Human Languages* (Proceedings Volume XI). Santa Fe Institute Studies in the Sciences of Complexity. Redwood City, California: Addison-Wesley.

Gell-Mann, M. 1994. *The Quark and the Jaguar: Adventures in the Simple and the Complex*. London: Little, Brown.

Gleick, J. 1987. *Chaos: Making a New Science.* New York: Penguin.

Glenn, S. M. and C. C. Cunningham. 1983. 'What do babies listen to most? A developmental study of auditory preferences in nonhandicapped infants and infants with Down's syndrome'. *Developmental Psychology* 19:332–7.

Glinert, L. 1993. 'Language as quasilect: Hebrew in contemporary Anglo-Jewry' in L. Glinert (ed.): *Hebrew in Ashkenaz: A Language in Exile.* New York: Oxford University Press.

Glucklich, A. 1997. *The End of Magic.* New York: Oxford University Press.

Goffman, E. 1974. *Frame Analysis: An Essay on the Organization of Experience.* Boston: Northeastern University Press (reprinted by Harmondsworth: Penguin).

Goffman, E. [1976] 1979. *Gender Advertisements.* London: Macmillan.

Gossen, G. H. 1976. 'Verbal dueling in Chamula' in B. Kirschenblatt-Gimblett (ed.): *Speech Play.* Philadelphia: University of Pennsylvania Press.

Goswami, U. 1995. 'Rhyme in children's early reading' in R. Beard (ed.): *Rhymes, Reading and Writing.* London: Hodder and Stoughton.

Goswami, U. 1997. 'Learning to read in different orthographies: phonological awareness, orthographic representations and dyslexia' in C. Hulme and M. Snowling (eds.): *Dyslexia: Biology, Cognition and Intervention.* London: Whurr.

Gould, S. J. 1985. *The Flamingo's Smile: Reflections in Natural History.* Harmondsworth: Penguin.

Gould, S. J. [1980] 1990. *The Panda's Thumb: More Reflections in Natural History.* Harmondsworth: Penguin.

Gould, S. J. 1992. 'On original ideas' in *Natural History* 92/1:26–33.

Gould, S. J. and R. C. Lewontin. 1984. 'The spandrels of San Marco and the Panglossian paradigm: a critique of the adaptionist programme' in E. Sober (ed.): *Conceptual Issues in Evolutionary Biology.* Cambridge, Massachusetts: Bradford Books/MIT Press.

Gray, J. 'Cultural content in the global ELT coursebook—mediation and transformation.' PhD thesis in preparation, London University Institute of Education.

Gregory, R. [1974] 1977. 'Psychology: towards a science of fiction' in *New Society* 23 May 1974, reprinted in M. Meek, A. Warlow, and G. Barton (eds.): *The Cool Web: The Pattern of Children's Reading.* London: Bodley Head.

Groos, K. 1901. *The Play of Man.* London: William Heinemann.

Gross, R. and R. McIlveen. 1998. *Psychology: A New Introduction.* London: Hodder and Stoughton.

Gruneau, R. S. 1980. 'Freedom and constraint. The paradoxes of play, games and sports'. *Journal of Sport History* 7:68–85.

Guéron, J. 1974. 'The meter of nursery rhymes: an application of the Halle-Keyser theory of meter'. *Poetics* 12/3:73–111.

Halliday, M. A. K. 1973. *Explorations in the Function of Language.* London: Edward Arnold.

Halliday, M. A. K. 1975. *Learning How to Mean.* London: Edward Arnold.

Halliday, M. A. K. 1976. (ed. G. Kress) *System and Function in Language.* Oxford: Oxford University Press.

Halliday, M. A. K. 1978. 'Antilanguages' in *Language as a Social Semiotic.* London: Arnold.

Halliday, M. A. K. 1985. *An Introduction to Functional Grammar.* London: Edward Arnold.

Handelman, D. 1996. 'Traps of transformation: theoretical convergences' in G. Hasan-Rokem and D. Shulman (eds.): 1996. *Untying the Knot: On Riddles and Other Enigmatic Modes.* New York and Oxford: Oxford University Press.

Harding, D. W. 1977. 'What happens when we read? (1) Psychological processes in the reading of fiction' in M. Meek, A. Warlow, and G. Barton: *The Cool Web: The Pattern of Children's Reading.* London: Bodley Head.

Harland, R. 1993. *Beyond Superstructuralism: The Syntagmatic Side of Language.* New York: Routledge.

Hasan, R. 1989. *Linguistics, Language, and Verbal Art.* Oxford: Oxford University Press.

Hasan-Rokem, G. and D. Shulman (eds.): 1996. *Untying the Knot: On Riddles and Other Enigmatic Modes.* New York and Oxford: Oxford University Press.

Healey, P. and R. Glanvill. 1992. *Urban Myths.* London: Virgin.

Heaney S. 1984. *Station Island.* London: Faber and Faber.

Hobsbaum, P. 1996. *Metre, Rhythm and Verse Form.* London and New York: Routledge.

Hockett, C. 1958. *A Course in Modern Linguistics.* New York: Macmillan.

Hodson, A. 1992. *Essential Genetics.* London: Bloomsbury.

Hogg, M. A. and G. M. Vaughan. 1998. *Social Psychology* (2nd edition.) London: Prentice Hall.

Howatt A. P. R. 1984. *A History of English Language Teaching.* Oxford: Oxford University Press.

Huizinga, J. [1944] 1949. *Homo Ludens.* London: Routledge and Kegan Paul.

Humboldt, W. von [1836] 1988. *On Language.* (Translated by Peter Heath.) Cambridge: Cambridge University Press.

Hunt, P. 1990. *Children's Literature: The Development of Criticism.* London: Routledge.

Hutchinson, T. G. M. and A. Waters. 1987. *English for Specific Purposes.* Cambridge: Cambridge University Press.

Hymes, D. 1972a. 'Models of the interaction of language and social life' in J. Gumperz and D. Hymes (eds.): *Directions in Sociolinguistics.* New York: Holt, Rinehart and Winston.

Hymes, D. 1972b. 'On communicative competence' in J.B. Pride and J. Holmes (eds.): *Sociolinguistics.* Harmondsworth: Penguin. (Original paper presented at the Research Planning Conference on Language Development in Disadvantaged Children, New York City, June 1966.)

Jacobson, H. 1997. *Seriously Funny: From the Ridiculous to the Sublime.* London: Viking.

Jakobson, R. 1960. 'Closing statement: linguistics and poetics' in T.A. Sebeok (ed.): *Style in Language.* Cambridge, Massachusetts: MIT Press.

Jones, S. 1993. *The Language of the Genes.* London: Harper Collins Flamingo.

Jones, S. 1997. *In the Blood: God, Genes and Destiny.* London: Flamingo.

Kaivola-Bregenhøj, A. 1996. 'Riddles and their uses' in G. Hasan-Rokem and D. Shulman (eds.): *Untying the Knot: On Riddles and Other Enigmatic Modes.* New York and Oxford: Oxford University Press.

Kauffman, S. 1995. *At Home in the Universe.* Harmondsworth: Viking.

Kelly, L. G. 1969. *25 Centuries of Language Teaching: 500 BC–1969.* Rowley, Massachusetts: Newbury House.

Keenan, J.M., B. MacWhinney, and D. Mayhew. 1977. 'Pragmatics in memory: a study of natural conversation'. *Journal of Verbal Learning and Verbal Behaviour* 16:549–60.

Kirschenblatt-Gimblett, B. (ed.): 1976. *Speech Play*. Philadelphia: University of Pennsylvania Press.

Klinger, E. 1971. *Structure and Functions of Fantasy*. New York: Wiley-Interscience.

Kramsch, C. and P. Sullivan. 1996. 'Appropriate pedagogy'. *English Language Teaching Journal* 50/3:199–213.

Krashen, S.D. 1981. *Second Language Acquisition and Second Language Learning*. Oxford: Pergamon.

Krashen, S.D. 1982. *Principles and Practice in Second Language Acquisition*. Oxford: Pergamon.

Krashen, S.D. 1985. *The Input Hypothesis: Issues and Implications*. London: Longman.

Krashen, S.D. and T.D. Terrell. 1983. *The Natural Approach: Language Acquisition in the Classroom*. Oxford: Pergamon.

Kristeva, J. [1974] 1980. 'The ethics of linguistics.' in *Desire in Language*. (Translated by T. Gora, A. Jardine, and L. Roudiez.) New York: Columbia University Press. (Reprinted in D. Lodge (ed.): 1988. *Modern Criticism and Theory*. London: Longman.)

Kristeva, J. 1989. *Language the Unknown*. (Translated Anne M. Menke.) New York: Columbia University Press.

Labov, W. 1974. 'The art of sounding and signifying' in W.W. Gage (ed.): *Language in its Social Setting*. Washington, DC: Anthropological Society of Washington.

Lantolf, J. 1997. 'The function of language play in the acquisition of L2 Spanish' in W.R. Glass and A.T. Pérez-Leroux (eds.): *Contemporary Perspectives on the Acquisition of Spanish. Volume 2: Production, Processing and Comprehension*. Somerville: Cascadilla Press.

Lantolf, J. and G. Appel. 1994. *Vygotskian Approaches to Second Language Research*. Norwood, NJ: Ablex.

Larsen-Freeman, D. 1991. 'Second language acquisition research: staking out the territory'. *TESOL Quarterly* 25:315–50.

Larsen-Freeman, D. 1997. 'Chaos/complexity science and second language acquisition'. *Applied Linguistics* 18/2:141–65.

Lecercle, J-J. 1990. *The Violence of Language*. London: Routledge.

Lecercle, J-J. 1994. *Philosophy of Nonsense*. London: Routledge.

Leech, G.N. l983. *Principles of Pragmatics*. London: Longman.

Lerdahl, F. and R. Jackendoff. 1983. *A Generative Theory of Tonal Music*. Cambridge, Massachusetts: MIT Press/Bradford Books.

Leslie, A.M. 1987. 'Pretense and representation: the origins of "theory of mind"'. *Psychological Review* 94:412–46.

Lewin, B. 1994. *Genes V*. Oxford: Oxford University Press.

Lewis, M. 1993. *The Lexical Approach*. Hove: Language Teaching Publications.

Lewontin, R.C. 1993. *The Doctrine of DNA: Biology as Ideology*. Harmondsworth: Penguin. (First published in Canada in 1991 as *Biology as Ideology*, Anansi Press.)

Li, C.N. 1992. 'Chinese' in W. Bright (ed.): *International Encyclopaedia of Linguistics*. New York, Oxford: Oxford University Press.

Littlewood, W. 1981. *Communicative Language Teaching*. Cambridge: Cambridge University Press.

Lo, T.W., K.W.K. Chu, C. Candlin, and A.M.Y. Lin. 1998. 'Language play and group dynamic of Hong Kong working class teenagers in and out of youth centres'. Paper presented at the *Sociolinguistics Symposium*. London University Institute of Education.

Locke, J. 1993. *The Child's Path to Spoken Language*. Cambridge, Massachusetts: Harvard University Press.

Long, M. 1983. 'Native speaker/non-native speaker conversation and negotiation of comprehensible input'. *Applied Linguistics* 4/2:126–41.

Long, M. 1985. 'A role for instruction in second language acquisition' in K. Hyltenstam and M. Pienemann (eds.): *Modelling and Assessing Second Language Learning*. Clevedon, Avon: Multilingual Matters.

Long, M. 1993. 'Assessment strategies for SLA theories'. *Applied Linguistics* 14/3: 225–49.

Long, M. 1996. 'The role of the linguistic environment in second language acquisition' in W.C. Ritchie and T.K. Bhatia (eds.): *Handbook of Second Language Acquisition*. New York: Academic.

Long, M. and G. Crookes. 1992. 'Three approaches to task-based syllabus design'. *TESOL Quarterly* 26/1:27–57.

Lovett, M.W., P.M. Chaplin, M.J. Ransby, and S.L. Borden. 1990. 'Training the word recognition skills of dyslexic children: treatment and transfer effects'. *Journal of Educational Psychology* 82:769–80.

Lozanov, G. [1971] 1978. *Suggestology and Outlines of Suggestopedia*. (Translated by M. Hall-Pozharkeva and K. Pashmakova.) London: Gordon and Breach.

Lyons, J. 1977. *Semantics* (2 vols.) Cambridge: Cambridge University Press.

Malim, T. and A. Birch. 1998. *Introductory Psychology*. London: Macmillan.

Malinowski, B. 1948. *Magic, Science and Religion, and Other Essays*. Boston, Massachusetts: Beacon Press.

Malof, J. [1970] 1978. *A Manual of English Meters*. Westport, Connecticut: Greenwood Press.

Malotki, E. 1983. *Hopi Time: A Linguistic Analysis of the Temporal Concepts in the Hopi Language*. Berlin: Mouton.

Martin, P. 1984. 'The whys and wherefores of play in cats' in P. K. Smith (ed.): *Play in Animals and Humans*. Oxford: Blackwell.

Maynard Smith, J. 1988. *Games, Sex and Evolution*. New York: Harvester Wheatsheaf.

McGhee, P.E. and A.J. Chapman (eds.): 1980. *Children's Humour*. Chichester: Wiley.

McGinn, C. 1997. *Ethics, Evil and Fiction*. Oxford: Oxford University Press.

McKie, R. 1988. *The Genetic Jigsaw: The Story of the New Genetics*. Oxford: Oxford University Press.

McNally, J. 1999. 'Creative misbehaviour: the use of German *Kabarett* within advanced foreign language learning classrooms'. Unpublished PhD thesis. King's College London.

McWhinney, B. 1996. *The CHILDES Database of Children's Language*. (CD-Rom.) Department of Psychology, Carnegie Mellon University.

Mead, M. 1928. *Coming of Age in Samoa: A Psychological Study of Primitive Youth for Western Civilisation*. London: Cape.

Medgyes, P. 1994. *The Non-Native Teacher*. London: Macmillan.

Mitchell, R. and F. Myles. 1998. *Second Language Learning Theories*. London: Edward Arnold.

Morreal, J. 1983. *Taking Laughter Seriously.* Albany: State University of New York Press.

Morris, D. 1967. *The Naked Ape.* New York: McGraw Hill.

Müller-Schwartze, D. (ed.): 1978. *Evolution of Play Behaviour.* Stroudsburg, Pennsylvania: Dowden, Hutchinson, and Ross.

Myers, D. G. 1998. *Psychology.* (5th edition) New York: Worth.

Nash, W. 1985. *The Language of Humour.* London: Longman.

Nelson, K. (ed.): 1989. *Narratives from the Crib.* Cambridge, Massachusetts: Harvard University Press.

Neumann, J. von and O. Morgenstern. 1944. *Theory of Games and Economic Behaviour.* Princeton, New Jersey: Princeton University Press.

Newman, M. 1986. 'Poetry processing'. *Byte*, February 1986:221–8.

Nunan, D. 1989. *Designing Tasks for the Communicative Classroom.* Cambridge: Cambridge University Press.

Nunan, D. 1998. 'Teaching grammar in context'. *ELT Journal* 25/2:101–9.

Nunan, D. and C. Lamb. 1996. *The Self-Directed Teacher: Managing the Learning Process.* Cambridge: Cambridge University Press.

Odier, D. 1970. *The Job: An Interview with William Burroughs.* London: Cape.

Ohta, A. S. 1998. 'The role of language play in the acquisition of foreign language by adult learners: evidence from the classroom'. Paper presented at the *Annual Conference of the American Association for Applied Linguistics*, Seattle.

Opie, I. 1993. *The People in the Playground.* Oxford: Oxford University Press.

Opie, I. and P. Opie. 1955. *The Oxford Nursery Rhyme Book.* Oxford: Oxford University Press.

Opie, I. and P. Opie. 1959. *The Lore and Language of Schoolchildren.* Oxford: Oxford University Press.

Opie, I. and P. Opie. 1985. *The Singing Game.* Oxford: Oxford University Press.

Opie, I. and P. Opie. 1997a. *Children's Games with Things.* Oxford: Oxford University Press.

Opie, I. and P. Opie. 1997b. *The Oxford Dictionary of Nursery Rhymes.* (new edn.) Oxford: Oxford University Press.

Oriard, M. 1991. *Sporting with the Gods: The Rhetoric of Play and Game in American Culture.* Cambridge: Cambridge University Press.

O'Halloran, K. A. 1997. 'Why Whorf has been misconstrued in stylistics and critical linguistics'. *Language and Literature* 6/3:163–80.

Pawley, A. and F. Syder. 1983. 'Two puzzles for linguistic theory: nativelike selection and nativelike fluency' in J. Richards and R. Schmidt (eds.): *Language and Communication.* London: Longman.

Pennycook, A. 1994. *The Cultural Politics of English as an International Language.* London: Longman.

Peters, A. 1983. *The Units of Language Acquisition.* Cambridge: Cambridge University Press.

Phillipson, R. 1992. *Linguistic Imperialism.* Oxford: Oxford University Press.

Piaget, J. [1926] 1959. *The Language and Thought of the Child.* London: Routledge and Kegan Paul.

Piattelli-Palmarini, M. 1989. 'Evolution, selection and cognition: from "learning" to parameter setting in biology and in the study of language'. *Cognition* 31:1–44.

Pike, K. 1954–60. *Language in Relation to a Unified Theory of the Structure of Human Behaviour.* (3 vols.) Glendale, California: Summer Institute of Linguistics.

Pinker, S. 1994. *The Language Instinct: The New Science of Language and Mind.* London: Allen Lane.

Pinker, S. [1997] 1998. *How the Mind Works.* London: Allen Lane.

Pinker, S. and P. Bloom. 1992. 'Natural Language and Natural Selection' in J. Barkow, J. Tooby, and L. Cosmides (eds.): 1992. *The Adapted Mind: Evolutionary Psychology and the Generation of Culture.* New York: Oxford University Press.

Pollack, R. 1995. *Signs of Life: The Language and Meanings of DNA.* Harmondsworth: Penguin.

Popper, K.R. 1972. *Objective Knowledge: An Evolutionary Approach.* Oxford: Clarendon Press.

Prabhu, N.S. 1984. 'Procedural Syllabuses' in T. E. Read (ed.): *Trends in Language Syllabus Design.* Singapore: Singapore University Press/RELC.

Prabhu, N.S. 1987. *Second Language Pedagogy.* Oxford: Oxford University Press.

Price, R. and S. Price. 1976. 'Secret Play Languages in Saramaka: Linguistic Disguise in a Caribbean Creole' in B. Kirschenblatt-Gimblett (ed.): *Speech Play.* Philadelphia: University of Pennsylvania Press.

Propp, V. [1928] 1968. *Morphology of the Folktale.* (Translated by L. Scott.) Austin: University of Texas Press.

RACTER. 1985. *The Policeman's Beard is Half Constructed.* New York: Warner Books.

Raffman, D. 1993. *Language, Music and Mind.* Cambridge, Massachusetts: MIT Press.

Rapp, A. 1951. *The Origins of Wit and Humour.* New York: Dunton.

Raskin, V. 1985. *Semantic Mechanisms of Humour.* Dordrecht: Reidel.

Raskin, V. 1992. 'Humor and Language' in W. Bright (ed.): *International Encyclopaedia of Linguistics.* New York, Oxford: Oxford University Press.

Reddy, M. 1979. 'The Conduit Metaphor' in A. Ortony (ed.): *Metaphor and Thought.* Cambridge: Cambridge University Press.

Redfern, W. 1984. *Puns.* Oxford: Blackwell.

Reynolds, P.C. 1972. 'Play, language and human evolution' in J. S. Bruner, A. Jolly, and K. Sylva (eds.): *Play—Its Role in Development and Evolution.* Harmondsworth: Penguin.

Richter, H. 1965. *Dada: Art and Anti-art.* London: Thames and Hudson.

Ridley, M. 1994. *The Red Queen: Sex and the Evolution of Human Nature.* Harmondsworth: Penguin.

Riley, J. 1996. *The Teaching of Reading: The Development of Literacy in the Early Years of School.* London: Paul Chapman.

Rosen, M. 1986. *Under the Bed.* London: Prentice Hall.

Russell, G. 1993. *The Social Psychology of Sport.* New York: Springer-Verlag.

Saint Augustine. [AD 398] 1961. *Confessions.* (Translated by R.S. Pine-Coffin.) Harmondsworth: Penguin.

Sapir, E. 1966. *Culture, Language and Personality: Selected Essays.* (Edited by D.G. Mandelbaum.) Berkeley: University of California Press.

Saussure, F. de. [1915] 1983. *Course in General Linguistics.* (Translated by Roy Harris.) London: Duckworth.

Schank, R.C. 1982. *Dynamic Memory.* Cambridge: Cambridge University Press.

Schank, R. C. and **R. Abelson.** 1977. *Scripts, Plans, Goals and Understanding.* Hillsdale, NJ: Lawrence Erlbaum.

Schumann, J. 1976. 'Second language acquisition research: getting a more global look at the learner'. *Language Learning* Special Issue Number 4:15–28.

Schumann, J. 1978a. *The Pidginisation Process: A Model for Second Language Acquisition.* Rowley, Massachusetts: Newbury House.

Schumann, J. 1978b. 'The acculturation model for second language acquisition' in R. Gingras (ed.): *Second Language Acquisition and Foreign Language Teaching.* Arlington, Virginia: Center for Applied Linguistics.

Schumann, J. 1980. 'Affective factors and the problem of age in second language acquisition' in K. Croft (ed.): *Readings on English as a Second Language.* Cambridge, Massachusetts: Winthrop.

Schwartzman, H. B. 1978. *Transformations: The Anthropology of Children's Play.* New York and London: Plenum Press.

Scott, P. and **C. Spencer.** 1998. *Psychology: A Contemporary Introduction.* Oxford: Blackwell.

Searle, J. R. 1969. *Speech Acts: An Essay in the Philosophy of Language.* Cambridge: Cambridge University Press.

Searle, J. R. 1975a. 'A taxonomy of illocutionary acts' in K. Gunderson (ed.): *Language, Mind and Knowledge. Minnesota Studies in the Philosophy of Science.* Vol. 7. Minneapolis: University of Minnesota Press.

Searle, J. R. 1975b. 'The logical status of fictional discourse'. *New Literary History* 6:319–32.

Selinker, L. 1972. 'Interlanguage'. *International Review of Applied Linguistics* 10: 209–31.

Selinker, L. 1991. *Rediscovering Interlanguage.* London: Longman.

Sheen, R. 1994. 'A critical analysis of the advocacy of the task-based syllabus'. *TESOL Quarterly* 28/1:127–47.

Sherzer, J. 1976. 'Play Languages: implications for (socio) linguistics' in B. Kirshenblatt-Gimblett (ed.): *Speech Play.* Philadelphia: University of Pennsylvania Press.

Sherzer, J. 1992. 'Verbal play' in W. Bright (ed.): *International Encyclopaedia of Linguistics.* Vol. 4. New York and Oxford: Oxford University Press.

Shippey, T. A. 1993. 'Principles of conversation in Beowulfian speech' in J.M. Sinclair, M. Hoey and G. Fox (eds.): *Techniques of Description: Spoken and Written Discourse.* London: Routledge.

Sigmund, K. 1995. *Games of Life: Explorations in Ecology, Evolution and Behaviour.* Harmondsworth: Penguin.

Sinclair, J. M. 1988. *New Directions in English Dictionaries.* Unpublished manuscript.

Sinclair, J. M. 1991. *Corpus, Concordance, Collocation.* Oxford: Oxford University Press.

Singer, J. L. 1975. *Daydreaming and Fantasy.* Oxford: Oxford University Press.

Skehan, P. 1998a. *A Cognitive Approach to Language Learning.* Oxford: Oxford University Press.

1998b. 'Processing perspectives on SLA and assessment'. Plenary Address, American Association for Applied Linguistics, Seattle, USA.

Skehan, P. and **P. Foster.** 1997. 'The influence of second language planning and task type on second language performance'. *Language Teaching Research* 1/3:185-212.

Smith, P. K. (ed.): 1984. *Play in Animals and Humans.* Oxford: Blackwell.

Sophocles. 1978. *Oedipus the King.* (Translated by Stephen Berg and Diskin Clay.) New York: Oxford University Press.

Speight, K. 1962. *Teach Yourself Italian.* London: Teach Yourself Books.

Spencer, H. 1898. *The Principles of Psychology.* Vol. II, Part 2. New York: D. Appleton.

Sperber, D. and D. Wilson. 1986. *Relevance.* Oxford: Blackwell.

Spolsky, B. 1989. *Conditions for Second Language Learning.* Oxford: Oxford University Press.

Starobinski, J. (ed.): 1971. *Les mots sous les mots: les anagrammes de Ferdinand de Saussure.* Paris: Gallimard.

Steiner, G. 1975. *After Babel.* Oxford: Oxford University Press.

Stewart, S. 1979. *Nonsense.* Baltimore: Johns Hopkins.

Stubbs, M. 1996. *Text and Corpus Analysis.* Oxford: Blackwell.

Sutton-Smith, B. 1979. *Play and Learning.* New York: Gardner.

Swales, J. 1990. *Genre Analysis.* Cambridge: Cambridge University Press.

Sweet, H. [1899]. 1964. *The Practical Study of Languages: A Guide for Teachers and Learners.* (Edited by R. Mackin.) Oxford: Oxford University Press.

Tannen, D. 1989. *Talking Voices: Repetition, Dialogue, and Imagery in Conversational Discourse.* Cambridge: Cambridge University Press.

Tarone, E. 1988. *Variation in Interlanguage.* London: Edward Arnold.

Tarone, E. 1997. 'Analyzing IL in natural settings: a sociolinguistic perspective on second language acquisition'. *Culture and Cognition* 30:137–49.

Tarone, E. 1999. 'Language play, interlanguage variation and second language acqusition'. Paper given at the Second Language Research Forum, University of Minnesota.

Tarone, E. and M. Broner. (forthcoming) 'Is it fun? Language play in a fifth grade Spanish immersion classroom'.

Tarone, E. and G. Yule. 1989. *Focus on the Language Learner.* Oxford: Oxford University Press.

Taylor-Parker, S. 1984. 'Playing for keeps: an evolutionary perspective on human games' in P. K. Smith (ed.): *Play in Animals and Humans.* Oxford: Blackwell.

Thompson, S.A. 1992. 'Functional grammar' in W. Bright (ed.): *International Encyclopaedia of Linguistics.* New York and Oxford: Oxford University Press.

Todorov, T. 1966. 'The typology of detective fiction' in T. Todorov. [1971] 1977. *The Poetics of Prose.* (Translated by Richard Howard.) Cornell University Press. Reprinted in D. Lodge (ed.): 1988. *Modern Criticism and Theory.* London: Longman.

Tolkien, J.R.R. 1964. 'On fairy stories' in *Tree and Leaf.* London: George Allen and Unwin.

Tooby, J. and L. Cosmides. 1992. 'The psychological foundations of culture' in J. Barkow, J. Tooby, and L. Cosmides (eds.): *The Adapted Mind: Evolutionary Psychology and the Generation of Culture.* New York: Oxford University Press.

Townsend, J.R. 1990. *Written for Children: An Outline of English-language Children's Literature.* (5th edition.) London: Bodley Head.

Turner, F. 1992. 'The neural lyre: poetic meter, the brain and time' in *Natural Classicism: Essays on Literature and Science.* Charlottesville: University of Virginia Press.

Tylor, E.B. [1879] 1971. 'The history of games' in E.M. Avedon and B. Sutton Smith: *The Study of Games.* New York: Wiley.

Ulmer, G. 1988. 'The puncept in grammatology' in J. Culler (ed.): *On Puns: The Foundation of Letters*. Oxford: Blackwell.

van Lier, L. 1994. 'Forks and hope: pursuing understanding in different ways'. *Applied Linguistics* 15/3:328–46.

van Lier, L. 1996. *Interaction in the Language Curriculum. Awareness, Autonomy and Authenticity*. London and New York: Longman.

Vygotsky, L.S. [1934] 1962. *Thought and Language*. (Translated by E. Haufmann and G. Vakar.) Cambridge, Massachusetts: MIT Press.

Vygotsky, L.S. [1933] 1976. 'Play and its role in the mental development of the child' in J. S. Bruner, A. Jolly, and K. Sylva (eds.): *Play—Its Role in Development and Evolution*. Harmondsworth: Penguin.

Waldrop, M. 1992. *Complexity: The Emerging Science at the Edge of Order and Chaos*. New York: Simon and Schuster.

Warlow, A. 1977. 'Kinds of reality: a hierarchy of veracity' in M. Meek, A. Warlow, and G. Barton (eds.): *The Cool Web: The Pattern of Children's Reading*. London: Bodley Head.

Watt, I. [1957] 1963. *The Rise of the Novel*. London: Peregrine.

Weiner, J. 1994. *The Beak of the Finch: Evolution in Real Time*. London: Vintage.

Weir, R.H. 1962. *Language in the Crib*. The Hague: Mouton.

Werth, P.W. 1976. 'Roman Jakobson's verbal analysis of poetry.' *Journal of Linguistics* 12: 21–73.

West, R. 1994. 'Needs analysis in language teaching'. *Language Teaching* 27/1: 1–19.

White, J. 1997. *Education and the End of Work: A New Philosophy of Work and Learning*. London: Cassell.

White, L. 1989. *Universal Grammar and Second Language Acquistion*. Amsterdam: Benjamins.

Whorf, B. [1940] 1956. 'Science and linguistics' in J. B. Carroll (ed.): *Selected Writings of Benjamin Lee Whorf*. Cambridge, Massachusetts: MIT Press.

Widdowson, H.G. 1975. *Stylistics and the Teaching of Literature*. London: Longman.

Widdowson, H.G. 1978. *Teaching Language as Communication*. Oxford: Oxford University Press.

Widdowson, H.G. 1979. *Explorations in Applied Linguistics*. Oxford: Oxford University Press.

Widdowson, H.G. 1983. *Learning Purpose and Language Use*. Oxford: Oxford University Press.

Widdowson, H.G. 1984. *Explorations in Applied Linguistics 2*. Oxford: Oxford University Press.

Widdowson, H.G. 1987. 'On the interpretation of poetic writing' in N. Fabb, D. Attridge, and C. McCabe (eds.): *The Linguistics of Writing: Arguments between Language and Literature*. Manchester: Manchester University Press.

Widdowson, H.G. 1989. 'Knowledge of language and ability for use'. *Applied Linguistics* 10/2:128–37.

Widdowson, H.G. 1990. *Aspects of Language Teaching*. Oxford: Oxford University Press.

Widdowson, H.G. 1992a. *Practical Stylistics*. Oxford: Oxford University Press.

Widdowson, H.G. 1992b. 'Aspects of the relationship between culture and language' in H. Antor and R. Ahrens (eds.): *Text-Culture-Reception. Cross Cultural Aspects of English Studies*. Carl Winter Universitaetsverlag.

Widdowson, H.G. 1994. '"Old song that will not declare itself". On poetry and the imprecision of meaning' in R. Sell and P. Verdonk (eds.): *Literature and the New Interdisciplinarity: Poetics, Linguistics, History.* Amsterdam: Rodopi.

Wilkins, D.A. 1976. *Notional Syllabuses.* Oxford: Oxford University Press.

Williams, G.C. 1996. *Plan and Purpose in Nature.* London: Weidenfeld and Nicolson.

Wills, C. 1994. *The Runaway Brain: The Evolution of Human Uniqueness.* London: HarperCollins Flamingo.

Wittgenstein, L. [1953] 1968. *Philosophical Investigations.* Oxford: Blackwell.

Wolfson, N. 1988. 'The bulge: a theory of speech behaviour and social distance' in J. Fine (ed.): *Second Language Discourse: A Textbook of Current Research.* Norwood, NJ: Ablex.

Wolfson, N. 1989. *Perspectives: Sociolinguistics and TESOL.* Cambridge, Massachusetts: Newbury House.

Index

Page-numbers in **bold type** denote main treatments; endnotes are indicated by *n*.